access to history

South Africa, 1948–94

From apartheid state to 'rainbow nation' *for Edexcel*

PETER CLEMENTS

access to history

South Africa, 1948–94

From apartheid state to 'rainbow nation' for Edexcel

PETER CLEMENTS

HODDER EDUCATION
AN HACHETTE UK COMPANY

The Publishers would like to thank the following for permission to reproduce copyright material:

Photo credits: p21 Drum Social Histories/Baileys African History Archive/Africa Media Online; **pp23, 27** Wikimedia Commons/ Public domain; **p34** Sipa Press/REX/Shutterstock; **pp43, 56** Drum Social Histories/Baileys African History Archive/Africa Media Online; **p73** Wikimedia Commons/CC BY-SA 4.0; **p75** Bettmann via Getty Images; **p78** Jan Hamman/Foto24/Gallo Images/Getty Images; **p80** Wikimedia Commons/Public domain; **p88** Rob C. Croes/Anefo/Nationaal Archief/via Wikimedia Commons/Public domain; **p108** Sowetan/Times Media via Africa Media Online; **p121** World Economic Forum (www.weforum.org) – Frederik de Klerk – World Economic Forum Annual Meeting Davos 1992, CC BY-SA 2.0; **p134** STRINGER/AFP/Getty Images; **p136** Peter Turnley/Corbis/VCG via Getty Images.

Acknowledgements: Abacus, *Long Walk to Freedom* by Nelson Mandela, 2013. African National Congress. BBC Books, *Beloved Country* by Daniel Reed, 1994; *The White Tribe of Africa* by David Harrison, 1981. Blackwell, *South Africa in the Twentieth Century* by James Barber, 1999. Cambridge University Press, *A Concise History of South Africa* by Robert Ross, 1999; 'Resistance and Reform 1973–1994' by Tom Lodge in the *Cambridge History of South Africa, Vol. 2 1885–1994*, 2011. Doubleday, 'A Miracle Unfolding' by Archbishop Desmond Tutu in *The Rainbow People of God: South Africa's Victory over Apartheid*, 1994. HarperCollins, *A History of South Africa* by Frank Welsh, 2000. HAUM, Cape Town and Pretoria, *Apartheid: A Socio-historical Exposition of the Origin and Development of the Apartheid Idea* by N.J. Rhodie MA and Professor Dr H.J. Venter, no date. Hurst & Company, *The Afrikaners: Biography of a People* by Hermann Giliomee, 2003. International Defence and Aid Fund for South Africa in cooperation with the UN Centre Against Apartheid, *Apartheid: The Facts*, 1983. James Currey, *A History of the ANC: South Africa Belongs to Us* by Francis Meli, 1989. Nelson Mandel Foundation. Paddington Press, *Biko* by Donald Woods, 1978. Pluto Press, *The ANC and the Liberation Struggle: A Critical Political Biography* by Dale T. McKinley, 1997. Sampson, Low, Marston & Co., *South and East African Yearbook and Guide for 1921*, 1921. South African History Online. Sutton Pocket Histories, *The African National Congress* by Saul Dubow, 2000. *The Times*, 'South Africa elections – from our own correspondent 26 May 1948'. University of California, Los Angeles Library.

Every effort has been made to trace all copyright holders, but if any have been inadvertently overlooked, the Publishers will be pleased to make the necessary arrangements at the first opportunity.

Although every effort has been made to ensure that website addresses are correct at time of going to press, Hodder Education cannot be held responsible for the content of any website mentioned in this book. It is sometimes possible to find a relocated web page by typing in the address of the home page for a website in the URL window of your browser.

Orders: please contact Bookpoint Ltd, 130 Milton Park, Abingdon, Oxon OX14 4SE. Telephone: +44 (0)1235 827720. Fax: +44 (0)1235 400401. Email: education@bookpoint.co.uk. Lines are open from 9 a.m. to 5 p.m., Monday to Saturday, with a 24-hour message answering service. You can also order through our website: www.hoddereducation.co.uk

First published in 2018 by
Hodder Education
An Hachette UK Company
Carmelite House, 50 Victoria Embankment
London EC4Y 0DZ

www.hoddereducation.co.uk

Impression number   10   9   8   7   6   5   4   3   2
Year   2022   2021   2020   2019

Cover photo: © Trinity Mirror/Mirrorpix/Alamy Stock Photo
Produced and typeset in Palatino by Gray Publishing, Tunbridge Wells
Printed in the UK by CPI Group (UK) Ltd

A catalogue record for this title is available from the British Library.

ISBN 978 1510423466

MIX
Paper from
responsible sources
FSC
www.fsc.org   FSC™ C104740

Contents

Dedication

Keith Randell (1943–2002)

The *Access to History* series was conceived and developed by Keith, who created a series to 'cater for students as they are, not as we might wish them to be'. He leaves a living legacy of a series that for over twenty years has provided a trusted, stimulating and well-loved accompaniment to post-16 study. Our aim with these new editions is to continue to offer students the best possible support for their studies.

CHAPTER 1

The response to apartheid, c1948–59

In 1948, South Africa comprised four broad ethnic groups, but all power was concentrated in the hands of a mainly European white minority who had settled there after colonising the country. This minority were themselves divided into Afrikaners, the Dutch and German settlers who spoke Afrikaans ('African Dutch'), and English speakers. The National Party, supported mainly by Afrikaners, took power in 1948 and implemented a policy of apartheid. While the foundations were laid quickly, the policy intensified later in the 1950s with the development of Bantustans or tribal homelands. The authorities supported this legislation with a raft of repressive measures. Many non-white South Africans protested against apartheid mainly by peaceful means, but the repression they encountered as a result prevented any success. The main anti-apartheid group, the African National Congress (ANC), was made up of members of different races. By the end of the decade, a new Africanist force, the Pan-Africanist Congress (PAC), had emerged, which believed that only people of colour could be involved in the struggles against apartheid.

These developments are examined under the following themes:

★ Life in South Africa, c1948

★ Reasons for the National Party victory, 1948

★ Codifying and implementing apartheid, 1948–59

★ African nationalism, 1948–59

Key dates

1899–1902	Second Boer War	1952	National Laws Amendment Act (also known as Abolition of Passes and Co-ordination of Documents Act)
1910	Creation of the Dominion of South Africa		
1912	Formation of the ANC		
1944	ANC Youth League (ANCYL) formed	1953	Bantu Education Act
		1955	Freedom Charter adopted
1948	National Party electoral victory	1956	Tomlinson Committee report on Bantustans
1949	Prohibition of Mixed Marriages Act		
1950	Population Registration Act		Women's pass protests
	Suppression of Communism Act	1956–61	Treason Trial
1951	Defiance Campaign	1957	Zeerust uprising
		1959	Formation of PAC

① Life in South Africa, c1948

▶ *What led to apartheid becoming law?*
▶ *How far was life in general different for the different ethnic groups in South Africa?*

KEY TERMS

Coalition A partnership between different political parties to try to win elections together.

Apartheid Strict separation of different racial groups. It is an Afrikaans word, meaning 'apart-hood'.

Afrikaners Descendants of immigrants to South Africa, mainly from the Netherlands and Germany.

Africans The original population of Africa.

Bureaucracy Members of the administration which implemented government policies.

White-collar Professional jobs such as administrators.

Segregation Separate facilities for members of different races.

In 1948 in South Africa, the National Party won 79 seats in Parliament during the election. It was a close-run race; the party's rivals, a **coalition** of the United and South African Labour parties, gained 71 seats (see page 11). The National Party supported the notion of **apartheid** and began to institute a system in which the different races in South Africa were segregated as much as possible.

Apartheid in practice

The concept of apartheid was predicated on four principles:

● South Africa comprised four racial groups, each with its own inherent and separate cultures (see page 4).
● White people were the civilised race and were entitled to absolute power over the interests of all.
● The white race was a single entity, despite comprising **Afrikaners** (see page 3) and English speakers. Black **Africans** (see page 4), meanwhile, were made up of different tribes that needed to be kept separate from each other in their own best interests. This was a particularly important concept as it implied Africans were different from each other: there was no single unified group of black Africans. This meant white people, a seemingly homogeneous group, could call themselves the majority group.
● The interests of white people should prevail. It was not necessary to provide separate but equal facilities (as would be seen in the USA in the early twentieth century). Because it was believed that the other races were inferior, the facilities provided for them could also be inferior. Other races would not appreciate the better facilities provided for whites.

Soon after 1948, laws were enacted which determined which race one belonged to, which in turn effectively determined one's whole expectations of life. Factors such as the thickness of one's hair were considered highly important by a growing **bureaucracy**. White South Africans benefited from apartheid as it guaranteed them the majority of the wealth of South Africa, the vast majority of the well-paid **white-collar** jobs, and pleasant, well-ordered lifestyles – while Africans suffered discrimination all their lives, and did the hard work in the mines and on the farms for little pay.

People increasingly spoke of grand and petty apartheid. Grand apartheid referred to the overall policy to keep the different races as separated as possible, for example by ensuring that they lived in different areas. Petty apartheid meant the day-to-day restrictions, such as separate facilities and restrictions – the **segregation** between the races.

Segregation preceded the National Party victory in 1948; as we shall see, extensive discriminatory policies aimed at maintaining **white supremacy** and treating non-white people as inferiors with limited rights of citizenship were already in place. However, the intellectuals behind National Party policy designed segregation under apartheid to protect both white superiority and survival. It developed on a scale almost unimaginable to those living in multiracial, multicultural societies today. In order to understand the significance of the National Party victory, we need to understand what went before.

A brief history of South Africa

Before European **colonisation**, South Africa was a vast area of 470,000 square miles (1.2 million km²) inhabited over thousands of years by different African peoples whom the settlers were to call **Bantus**. The first wave of Europeans, mainly employees of the Dutch East India Trading Company, arrived in 1652. They met the **indigenous** San and the Khoi, who understandably feared the arrival of these interlopers, particularly as settlers, mainly from the Netherlands and Germany, began to arrive to farm and use slaves trafficked from elsewhere in Africa. The settlers, calling themselves **Boers**, began to fan out, moving north and west and meeting the more powerful Xhosa population, who equally resented their presence.

Early European colonialism

The British arrived as a result of the **French Revolutionary and Napoleonic Wars**. The San and the Khoi had more or less been exterminated by warfare and disease, and the Xhosa were gradually defeated by the British Army with its more sophisticated military technology. The nineteenth century saw the Africans losing more and more land to settlers.

The Afrikaners

The relationship between the Boer settlers and British was always uneasy, and worsened when the British abolished slavery within the British Empire in 1833. Many of the Boer settlers who kept slaves then moved into the vast **hinterland** away from British rule. This was called the **Great Trek** and had enormous ramifications in the subsequent history of South Africa. The hinterland into which they moved appeared largely uninhabited, largely because of local wars and famine of which they knew nothing. The myth developed that they had moved into an empty land. Afrikaners subsequently used this to suggest Africans had no right to the land of South Africa, and that Africans had moved into these areas at roughly the same time as the Boers themselves.

The **Covenant** of 1838 was another myth used to justify their possession of the land. When the Boers encountered the powerful Zulu nation, conflict was inevitable. On the eve of the Battle of Blood River against the Zulus in 1838, the Boers were alleged to have a Covenant with God asking for victory. This

KEY TERMS

White supremacy A belief in the right of white people to govern and the inferiority of non-white people.

Colonisation Settling in an area and taking control over it and its people, often through force and exploitation.

Bantus African people who speak a common group of languages. In the apartheid era white people used the term to refer to Africans in a derogatory manner.

Indigenous Native to an area.

Boers A Dutch word; the name given to the settlers from the Netherlands and Germany.

French Revolutionary and Napoleonic Wars A series of wars fought between France and Britain and their respective allies between 1792 and 1815 in which France was defeated.

Hinterland Land in the interior of a country.

Great Trek Movement of Boer farmers into the vast South African interior, away from British rule, which began in 1834.

Covenant Solemn oath or agreement; in this sense, the agreement apparently made between God and the Boers in 1838.

subsequently became the basis of the Boer belief that God had granted them the land of South Africa.

The gold rush and Boer Wars

The Boers founded two **Republics**: the Transvaal and Orange Free State (see map on page 6). Diamonds and gold were discovered in great quantities in the Transvaal in 1867 and 1886. This led to a **gold rush** and eventually to the **second Boer War** between the Boers and the British in 1899. When Britain emerged the victor in 1902, it eventually absorbed the two Boer Republics in a new Union of South Africa in 1910. This was made up of the two predominantly Afrikaner areas, and the British-dominated **Cape** and Natal, which had been British colonies. The Union of South Africa became a self-governing **dominion** within the British Empire.

Race, segregation and discrimination in 1948

The different races of South Africa were strictly segregated. With only a few exceptions, white people were the only ethnic group who could vote. Black Africans, in particular, were treated as cheap labour, unable to compete with white people for whom the best jobs were reserved.

In 1948, the majority of South Africa's population were black Africans, descended from the indigenous inhabitants. By 1948, they had been dispossessed of most of their land, could not vote and were subject to widespread discrimination. Successive governments not only kept them as far as possible away from the white population, but tried to keep them separate from each other – a type of divide and rule. Africans were expected to think of themselves as Zulu, or Xhosa, rather than of one race. While many white people wanted black Africans confined to the reserves allocated to them (see below), most saw the need for cheap labour and supported laws exploiting them for this purpose.

The other main ethnic groups were:

- Coloured people, or descendants of mixed marriages, who lived mainly in Cape Province. Some could still vote.
- Indians were descendants of 150,000 people imported by the British during the nineteenth century who had been introduced largely as agricultural labourers. Many later found work as administrators and founded a prosperous merchant class of traders and shopkeepers. They lived mainly in the province of Natal.
- White people were comprised of Afrikaans and English speakers, with tensions between them (see page 9). Until 1948, Afrikaners felt that English speakers dominated both economically and politically.

KEY TERMS

Republic Country without a monarch at its head, usually led by a president.

Gold rush Rapid migration of people to an area to find gold and become rich.

Second Boer War War between Britain and the Boers between 1899 and 1902 with the Boers seeking to assert their complete independence from Britain, which, in turn, wished to extend its influence to gain control over the gold and diamond industries in the Transvaal.

Cape The southernmost province of South Africa, originally Cape Colony, part of the British Empire.

Dominion Largely self-governing country within the British Empire, recognising the monarch as head of state.

Table 1.1 Population figures, 1946

Ethnic group	Population
Black Africans (many different groups)	7,830,559
White	2,372,044
Coloured	928,062
Indian	285,260

Source: based on data quoted in William Beinart, *A History of South Africa*, Oxford University Press, 1994, page 262.

Table 1.2 Discriminatory legislation, 1910–36

1911 Mines and Works Act and 1911 Natives' Labour Regulation Act	• Mines and Works Act: excluded Africans from most skilled jobs in the mines, which were reserved for white people • Natives' Labour Regulation Act: set down working conditions for Africans. They were to be recruited in rural areas, fingerprinted and issued with pass books which gave them permission to enter their areas of work. This was one of the Acts known as the pass laws (see box, page 6)
1913 Natives Land Act	• Restricted African ownership of land to seven per cent of South Africa. The government argued this figure was equivalent to African land holdings before the whites occupied the hinterland (see page 3) • Many Africans were now forced to work for white farmers – or leave to work under the temporary contracts in the mines and cities. This was necessary because the homelands such as Zululand and Transkei soon became overcrowded • Most of the land Africans were allowed to keep was of the poorest quality – the land white people had not taken
1923 Natives (Urban Areas) Act	• Africans should remain in cities only to administer to the needs of the white inhabitants, for example, as domestic servants • Africans employed in industry or mining were expected to live in townships specially built for them on the outskirts of the cities, and to leave when their contract ended
Industrial Conciliation Act 1924	• Restricted the right of Africans to organise themselves into trade unions and negotiate their terms of employment. They were given no rights as employees
1927 Native Administration Act	• Set up the Department of Native Affairs, or Native Affairs Department (NAD), to control all matters relating to Africans. They were thereby separated in law from all other South Africans and had no civic rights outside this structure
1936 Native Trust and Land Act	• Extended the amount of tribal reserves to 13.6 per cent of the total from the original seven per cent in the 1913 Natives Land Act. Africans were not allowed to buy any land outside the tribal reserves
Representation of the Natives Act 1936	• Approximately 10,000 Africans had been able to vote in the Cape on the same basis as white people (in other words, if they owned sufficient property, they could vote). This Act removed such rights. Africans were effectively disenfranchised and were treated as foreigners with no rights of permanent residence outside the designated tribal reserves • African leaders in the Cape – about 4000 – were allowed to vote for four white representatives to the Senate. A Native Representative Council was created of six white officials, four nominated and twelve elected Africans to represent the views of Cape Africans in Parliament

A note on 'coloured'

In most countries, the used of 'coloured' to describe a black or mixed race person is old-fashioned and derogatory. In the context of South Africa, and this book, 'coloured' refers very specifically to a social categorisation of people. From 1950 to 1990, under apartheid, 'coloured' was legally defined as 'a person of mixed European ("white") and African ("black") or Asian ancestry.'

Figure 1.1 South Africa and the tribal homelands in 1948.

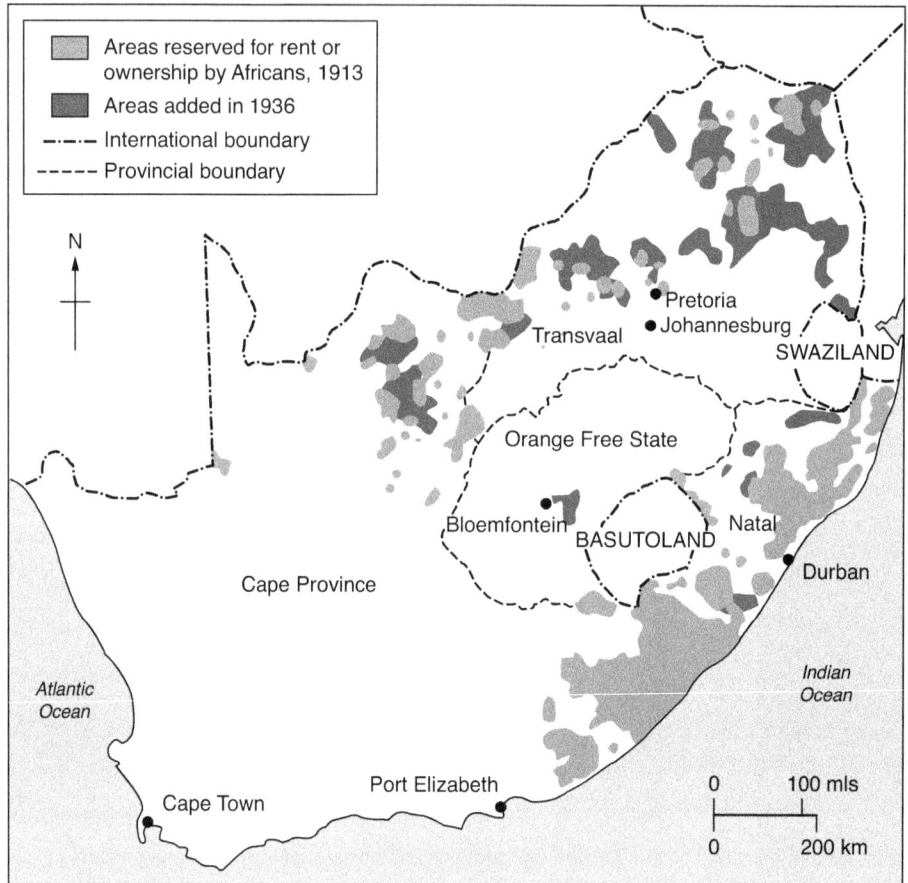

Segregation in legislation

Both Afrikaners and English speakers agreed in their perception that Africans were racially inferior. They also highlighted the fundamental contradiction in segregation legislation: white people tried to exclude Africans from 'white South Africa', but needed them at the same time to do the work they themselves did not want to do. Therefore, because black African labour was needed, laws such as the 1913 Natives Land Act were passed, in part to encourage them to leave the rural areas to work in industry and especially in the mines.

Pass laws

The pass laws were developed over the nineteenth and early twentieth centuries to control the movement of Africans and manage migrant labour. They operated a type of internal passport system (the pass book) to control where Africans could live, work and visit. While each South African province had its own system of pass laws, they were formalised and centralised by the Abolition of Passes and Co-ordination of Documents Act 1952 (see page 20). The pass laws became the lynchpin of apartheid.

Discrimination

Overall, in 1948, black Africans were overwhelmingly the largest ethnic group but all political and economic power was effectively monopolised by white people. As a result, all non-white groups faced discrimination – neither Indians nor the vast majority of coloured people could vote, and both groups faced petty apartheid restrictions. It is worth re-emphasising here that the foundations of apartheid pre-dated the 1948 National Party victory and most white groups were united in supporting white supremacy.

White justification for discrimination and segregation

Most white people had racist views which varied between Africans being lazy, untrustworthy and, if given the opportunity, dangerous. They considered black people most content in rural areas, tending to their farms and cattle, away from the temptations of urban life. These views were largely based on two factors:

- ignorance, and fear of the consequences for their own position and indeed safety if Africans were given political or economic rights
- a need to feel reassured that separation from white people was in the Africans' best interests – that they were happy and contented in a simple **pastoral environment**.

Urbanisation and industrialisation; townships and rural society

Although mainly rural, white South Africa grew more urban and industrial as the twentieth century developed. This was the result, in particular, of the growth in the mining industry, for example gold, diamonds and precious metals, on which South Africa relied for much of its wealth. Elsewhere, the South African economy remained mainly agricultural.

As mentioned, there was a tension between the desire to prevent Africans moving into areas reserved for white people and the need for cheap labour. In theory, Africans worked on temporary contracts and had to return to the tribal areas allocated to them when these contracts ended; in practice, it is estimated that in the period 1919–39 every African man went to work for white people at some point during his life. By 1946, 23 per cent of Africans were living in urban areas as opposed to 75 per cent of white people, 61 per cent of coloured people and 71 per cent of Indians.

Townships

Transient workers lived either in single-sex barracks or in townships: special settlements on the edge of urban areas, with basic homes for urban African workers. These were often overcrowded, insanitary and squalid, and were to continue so until the end of the apartheid period.

KEY TERM

Pastoral environment
Rural life based on small-scale agriculture.

Rural society

Most Africans lived in their homelands, such as Transkei and Zululand, which were increasingly overcrowded and poor. They could not sustain their populations. Many critics saw them simply as reserves where Africans were held until required by whites: in 1936, as many as half the able-bodied male population was absent at any one time. Rural society in the tribal reserves was dominated by traditions and culture and governed by chieftains from the most powerful families. Nelson Mandela (see page 27) came from one such ruling elite in the Transkei reserve. The economies were almost completely rural.

SOURCE A

Extract from the *South and East African Yearbook and Guide for 1921*, Sampson, Low, Marston & Co., 1921, page 195.

*Although these are altered somewhat in the last present day, the social customs of the Bantus, which have always allotted to the women all work except cattle tending and hunting, still permit the man who has acquired a wife to live in almost complete idleness. It might be supposed that contact with civilised life would have early created a desire for what we are accustomed to look upon as the comforts and necessities of civilisation but although some change has taken place in recent years, the visitor to a **Kaffir kraal** cannot fail to notice how little influence the white man's mode of living still has on the natives' surroundings and how capable they are of providing for their own limited wants and comforts.*

Family responsibilities, so potent in Europe count not at all. Land is generally held on the Communal system and, while wealth is impossible, real poverty is unknown.

A bevy of growing daughters, so far from causing sleepless nights, are the father's most valuable asset. He is not called upon to find dowries for them; on the contrary his sons-in-law pay him handsomely on their marriage.

> ? What can you infer from Source A about the author's attitude towards the lives of Africans?

> **KEY TERMS**
>
> **Kaffir** A derogatory name given by Afrikaners to black Africans.
>
> **Kraals** African collections of farms where families or close members of tribal groups would live together.

Afrikaner culture and politics

Afrikaners were descended from the Boers (see page 3); their language, Afrikaans, is derived from German and Dutch. As time went on, Afrikaners developed their own culture, separate from British or European. They were conscious that, unlike the British, they had no 'mother country' as such, and nowhere to go to should their life in South Africa fail: some commentators called them the white tribe of Africa.

As a people, Afrikaners were characterised by the following:

- Hard work, mainly farming land that was often naturally infertile.
- A stern puritanical Christianity (believing in the literal truth of the Bible) and rejection of 'pleasures of the flesh', such as alcohol.

- Extreme racism: believing that people of colour were inferior. Some even believed these people had been cursed by God. This was reinforced by the teachings of the **Dutch Reformed Church** to which most adhered.
- A '**laager mentality**' exemplified by their determination to proceed with apartheid and white supremacy despite internal and later, international opposition: indeed, the greater the opposition, the greater the determination.

Political parties before the Second World War

All the political parties vying for power were composed almost exclusively of white Africans. Afrikaners, however, often felt excluded from power: the most successful parties were dominated by English speakers and legislated, the Afrikaners believed, in the interests of these citizens – although they did pass segregationist legislation which benefited all white groups (see page 6).

However, during the interwar years (between 1919 and 1939), Afrikaners developed their own identity and institutions: these included the **Broederbond**, a hugely influential movement set up in 1918 and dedicated to promoting their interests. During the apartheid era, from 1948 to 1994, every South African leader was a member of the Broederbond. After various struggles and mergers, the main Afrikaner party emerged as the National Party. The National Party promoted Afrikaner identity and values, and was intent on imposing a system of apartheid, white supremacy and reducing ties with Britain.

The influence of Britain

South Africa had been a dominion within the British Empire since 1910. English-speaking parties dominated South African government during the interwar years, although they were just as racist and segregationist as the National Party, producing the raft of discriminatory laws to maintain white supremacy. Afrikaners, however, resented British influence:

- They had been defeated in the second Boer War of 1899–1902 (a war fought to expel the British) and resented the settlement which saw South Africa created as a British dominion.
- They had resented South Africa supporting Britain in the First World War: many had strong ties to Germany.
- They resented English speakers' dominance in the economy.

1910 Constitution

As a dominion, the British government appointed a governor general and a two-house legislature, the Parliament, comprising the Senate and House of Assembly. The 50 Senators in the Senate were appointed either by the governor general or by the Regional Assemblies of the four provinces of Cape Province, Natal, Orange Free State and Transvaal (see map on page 6). The membership of the House of Assembly was usually elected every five years. The two main

KEY TERMS

Dutch Reformed Church The Afrikaner Church which supported apartheid.

Laager mentality The belief among Afrikaners of the need to stick together in the face of outside criticism: the analogy refers to how Boers would defend themselves within camps (laagers) if attacked by Africans during the period of settlement.

Broederbond Hugely influential Afrikaner organisation promoting apartheid and Afrikaner hegemony.

parties were the Unionists, dominated by English speakers who sought to maintain close ties with Britain, and the National Party, comprised mainly of Afrikaners who sought a more independent path with the ultimate goal of a republic. Any legislation to change the 1910 constitution needed a two-thirds majority in a joint sitting of both legislative Houses to pass.

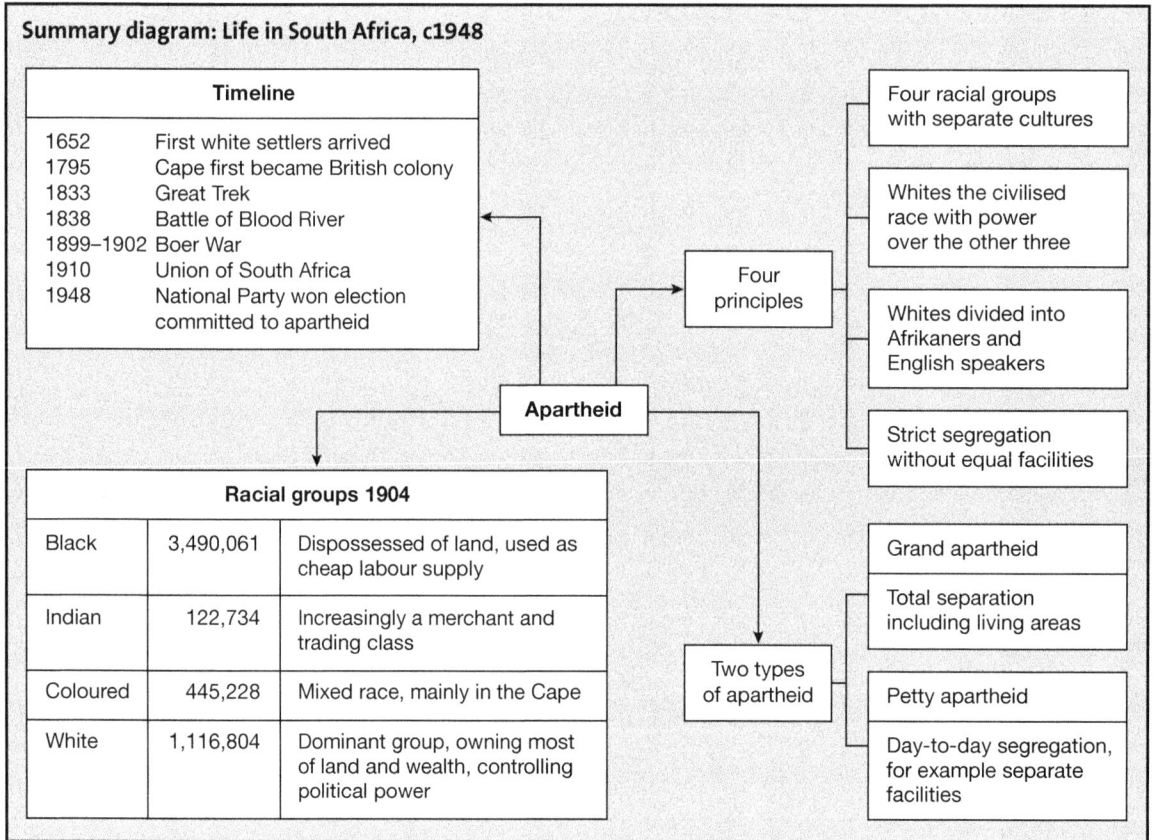

Summary diagram: Life in South Africa, c1948

Timeline

1652	First white settlers arrived
1795	Cape first became British colony
1833	Great Trek
1838	Battle of Blood River
1899–1902	Boer War
1910	Union of South Africa
1948	National Party won election committed to apartheid

Four principles

- Four racial groups with separate cultures
- Whites the civilised race with power over the other three
- Whites divided into Afrikaners and English speakers
- Strict segregation without equal facilities

Apartheid

Racial groups 1904

Black	3,490,061	Dispossessed of land, used as cheap labour supply
Indian	122,734	Increasingly a merchant and trading class
Coloured	445,228	Mixed race, mainly in the Cape
White	1,116,804	Dominant group, owning most of land and wealth, controlling political power

Two types of apartheid

- Grand apartheid
- Total separation including living areas
- Petty apartheid
- Day-to-day segregation, for example separate facilities

2 Reasons for the National Party victory, 1948

▶ *How did the National Party win control of South Africa's Parliament?*

In the 1948 elections, the National Party won 79 seats to the United Party's 71. The new government under **D.F. Malan** was committed to an extensive policy of apartheid, in which the races were segregated as much as possible. The National Party was to win every further election until the demise of apartheid in 1994. This section explains how the Second World War's impact on the economy, and its cultural impact, divided Afrikaners and contributed to increasing Afrikaner nationalism.

> 🔑 **KEY FIGURE**
>
> **D.F. Malan (1874–1959)**
> The National Party prime minister who introduced the apartheid state before retiring in 1954.

The impact of the Second World War on the economy

The need for labour meant many of the laws relating to the employment of Africans were relaxed: of the 125,000 extra workers employed in manufacturing during the war years, just 25 per cent were white people. Although Africans received far less pay than white people, many Afrikaners feared Africans would take their jobs once the war was over.

Table 1.3 Election results to the House of Assembly, 1948–89

Year	National Party	United Party	Others	Prime minister	Notes
1948	79	71	0	D.F. Malan	Both National and United Party had coalition partners
1953	94	57	5	D.F. Malan, retired 1954 J.G. Strijdom	
1958	103	53	0	J.G. Strijdom, died 1958 H. Verwoerd	
1961	105	49	0	H. Verwoerd	
1966	126	39	1	H. Verwoerd, assassinated 1966 J. Vorster	
1970	117	47	1	J. Vorster	
1974	134	41	6	J. Vorster	
1977	134		34	J. Vorster retired, P.W. Botha	United Party had dissolved itself
1981	131		34	P.W. Botha	
1987	124		43	P.W. Botha, retired through ill health 1989	First House of Assembly elections under the 1983 constitution: Botha was executive president
1989	94		72	F.W. de Klerk	

KEY FIGURE

Jan Smuts (1870–1950)
Former Boer general and prime minister who led the United Party. He was a well-respected international figure at the time.

In a speech in January 1942, the leader of the ruling United Party, **Jan Smuts**, suggested that the policy of racial segregation had been a failure for Africans, citing statistics of African poverty and infant mortality. Afrikaners particularly feared that the United Party, under the guidance of Deputy Prime Minister Jan Hofmeyr, was preparing a more moderate race policy. Hofmeyr, in particular, encouraged the education of Africans to provide a more skilled workforce, and relaxed the pass laws in 1942 to facilitate employment in urban areas. In a speech to the moderate Institute of Race Relations in Cape Town in January 1942, Prime Minister Jan Smuts had even gone so far as to argue that the policy of racial segregation had been a failure for Africans, citing statistics of African poverty and infant mortality as examples. His government made tentative efforts to improve their situation, introducing unemployment insurance schemes and free school meals. In 1946, a Commission to investigate the possibility of a National Health Service even recommended a non-discriminatory healthcare system – although this was not taken any further.

The growth of Afrikaner nationalism and Nazi support

During the Second World War, while many joined with English speakers in supporting the Allies (half the white South African male population of military age, 180,000 men, joined the Allied forces), some Afrikaners actively worked for a Nazi victory, for example by broadcasting and publishing pro-Nazi material. Hendrik Verwoerd (see page 23), the future prime minister, became the editor of *Die Transvaler*, the newspaper of the National Party. This became notorious during the war not only for its pro-Nazi stance but also for its anti-Semitism.

Many Afrikaners joined the openly pro-fascist Greyshirt movement, or supported the Oxwagon Sentinel, formed after the Battle of Blood River centenary (see below) and modelled on the Nazi Party. It claimed 250,000 members by 1939. Many were interned as potential traitors during the war years.

United Party moderation of race policies

As the party in government at the time of wartime victory in 1945, the United Party expected to remain in power. However, it was faced with various problems:

- The outgoing prime minister, Jan Smuts, was old and tired. As an international statesman he had been heavily involved in both the Allied leadership during the war and the post-war peace settlements. As a result, many white South Africans felt he was out of touch with developments in South Africa.
- The election campaign lacked lustre and seemed empty of new ideas.
- The United Party seemed particularly weak on race relations, which the Nationalists were able to exploit to good effect, winning English-speaking votes as a result.

Post-war reunity among Afrikaners

Once the war was over and Germany defeated, Afrikaners tended to unite again under the National Party banner, which emphasised their common interests:

- They did not trust the English-speaking parties.
- In 1938, the Voortrekker monument, celebrating the centenary of the Battle of Blood River, was built: it created a real sense of Afrikaner identity.
- Afrikaner finance concerns were set up to help Afrikaners start their own businesses.
- The Dutch Reformed Church provided Afrikaner schools and cultural activities to develop a pride in Afrikaner identity.

National Party policy on race

Many white South Africans distrusted the United Party on its race policies. During the election campaign, Smuts suggested the influx of Africans into white areas for employment should continue. Although he emphasised that Africans should continue to live in strictly segregated and regulated communities, the National Party went one step further with their own simple and easily comprehensible policy – apartheid, with separation of the races as far as possible. Africans should only be allowed in South Africa as guest workers, and otherwise be confined to their reserves. Of course, all the complexities of this policy had not been worked through, and there were considerable divisions as to the practicalities of separation, but the basic premise was straightforward – and appealed to many English speakers as well as Afrikaners.

SOURCE B

Extract from *The Times*, 'South Africa elections – from our own correspondent 26 May 1948'. *The Times* is a well-respected and authoritative British newspaper.

The Nationalists have been … assiduous in exploiting against the Government every little discomfort, every possible cause of fear … they are even trying to proselytise [convert] English speaking voters on the plea that they were temporarily putting their republicanism into cold storage in order to secure the collaboration of both European groups in solving the native problem for all time.

This then is the theme of their electioneering, and the main target of their attack is Mr. J.H. Hofmeyr, the deputy prime minister. Mr. Hofmeyr … has repeatedly said … that discrimination on grounds of race alone is morally wrong …

The Nationalists argue that Mr. Hofmeyr will advocate a policy of economic and political equality for all races which must lead to social equality, intermarriage and the end of white race and white civilization in South Africa. The overtones and undertones of this argument are calculated to give the ignorant and prejudiced the impression that almost as soon as Mr. Hofmeyr comes to power, natives will be asking for their sister's hand in marriage.

Why, according to Source B, are the Nationalists attacking Mr Hofmeyr?

Afrikaners developed the National Party by organising at local levels to win support and developing strategies for the achievement of power. In particular, Albert Hertzog's mineworkers' union was effective in local organisation in the Transvaal, while strong local organisations were built up in the Cape, influenced by a future prime minister, P.W. Botha. During the election the nationalists won six seats in the gold-mining areas of Witwatersrand where Hertzog's miners had played a key role in organising the electoral campaign.

Weighting of the constituencies

Despite all these factors, the most important reason why the Nationalists won may have been a technical one – that the rural constituencies, where most of their supporters still lived, were weighted more heavily in terms of representation than the urban ones – in fact, 15 per cent more. This meant that it needed fifteen per cent more votes to win a seat in an urban area than a rural one. In the election, the United Party won 50 per cent of the popular vote and the nationalists 40 per cent. However, because of this weighting, the nationalists still won because they won more constituencies – 79 to the United Party's 71.

International pressures for change

The immediate international response to the National Party victory was muted because many European countries, such as Britain and France, still had empires in which the indigenous populations were subservient. South Africa was surrounded by pliant neighbours, such as Rhodesia (present-day Zimbabwe), part of the British Empire, and Angola and Mozambique governed by Portugal. South Africa was itself in charge of South West Africa (later called Namibia).

However, international criticism did grow, particularly as anti-colonial movements developed. Most criticism was from individuals and specific groups rather than the governments of influential countries.

The United Nations

The first international discussion on apartheid had been initiated by India, which was concerned about the treatment of Indians in South Africa as early as 1946. Thereafter, the **United Nations General Council** condemned apartheid every year from 1952. However, the USA was very influential within the **United Nations** (UN), especially in its **Security Council**. South Africa avoided pressure to change because it was seen as a reliable ally against the growth of **communism**, and profitable for investment. The situation was to change significantly by the end of the 1950s but, initially at least, the South African government was free to act without international coercion.

KEY TERMS

United Nations General Council The legislature of the United Nations.

United Nations Formed in 1945, largely to solve international disputes and problems.

Security Council The executive of the UN, responsible for international peace keeping.

Communism Belief that the planning and control of the economy and society should all be controlled by the state. People should be rewarded according to the value of their contribution to society. Nationalist politicians opposed in particular the belief that all should have equality of opportunity regardless of ethnicity.

Summary diagram: Reasons for the National Party victory, 1948

National Party Coalition (HNP and Afrikaner Party)	vs	United Party Coalition (UP and SALP)

Apartheid: separation of races into distinct groups		Segregation but recognised need for cheap African labour

Apartheid policy		Segregation policy

79 seats		71 seats

Why they won		**Why they were defeated**
• Energetic campaign • Accused United Party of promoting racial integration • Weighting in rural areas more likely to support National Party		• Poor campaign • Smuts old and tired • Weak policies, for example on race

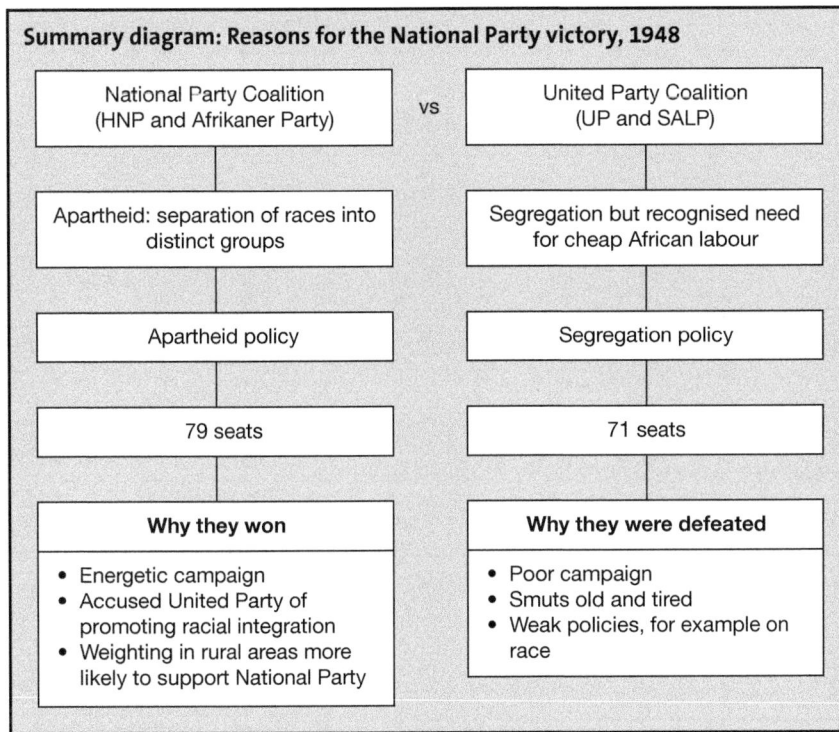

3 Codifying and implementing apartheid, 1948–59

▶ *How far was apartheid implemented in the period 1948–59?*

The years 1948–59 saw the effective application of apartheid in all its forms and the development of the National Party as the natural party of government in South Africa.

Strengthening the National Party

The new government had two overarching aims:

- To impose white supremacy through an all-embracing system of apartheid.
- To end political ties with Britain and form a republic (see pages 48–50).

Grand and petty apartheid

The National Party strategy envisaged a total system of apartheid. Many examples of segregation had preceded their electoral victory, for example the carrying of passes. Now, however, it was all formalised in national law. There were two broad types of apartheid:

- *Grand apartheid.* This was the overall strategy of keeping the different races separated as much as possible; for example, by ensuring they lived in separate areas.
- *Petty apartheid.* This was the day-to-day restrictions, such as separate facilities, for example public amenities and transport waiting rooms. Many Africans found this more wearying than grand apartheid.

The National Party did not have precise blueprints for the implementation of apartheid, for example the practical application of grand and petty apartheid throughout the country in all areas of activity. Its main ambition in the early years of government was to stay in power. However, apartheid was the centre of its platform. The National Party maintained its support and achieved its vision of apartheid through the strategies considered below.

Increasing Afrikaner influence in the state apparatus

The state became increasingly dominated by Afrikaners. As English-speaking civil servants retired, for example, they were replaced by Afrikaners. This was achieved in part by patronage – those in important positions appointed people they favoured – and justified by the assertion that senior civil servants should be bilingual. By 1959, only six out of 40 heads of government departments were English speakers. As the government grew in terms of power and activities, and state organisations developed, such as the Electricity Supply Corporation, key posts went to Afrikaners. This trend was especially noteworthy in the security forces.

Broederbond

The Broederbond (see page 9) grew in influence to such an extent that it almost became the government. All senior National Party politicians and government officials were expected to maintain close ties with it. Its policy documents effectively became government thinking.

Extension of voters

Conscious of its narrow majority in Parliament, the government created six more seats in South West Africa (Namibia), where residents would be expected to vote for the Nationalists. In South Africa, the average number of voters in a constituency was 24,000; each of the new six seats contained between 9000 and 12,000 voters, so this nationalist stronghold held twice the number of seats it would otherwise have been entitled to.

The disfranchisement of coloured voters (the Separate Representation of Voters Act 1951)

The government sought an all-white electorate and introduced a measure to abolish the right of coloured South Africans to vote. This right was protected by the 1910 Constitution (see page 9). The measure to abolish it required a two-thirds majority in a joint sitting of both Houses of Parliament. Against the rules of the court, the National Party introduced their Separate Representation of Voters Bill (1951) separately into each House instead. The United Party successfully contested this. However, after its 1953 electoral victory, the government enlarged the senate from 48 to 89 members (the Senate Act 1955) to ensure that the National Party had the required majority. The measure became law, with coloured Cape voters disenfranchised in February 1956.

Subsequently, the party grew in support: by the elections of 1958 and 1961 it had a majority of over 50 seats, which it was able to maintain throughout the apartheid period (see page 11). This was due both to party organisation and control, and to the development of a bureaucracy which became dominated by Afrikaners. This was particularly true of the Department of Native Affairs, which administered apartheid. Its budget doubled from £3,087,000 in 1946 to £7,205,250 by 1960. The security forces also grew significantly (see pages 45 and 67). Many Afrikaners quite simply were tied to the continuation of National Party government because they relied on it for their livelihoods.

Apartheid laws

Although apartheid intensified during the premiership of Hendrik Verwoerd in the later 1950s, the foundations were created in the years following the National Party's victory in 1948. There were eventually to be more than 300 such laws.

Divide and rule

The intention was always to divide and rule: to keep the different races as far part as possible, and keep Africans divided into their different tribal units to emphasise their own nationalities. Townships themselves were often divided into tribal areas; **Bantustans** were exclusive for members of different tribal groups. The idea of Africanism was complete anathema to white people. If Africans were divided into their tribal groups, as opposed to all being united under 'African', white people would no longer be a minority group. The intention was to keep all racial groups as separate from each other as possible.

While many Acts were introduced to cover every possible aspect of racial division, often building on ones already in existence, the cornerstone was the 1950 Population Registration Act.

Population Registration Act 1950

This Act designated the ethnic category of everyone, divided initially into 'black', 'white' and 'coloured', with 'Indian' added later. It insisted the different groups be kept strictly separate. Everyone was registered according to their ethnic group and issued with an identity card. Later amendments to the Act in 1964 and 1967 placed greater stress on appearance and **genealogy** to prevent light-skinned members of other groups passing themselves off as white.

> **KEY TERMS**
>
> **Bantustans** African homelands or tribal reserves.
>
> **Genealogy** Study of one's family, to identify one's roots.

Prohibition of Mixed Marriages Act 1949 and Immorality Act 1949

Unsurprisingly, mixed marriages were rare, although, bizarrely, they were not illegal: however sexual relations within such marriages were, according to the 1927 Immorality Act. In 1949 and 1950, mixed marriages and sexual relations between members of different ethnic groups were made illegal. White people could be imprisoned for disobeying the latter, although their punishment was not usually as severe as for members of other groups, including their sexual partners.

Group Areas Act 1950

This Act authorised the government to designate a particular area for occupation by one particular ethnic group. Members of other ethnic groups in this area were to be forcibly evicted. The Act was responsible for the forcible eviction of 3.5 million Africans between 1951 and 1986, with over 1 million of these being deported from urban areas into the tribal areas or Bantustans (see pages 20 and 26). One of the most noted results of the Group Areas Act was the destruction of the mixed race suburb of Sophiatown in Johannesburg.

Sophiatown

Sophiatown was the only place in South Africa where Africans were allowed to own property. Its population also included Indians and some white people who had lived there before its designation as an African area, so it was a truly multi-ethnic area. In 1953, it had an official population of 39,186, although some estimates place it as high as 60,000. Population density may have been as much as 150 people per acre. Often, many families lived in one room. Over 70 per cent of the dwellings in Sophiatown could be classed as slums. This was because as more and more people moved in, attracted to its vibrant life and proximity to the city centre of Johannesburg, residents began to build sheds – sometimes called stands – in any available space on their properties. Apart from the housing situation, white people had been complaining for years about Sophiatown, particularly as their own suburbs, such as Westdene and Newlands, encroached upon it.

Forced removals

The 1950 Group Areas Act gave the government control over relocations. In 1953, it began building a new township, Meadowlands (in the area now called **Soweto**). The Natives Resettlement Act, a year later, enabled the government to specifically move Africans from anywhere in and next to Johannesburg to any other area. Thus, the stage was set: notices were given for the eviction and removal of the first of Sophiatown's residents. On 10 February 1955, a day of heavy rain, these were ruthlessly effected.

Many observers have argued that resistance to the removals was hopeless in the face of the force the authorities were prepared to use. Nelson Mandela, writing in 1994, argued that resistance failed in Sophiatown because of government resolve.

KEY TERM

Soweto An acronym for South Western Townships (African townships on the edge of Johannesburg).

SOURCE C

Extract from Nelson Mandela, *Long Walk to Freedom*, Abacus, 2013, pages 193–4. Mandela was a leading anti-apartheid activist who became the first president of a democratic South Africa in 1994 (see page 27 for a detailed profile).

*We never provided the people with an alternative to moving to Meadowlands. When the people in Sophiatown realized we could neither stop the government not provide them with housing elsewhere, their own resistance waned and the flow of people to Meadowlands increased. Many tenants moved willingly, for they found they would have more space and cleaner housing in Meadowlands. We did not take into account the different situations of landlords and tenants. While the landlords had reasons to stay, many tenants had an incentive to leave. The ANC [African National Congress] was criticized by a number of **Africanist** members who accused the leadership of protecting the interests of the landlords at the expense of the tenants.*

The lesson I took away from the campaign was that in the end, we had no alternative to armed and violent resistance. Over and over again, we had used all the nonviolent weapons in our arsenal – speeches, deputations, threats, marches, strikes, stay-aways, voluntary imprisonment – to no avail, for whatever we did was met by an iron hand. A freedom fighter learns the hard way that it is the oppressor who defines the nature of the struggle, and the oppressed is often left no recourse but to use methods that mirror those of the oppressor. At a certain point, one can only fight fire with fire.

> How useful is Source C in explaining the futility of resistance to the Sophiatown removals?

> **KEY TERM**
>
> **Africanist** Refers to Africanism, the policy of black Africans to fight against apartheid without help from other ethnic groups.

Reasons for the removals

The government gave various reasons for the forced removal of mixed areas, notably that the different races were not able to live together peacefully, and that they needed to clear the slums. Undoubtedly, much of Sophiatown and, indeed, many other non-white areas were slums because little was ever invested in their infrastructure. There was, however, no evidence to suggest the races could not get along together in Sophiatown. Indeed, it may be because the races seemed to live harmoniously together that it became a crushing issue for the authorities. However, ultimately the prime motive for its destruction was to keep people of colour in certain areas and, particularly for Africans, in townships where transience (the temporary nature of African residence in white South Africa) was emphasised. The true *homes* of Africans were meant to be in the tribal homelands.

Triomf

After the first dispersals, Sophiatown was gradually emptied as new quarters were made ready in Meadowlands. Although the final residents were not removed until 1959, Sophiatown remained largely a wasteland for years during and after the removals. Its name was removed from maps, and in 1962 it became an all-white suburb called Triomph or Triomf: Afrikaans for 'triumph' – the name was an insult to non-white people and a powerful assertion of the government's resolve.

Bantu Authorities Act 1951

This Act reiterated the assertion that the home areas for Africans, and the only places they were entitled to live, were their 'tribal reserves' set out in the 1911 and 1936 legislation. As Africans were now treated as foreigners in white South Africa, the Native Representative Council established in 1936 (see page 5) was abolished. The tribal reserves were to be governed by tribal leaders designated by the government. However, these could be deposed if they proved uncooperative (see page 35). Many chose to comply because it allowed them to maintain some authority, and the alternative such as direct rule from Pretoria might be worse. Tribal leaders were ostensibly responsible for allocation of land, development programmes and welfare policies. Yet, the problem remained that the homelands were never going to be self-sufficient.

Taken together, the laws regarding residence and the governance of tribal reserves emphasised that Africans had no permanent place in white South Africa and that their presence was only tolerated as a source of cheap labour. The Group Areas Act reiterated that different ethnic groups should live away from each other and any interaction between them should be kept to a minimum.

Pass laws and education

Apartheid treated black Africans as a subservient race only tolerated as guest workers in white South Africa. Two of the means by which this was focused on a day-to-day level were through pass laws and education.

Pass laws: the Native Laws Amendment Act 1952

This Act was also known as the Abolition of Passes and Co-ordination of Documents Act. It standardised the use of passes by Africans throughout South Africa by officially abolishing existing passes and replacing them with reference books. Previously, the precise details of what information Africans needed to carry with their passes varied between provinces. The Act now stated specifically:

- All Africans had to carry reference books at all times. This included all men and women: the latter had previously been excluded from pass laws.
- Neither African men nor women could remain in urban areas for 70 hours after their permits had expired.
- No African could live permanently in an urban area unless they had been born there, or lived there for over fifteen years, or been with the same employer for over ten years.
- National reference books were issued, replacing the regional ones. The pass contained a photograph, employment record and personal details such as marital status. It was a criminal offence not to carry it.

Impact of the Act

In effect, the Act's purpose was to standardise the use of passes throughout South Africa. The abolition of passes and their replacement with reference books was simply a matter of form. The use of passes in practice became even more rigorously enforced and most people still called them passes rather than reference books.

Some historians, for example William Beinart (1994), have seen this Act as particularly important in the control of Africans. While other groups had to carry identity cards, Africans needed this complex and bulky document with them at all times. One member of the Black Sash (see page 33) recalled being shocked by an African woman who explained why she, and hundreds of other African females, always had their babies with them: if they left their breastfeeding babies with child-minders, and were found to have any problems with their passes by the police, they could be arrested and deported to a homeland, and would have to leave their baby behind.

One legal expert, Professor Julius Lewin of Witwatersrand University, reported that the pass system was so complex that no African could obey it even if he had wanted to. If any African was stopped by an officer pedantic enough he would inevitably be able to discover some infringement. This was particularly the case when one considers that many Africans were at best semi-literate and unable to read much of the information in their passes. In the early 1950s, there were 968,593 arrests for violations of the pass laws with 861,269 convictions.

SOURCE D

Photograph of police checking passes in Johannesburg train station, 1956.

What does the photograph in Source D suggest about the use of passes?

SOURCE E

Extract from N.J. Rhodie MA and Professor Dr H.J. Venter, *Apartheid: A Socio-historical Exposition of the Origin and Development of the Apartheid Idea*, published by HAUM, Cape Town and Pretoria, no date (probably late 1950s), page 218. This work attempted to justify apartheid.

Any apartheid measure can be difficult to implement if the Bantu is not subjected to an effective system of identification. The Central Reference Bureau, which was established on 2nd January 1953, as a direct result of the Natives (Abolition of Passes and Co-ordination of Documents) Act of 1952, to a considerable degree satisfies this need. The Bureau makes provision for an identification booklet called a 'reference book' in which is consolidated all the information which was previously contained in several separate documents. On 1st February 1958, the reference book system was begun officially for all male Bantu over the age of 16 years. During the three months between 1st February, and 30th April 1958, 3,281,192 reference books were issued to Bantu males. During the same period, 825,509 Bantu women applied for reference books of their own accord. The creation of the Central Reference Bureau is not to stigmatise the Bantu with its identification system but simply to make easier their administration on an apartheid basis.

Education: Bantu Education Act 1953

This was largely the brainchild of Minister for Native Affairs Hendrik Verwoerd and the Eiselen Commission he appointed in 1949 to investigate African education.

Education before the National Party victory

The vast majority of education for Africans was provided by Church-run **mission schools**. In 1945, there were 4360 mission schools and 230 government-run ones. The state spent sixteen times as much on education for white children as it did for Africans.

By 1948, the system was breaking down. With poor funding, often dilapidated buildings and insufficient resources, the schools could no longer maintain their functions. The rise in African populations and urbanisation meant they were vastly overcrowded and regularly had to turn prospective pupils away. The reality was that less than 33 per cent of African children attended school at all.

The Eiselen Report

As minister of native affairs, Verwoerd worked very closely with the department secretary, Werner Eiselen, an anthropologist, expert on native affairs and author of many tracts on the need for apartheid. In 1949, Eiselen was charged with investigating African education and making recommendations for its development. He believed it was important to protect Africans from Western influences, which he believed harmed their culture. He felt that Africans could

Hendrik Verwoerd

1901	Born in the Netherlands but family moved to South Africa
1912	Family moved to Rhodesia
1927	Appointed professor of applied psychology at the Afrikaner University of Stellenbosch
1937	Became editor of National Party newspaper *Die Transvaler*
1950	Appointed minister of native affairs
1958	Became prime minister and intensified apartheid
1960	Survived first assassination attempt
1966	Assassinated

Early life and academic career

Verwoerd was born in the Netherlands in 1901 and moved to South Africa two years later. He may have seen himself as something of an outsider, and wanted to prove himself as the epitome of Afrikaner values. His father was a building contractor who became a missionary. Much of Verwoerd's early life was spent among English speakers, first in the Cape and then in the British colony of Rhodesia, now Zimbabwe, where he was marked out for his Afrikaner accent.

Verwoerd became professor of applied psychology at the University of Stellenbosch and editor of *Die Transvaler*, the Transvaal newspaper aimed at an Afrikaner audience. During the Second World War it became notorious not only for its pro-Nazi stance but also for its anti-Semitism.

Minister of native affairs

As minister of Bantu affairs, Verwoerd was particularly associated with the Bantu Education Act, which prepared Africans for their lowly station in white South Africa. Verwoerd very famously asked, 'What is the point of teaching a Bantu child mathematics when he cannot use it in practice?' In fact, his ideas on race owed much to eugenics, which advanced the concept of racial hierarchy and the dangers of **miscegenation**. Verwoerd genuinely believed Africans would be happier developing at their own inferior level and celebrating their own culture. He did not believe in complete separation because he recognised white South Africa needed Africans as a source of unskilled labour. However, he insisted their position in white South Africa could only be transient, dependent on their having employment.

Prime minister

Verwoerd became prime minister in 1958 and intensified apartheid notably through the creation and development of Bantustans or tribal homelands. He believed these should one day be independent nations. He also oversaw the move to a republic in 1960 and withdrawal from the Commonwealth. Verwoerd's period in office saw the beginning of the most confident period of apartheid and economic prosperity for white South Africans. Verwoerd survived one assassination attempt in 1960 but succumbed to a second in 1966.

best develop as a people within their own pastoral traditions: he argued that apartheid, in fact, protected Africans from harmful Western influences. This idea, to a large extent, was reflected in his report, which advocated:

- a curriculum based on the limited skills Africans needed to function as a reservoir of cheap labour
- the growth in political control of education by the government through the eventual creation of a Department of Bantu Education.

The report laid the foundation for the subsequent legislation through its emphasis on strict apartheid in education and the limited curriculum for African children.

KEY TERM

Miscegenation Mixing of different racial groups through marriage and sexual relations.

The Bantu Education Act brought about the following:

- The removal of control of African education from the Ministry of Education to the Ministry for Native Affairs.
- An end to state subsidies for mission schools, so most were forced to close.
- An expansion of the government-run system and setting of a limited vocational-based curricula. The work of the Department of Native Affairs grew significantly; the Act, for example, gave it the management of 26,000 African teachers. In 1958, a separate Department of Bantu Education was created to meet this increased workload.

Verwoerd said, 'What is the purpose of teaching a Bantu child mathematics?' He meant that it was harmful to give Africans ideas above their station; all it would achieve was anger and discontent that their expectations could never be realised.

Impact of the Bantu Education Act

While everyone agreed that education needed to be reformed, few were satisfied with this solution. African National Congress (ANC) leader Professor Z.K. Matthews of Fort Hare University (see page 25) said, 'Education for ignorance and inferiority in Verwoerd's schools is worse than no education at all.'

All the Churches with the exception of the Dutch Reformed Church opposed the Bantu Education Act. Nevertheless, the government insisted, saying that mission schools must either be handed over to the government by December 1954 or accept a decrease in subsidies until they ceased altogether and the schools became fully independent. The vast majority of mission schools closed, although the Roman Catholic Church, **Seventh Day Adventists** and some Jewish groups kept theirs open. Some Africans began to operate their own unofficial schools in garages and living rooms. Sixty-seven out of 70 pupils at one unofficial school even managed to pass their Standard 6 exams. When the government passed a law to outlaw unofficial education for Africans, they were renamed 'Cultural Clubs' to avoid being illegal, but lack of funds forced most of them to close.

Most Churches complied with the terms of the Act and handed over their schools because they wanted to keep African children off the streets (see page 42). However, Bishop of Johannesburg Ambrose Reeves refused and reopened Anglican schools as private institutions, charging fees of 50 pence per month. However, most parents could not afford even this, and the huge waiting lists meant that many children were turned away.

Protests against the Act

Many Africans had no wish to send their children to schools where they would be taught white superiority and the limited role of the African.

The ANC lacked the resources to provide alternative education for all but a few. Nevertheless, the annual ANC conference at Durban in December 1954 voted

KEY TERM

Seventh Day Adventists
Religious group who see Saturday as the Sabbath.

for an indefinite boycott of the new government-run schools. Verwoerd said in return that all schools affected by a boycott would be closed on the grounds that if children did not want to attend, the schools were unnecessary. Any children boycotting schools would not be readmitted. As a result, the boycott was only partially successful. In the East Rand in Johannesburg, where ANC support was particularly strong, thousands stayed home and **pickets** forced those who wanted to go to school to leave. In most areas, however, the schools continued as normal. The potential consequences of a boycott, for example the closure of affected schools or children never being able to attend school in the future, were too severe.

As the boycott fizzled out, the government did relent and allow those who wanted to attend their schools. Nevertheless, in the long term, they may have unwittingly politicised many children by the frustrations generated by the poor-quality education on offer and the resultant lack of opportunities. Most African children and their parents realised their education was inferior to that of white students and was being used as a weapon to limit their opportunities for advancement in the apartheid society.

Extension of Universities Act 1959

There were four English-language universities, four Afrikaner universities and one specifically for non-white students, Fort Hare, in South Africa during the 1950s. At Fort Hare, coloured, Indians and African students studied in an integrated environment under both white and non-white lecturers; its non-discriminatory principle was highly valued and defended. Three of the English-speaking universities also took non-white students and indeed employed some non-white lecturers; in 1954, **Robert Sobukwe** was employed to teach African studies at the University of Witwatersrand. All universities were dependent on government subsidies. Unsurprisingly, the National Party's government remained unhappy about Africans, in particular, studying to degree level and beyond. Therefore, in 1959, the Extension of Universities Act was passed to ban the English-language universities from accepting African students. By way of recompense, three new strictly segregated colleges were opened for coloured, Indian and Zulu students, and another for Africans in the Transvaal. Fort Hare remained under a new and more conciliatory Principal for Xhosa-speaking students only.

The Tomlinson Report and Bantustans

The Tomlinson Commission in 1956 reported on how the homelands might be developed. Its report reasserted the following:

- Homelands could never support more than two-thirds of their populations, and advised more land be allocated.
- Policies of **betterment** be developed to combat problems such as soil erosion. It was estimated that the cost of this would be at least £100 million.

- The agricultural workforce should be reduced. Industrial concerns could be developed just outside the borders and towns developed just within, so homeland residents could commute for employment.

The government broadly accepted the report's findings, although it had no intention of providing more land, and disliked the recommendations concerning industrial developments, because, by the use of cheap labour, such ventures would undercut white-staffed competitors.

Bantu Self-government Act 1959

This set up eight self-governing homelands in which black Africans were to be citizens. By making these homelands 'independent', removing them officially from South African statistics, Afrikaners and English-speaking white people would effectively be the largest ethnic group in South Africa.

The 1951 Bantu Authorities Act (see page 20) and the subsequent Bantu Self-government Act of 1959 provided the key for grand apartheid, however, and from this developed the ambitious policy of Bantustans as separate and independent countries (see page 65).

Political suppression and the Treason Trial

South Africa remained a democracy for white voters, and white opposition parties were tolerated so long as they were peaceful and did not attempt to recruit black Africans. However, any opposition from non-white groups was often brutally suppressed, and the security forces deployed both physical and psychological pressure. Different groups had protested against apartheid since its inception, and women and youth groups were involved besides adult men (see page 32). The main legal authority for repression in the 1950s was the Suppression of Communism Act 1950.

Suppression of Communism Act 1950

The government genuinely believed Communist agitators were behind the majority of protests against apartheid. In suppressing communism, white South Africa was seen by the Western powers and the USA, in particular, as a reliable ally in the **Cold War**.

This Act defined communism as any scheme aimed 'at bringing about any political and social and economic change within the Union by the promotion of disturbance and disorder':

- Communism was, therefore, a euphemism for any form of unrest, and the Act could be used to imprison anyone for anything the authorities deemed subversive.
- The authorities could also ban organisations and individuals from contacting others for periods of up to five years by the use of **banning orders**. For many, this meant house arrest.

KEY TERMS

Cold War The hostility between the USA and the Union of Soviet Socialist Republics (USSR, or Soviet Union) in the post-Second World War era; this manifested itself in methods such as propaganda and gaining allies through economic aid.

Banning orders Measures restricting one's movements, limiting one to a certain specifically defined area or house arrest.

Nelson Mandela

1918	Born in Transkei into the Thembo royal family
1939	Entered Fort Hare University
1940	Expelled from university
1941	Moved to Johannesburg and began to train as a lawyer
1943	Joined ANC and co-founded the ANC Youth League
1952	Became involved in the Defiance Campaign; co-founded first African law firm in South Africa
1955	Key defendant in the Treason Trial
1961	Organised *Umkhonto we Sizwe* or Spear of the Nation (MK)
1964	Sentenced to life imprisonment following the Rivonia Trial
1990	Released and worked towards a peaceful post-apartheid settlement
1994	Became first fully democratically elected president
2013	Died

Early life and career

Mandela was born into a Thembo royal family of Transkei, where his father was adviser to the king. He entered Fort Hare University in 1939 but was expelled for, among other things, organising a protest about the quality of the food. Mandela fled to Johannesburg in 1941 to avoid an arranged marriage. He began to train as a lawyer and in 1952 co-founded, with Oliver Tambo, South Africa's first African law firm.

ANC activist, 1943–64

Mandela became increasingly politicised, joined the ANC and co-founded the ANC Youth League, which demanded more active protest, in 1943. In 1952, he helped organise the Defiance Campaign and in 1956 became a leading defendant in the Treason Trial. Despairing that peaceful protest would ever be successful, Mandela formed the MK in 1961 to begin an armed struggle. He was subsequently arrested and sentenced to life imprisonment in 1964, following the Rivonia Trial.

Imprisonment, release and presidency

Mandela remained a prisoner for 27 years, but during the 1980s, as apartheid faltered, was increasingly seen as one of the few people with stature enough to effect a peaceful transition to democracy. Mandela was released in 1990, and worked tirelessly to make this possible. In 1994, he became the first fully democratically elected president of South Africa, and was credited with uniting South Africa and ensuring that democracy became embedded. He lived until 2013, venerated as a world statesman.

The Act was to have a significant impact on the Communist Party of South Africa (CPSA) (see page 30).

Further repression

The government also passed other Acts of repression:

- In 1953, the Public Safety Act allowed the government to call a state of emergency for twelve months in the first instance, with powers to renew it indefinitely.
- The Criminal Law Amendment Act of 1953 stated that anyone accompanying a person found guilty of a crime would automatically be assumed guilty as well, and have to prove their innocence.
- The Censorship Acts in 1955 and 1956 censored any criticism in reports and literature that were being imported into South Africa.

- In 1956, the Riotous Assemblies Act outlawed any meetings which might engender hostility between the races, and prevented any 'banned' persons from addressing public meetings. This had been passed to prevent meetings such as the 1955 Congress of the People, which had led to the Freedom Charter (see page 33).

The main intention was to isolate would-be protesters and prevent seditious material from reaching their potential audience – with repression when it did.

The Treason Trial, 1956–61

Many different groups of all races had protested against the implementation of apartheid. At a People's Congress in Kliptown, in June 1955, these groups drew up a Freedom Charter, demanding equal rights for all in South Africa (see page 33).

KEY TERM

High treason Plotting to overthrow the state.

Eighteen months after the ratification of the Freedom Charter, on 5 December 1956, the authorities arrested 156 of those who had attended the Kliptown meeting and charged them with **high treason**. Those arraigned included the entire leadership of the ANC and most of that of the other opposition groups. After five months, they were accused of conspiring to overthrow the government and replace it with a Communist regime. The ensuing Treason Trial dragged on for five years.

From 1957 onwards, some defendants were released for lack of evidence and indictments were withdrawn against 73 defendants. The trial against the remaining 30 defendants finally began in August 1959. While the defendants were in court, they could find little time for either for covert activities or earning their livelihood. Nelson Mandela's and Oliver Tambo's law firm effectively went out of business during the trial (see pages 27 and 88 for their profiles).

In March 1961, the trial ended with the acquittal of all the defendants. The prosecution had failed to present a convincing case throughout the trial, and there was no evidence that any of those accused had ever been guilty of treason. However, there was no sense of rejoicing among dissidents.

Summary diagram: Codifying and implementing apartheid, 1948–59

```
                    Prohibition of Mixed              Bantu
                    Marriages Act 1949 and       Education Act 1953
                    Immorality Act 1950
                                                                              Extension of
  Separate Representation                                                  Universities Act 1959
    of Voters Act 1951                           State to control
                                                 African education
                                                                           University education
  Removal of coloured voters                                                   segregated
  from Cape electoral register

                                                                           Group Areas Act 1950
   Population Registration              Apartheid
        Act 1950                        legislation                      • Areas designated for specific
                                                                           racial groups
                                                                         • Sophiatown removals 1955
    Everyone registered
    according to race

                                                                          Bantu Authorities Act 1951
   Native Laws Amendment         Bantu Self-government Act
        Act 1952                          1952                           Africans should live in tribal homelands
                                                                         except if employed in white areas
  Closer regulation of passes and    Set up eight 'self-governing'
  conditions of residence in          homelands for Africans
         white areas
```

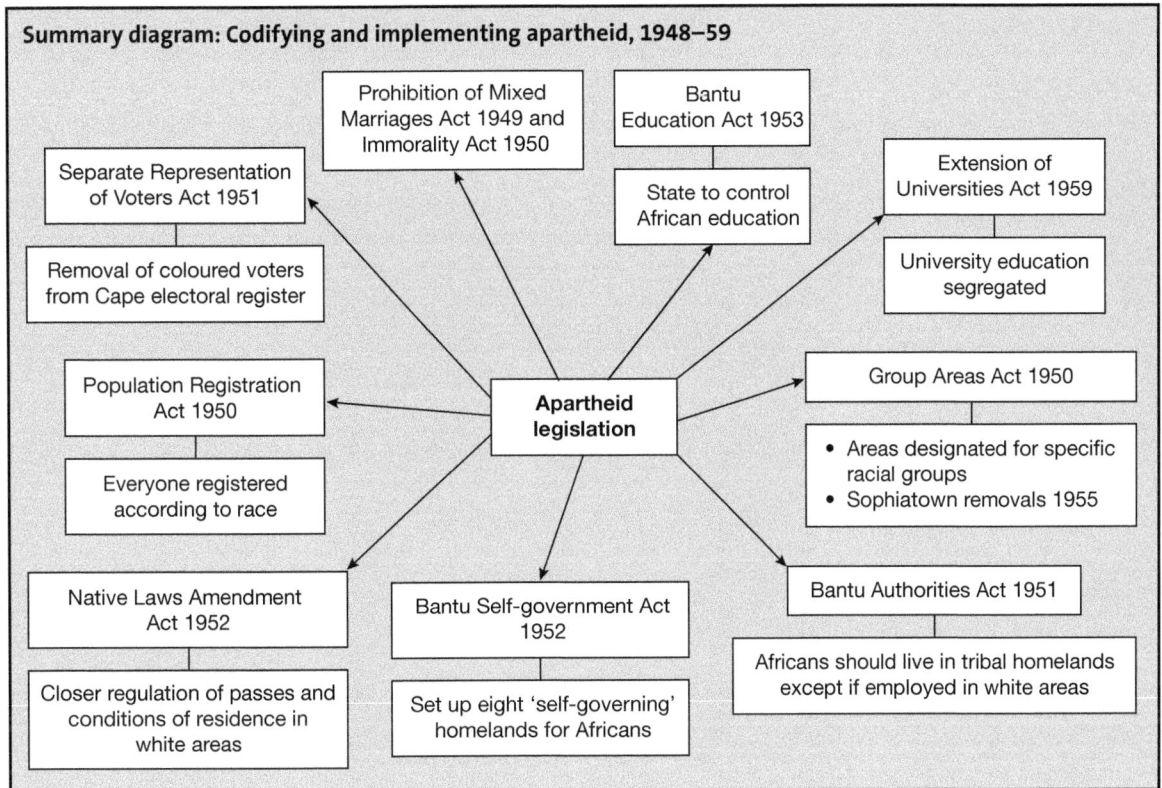

4 African nationalism, 1948–59

▶ *How successfully did Africans and other ethnic groups protest against apartheid in the period 1948–59?*

Africans and other ethnic groups had protested against segregation and discrimination since the beginnings of South Africa. While each racial group had its own organisations, some, notably the ANC, embraced all South Africans. In 1948, there were several key protest groups, all of whom adopted a policy of peaceful protest. By 1959, they were becoming increasingly militant in the face of frustrations with their lack of success and increasing government repression.

Political opposition in 1948

The main African opposition was led by the ANC. This had been formed in 1912 by a middle-class elite and had concentrated on debate and argument. However, it always supported campaigns to improve the lives of Africans and did attract **grass-roots support**.

🔑 **KEY TERM**

Grass-roots support
Backing at a local level.

KEY TERMS

Passive resistance Non-violent opposition.

Trade unions Worker-based organisations which aimed to improve working conditions for their members and sometimes became involved in anti-apartheid activities.

Civil disobedience Refusal to follow the law, such as refusing to carry passes.

KEY FIGURES

Alfred Xuma (1893–1962)

It was under Xuma's presidency of the ANC (1940–49) that the ANC Youth League was formed, but he was increasingly criticised as being out of touch with rank-and-file members, and felt to be too conservative.

Walter Sisulu (1912–2003)

Anti-apartheid activist and long-time associate of Nelson Mandela, with whom he shared 27 years' imprisonment on Robben Island: he was the founder of the ANC Youth League.

The South African Indian Congress (SAIC) had been founded in 1919 to support the promotion of rights of Indians and oppose segregation. It advocated **passive resistance** and sought to work with the ANC and other groups in a common front. To this end, an alliance was made with the ANC in March 1947: the so-called 'three doctors' pact' (as all the leaders had doctoral qualifications).

The Communist Party of South Africa (CPSA) was a multi-ethnic party founded in 1921 with the aim of organising Africans into **trade unions** and unite with white trade unionists on the basis of class rather than race. The CPSA often worked closely with the ANC, giving rise to the government accusation that the ANC leadership was itself Communist. After the Suppression of Communism Act (1950), the CPSA dissolved itself and became an illegal organisation, renaming itself the South African Communist Party (SACP). Its policy was that South Africa must become a state where all races were treated equally before communism could be successful there. Therefore, it continued to work with anti-apartheid groups, notably the ANC.

Cooperation between groups

By the mid-1930s, all non-white groups saw the need to cooperate in joint campaigns, but because of the restrictions on travel caused by the pass laws, simple communication was difficult enough, let alone joint action. In December 1935, 400 delegates did meet in Bloemfontein to establish the All-African Convention (AAC), which emphasised both loyalty to South Africa and its opposition to segregation. By the late 1940s, the scene was set for more radical and direct action campaigns, particularly in response to grand apartheid.

The revival of the ANC

From 1940, under the leadership of **Alfred Xuma**, the ANC began to work more closely with other organisations, such as the SAIC, to develop a policy of non-cooperation involving **civil disobedience**. Again, it also developed support at local levels, for example supporting the 1946 mine-workers' strike, which saw as many as 100,000 on strike and brutal repression by the security forces. However, it was still seen largely as an organisation run by and for urban elites. Younger members were questioning the pace of its activities, as compared with the more direct action, as exemplified by the unionists who were to organise the 1946 strike. In short, the ANC seemed to follow rather than lead developments in the struggle against apartheid.

The pace of ANC activities and frustrations over its demands being ignored by successive governments led to the growth of more radical movements within the organisation.

The ANC Youth League

In 1943, **Walter Sisulu** formed the ANC Youth League (ANCYL), which included a new generation of leaders such as Nelson Mandela, Oliver Tambo and

Robert Sobukwe (see page 25). The ANCYL sought a broader organisation with mass support. In its manifesto, the ANCYL advocated direct action rather than protests and discussion. It emphasised the community-based culture of Africans which could be built on to promote mass action. After the 1949 ANC conference, leaders of the ANCYL took control of the organisation, capturing key positions. Walter Sisulu, for example, became the first full-time ANC secretary.

Africanism

Some leaders felt the ANC should recruit only Africans, while others, such as Mandela and Tambo, felt the ANC should effectively be multi-ethnic and welcomed support from all groups, notably the Communists. This notion of Africanism was to be vital in the development of the anti-apartheid struggle.

The Basic Policy and Programme of Action

In 1948, partly as a response to the National Party electoral victory, the ANCYL created the Basic Policy, which proposed three positions:

- that Africans should unite as one group rather than members of different tribes
- that Africans had the right to the wealth and prosperity of Africa
- that Africans should accept the help of other sympathetic groups.

This was formalised in 1949 into a Programme of Action, emphasising the need for direct action against apartheid and stressing:

- the absolute rejection of white domination in South Africa
- a pro-African policy, which meant supporting African nationalism both within South Africa and in liberation campaigns against colonialism throughout the continent
- an assertion of pride in being African in the face of white assertions of racism and African inferiority
- a demand for mass and direct action to oppose apartheid.

The Defiance Campaign, 1952

The Defiance Campaign was the first large-scale example of direct action by the ANC. It was to be non-violent and divided into two stages:

- an initial stage of local protest in which supporters would break the law, for example, by refusing to carry passes and invite themselves for arrest – the idea being that the sheer numbers of those arrested would exceed the authorities' ability to cope and also show the weight of opposition to apartheid
- an extension of mass defiance with nationwide strikes and protests.

Over 10,000 people attended the inaugural meeting in Durban. The size of this crowd showed that the ANC was reaching a wide audience. Indeed, its membership rose from an estimated 4000 to over 100,000 after the campaign.

Results of the Defiance Campaign

Any significant, organised protest rattled the government. In the six months of the campaign, 8500 participants were indeed arrested for various acts of defiance – but the vast majority of 8 million Africans did not become involved. Nevertheless, the government subsequently passed a raft of measures to make civil disobedience a crime (see pages 27–8) and the campaign organisers, including Nelson Mandela, were inevitably arrested.

The end of the campaign

The Defiance Campaign formally ended in January 1953, having lasted for six months. It never moved beyond one mass protest in the eastern Cape, and there was little participation in rural areas.

One could argue that the campaign had only limited success, yet, by its end:

- The ANC had become a mass organisation led by committed and experienced activists.
- The ANC realised it could embarrass the government by tactics of protest and non-participation, but not topple it – in other words, campaigns such as Defiance would not be successful in themselves if their goal was to abolish apartheid, no matter how many people participated in them.

Women's pass protest, 1956

Women had always been involved in anti-apartheid protest. The Bantu Women's League, for example, had joined the ANC as early as 1918, and the ANC Women's League was formally inaugurated in 1948. The women's pass protest of 1956, however, saw a movement almost exclusively organised and put into action by women.

The Federation of South African Women (FSAW), formed in April 1954 by anti-apartheid activists such as Helen Joseph, and the president of the ANC Women's League, Lilian Ngoyi, organised a significant women's protest movement to protest against women having to register for passes and carry pass books, a new amendment to the pass laws (see page 20). On 9 August 1956, now known as Women's Day in South Africa, 20,000 women marched on Pretoria with a petition bearing 100,000 signatures. The government buildings were largely empty; they were received by Premier Strijdom's secretary but sent away with no promises for reform.

The protests continued: 1000 women protested in Lichtenburg in the western Transvaal when officials tried to register them, and the police fired into the crowd, killing two. At Nelspruit in eastern Transvaal, a group of women attacked the official charged with their registration. Five were arrested; 300 marched on the local police station to demand their release – the police response again was brutal. By March 1960, 3,020,281 or 75 per cent of the total African female population had been issued with passes but the fact of accepting them did not end their protests (see page 35).

Black Sash

One effect of the women's protest against passes was the radicalisation of the white protest group Black Sash, which supported this action and also began to open advice centres for non-white Africans. Black Sash arranged bail for arrested women who otherwise would not be allowed to return home to look after their children. The group also built up a pool of lawyers who would represent African women for minimal fees – and gradually the group built up trust among Africans who previously had been universally wary of white people offering to help them.

The creation of a Freedom Charter

The ANC and other protest organisations held meetings nationwide in the early 1950s to hear people's demands and grievances. These included a key meeting in 1954 where it was decided to create a charter of universal rights, based on what the African people wanted. With so many protest leaders caught up in trials and banning orders, this process took a long time. Eventually, a committee drew up the Freedom Charter which was to be presented to a People's Congress. This took place at Kliptown near Johannesburg between 25 and 26 June 1955 and was attended by 3000 representatives of all the opposition groups. The different groups came together and began to call themselves the Congress Alliance, which ratified the Freedom Charter.

SOURCE F

Extract from the preamble to the Freedom Charter, quoted in Francis Meli, *A History of the ANC: South Africa Belongs to Us*, James Currey, 1989, page 210.

We the people of South Africa declare for all our country and the world to know:

- *That South Africa belongs to all who live in it, black and white, and that no government can justly claim authority unless it is based on the will of the people;*

- *That our people have been robbed of their birthright to land, liberty and peace by a form of government founded on injustice and inequality;*

- *That our country will never be prosperous or free until all our people live in brotherhood, enjoying equal rights and opportunities;*

- *That only a democratic state, based on the will of all the people can secure to all their birthright without distinction of colour, race, sex or belief;*

- *And therefore we, the people of South Africa, black and white together – equals, countrymen and brothers – adopt this Freedom Charter. And we pledge ourselves to strive together, sparing neither strength nor courage, until the democratic changes here set out have been won.*

What can you infer from Source F about the aims of the Freedom Charter?

SOURCE G

? What can you infer from Source G about the scale of the Treason Trial?

TREASON TRIAL

A montage of those accused in the Treason Trial, 1956.

The significance of the Freedom Charter

The Freedom Charter was a statement of ideals and aims rather than a strategy. Much of its significance was in its preamble.

Rural resistance

The ANC admitted it had more support in urban areas, but during the 1950s there were many cases of rural unrest. These were often spontaneous and unplanned, making them more difficult to control or suppress.

Potato boycott, 1957–59

This was an ANC-sponsored boycott on buying potatoes because of the harsh conditions endured by potato workers. Potatoes rot quickly, and stocks piled up as people refused to buy them. In August 1959, farmers began to improve working conditions and the boycott was hailed as a success.

Zeerust uprising, 1957

This uprising was precipitated by the imposition of passes for women living in the Zeerust area of western Transvaal, as introduced in the 1952 Native Laws Amendment Act. When the local chief was ordered to enforce this measure, he refused and was dismissed. The result was widespread protest. Men and women living in Johannesburg chartered buses to join in the protest. They were subsequently arrested by the security forces and blamed for the unrest. The authorities were enraged when most were acquitted. The women in Zeerust meanwhile were forced to carry their passes by a special police squad.

East Pondoland

The local chief of this region, Chief Botha Sigcau, who sided with the government, was accused of corruption, for example in selling mineral rights. Local people insisted on his dismissal and violent clashes took place, led by the **Intaba movement**. As part of the protest, locals boycotted white-owned stores. The chief survived, however, with help from the security forces, and the protests were called off in January 1961 (see page 53).

Rural unrest and the lack of ANC influence in non-urban areas helped garner support for the newly formed Pan-Africanist Congress (PAC).

The Pan-Africanist Congress

Robert Sobukwe had been an ANCYL leader but he disagreed with the **integrationist** approach and was a firm supporter of Africanism (see page 19). In 1957, he helped form the Pan-Africanist Congress (PAC).

> **🔑 KEY TERMS**
>
> **Intaba movement**
> Resistance movement in East Pondoland. *Intaba* is a Zulu word for 'mountain'.
>
> **Integrationist** One who believes that all races, including white people, should be involved in the fight against apartheid.

The PAC philosophy

The PAC blamed the failures of the ANC on its willingness to work with other groups. In particular, it rejected the Freedom Charter, largely because of its emphasis on equal rights: many within the PAC rejected equal rights for whites, whom it accused of exploiting and oppressing black Africans. From its inception, the PAC believed Africans could only act successfully by themselves. Many members – although not Sobukwe himself – saw white people as the enemy, who must be expelled from South Africa. It also opposed communism, and associated itself with other independence movements in Africa, fighting colonialism.

The fundamental difference between the ANC and PAC was over the Africanist policy. The ANC insisted all ethnic groups could participate in the struggle against apartheid and all ethnic groups had an equal role to play in a post-apartheid society.

The formation of the PAC in April 1959 did not take the ANC leaders by surprise – they had already expelled one of its founders, **Potlako Leballo**, from the ANC for his Africanist views – but they disagreed profoundly with its philosophy. As they understood it, the PAC saw the liberation of South Africa from apartheid in the same context as anti-colonial movements throughout Africa: Africa belonged to black Africans who must fight alone for their liberation. The ANC had no problem with this view in relation to countries such as Ghana and Kenya, which were fighting for independence from colonial masters. The ANC felt, however, that it was inappropriate for South Africa, where 'Africans' were not exclusively black. Extremists in PAC argued that there was no place in Africa for white people or Asians, whereas the ANC embraced all groups who would support their struggle whatever their ethnicity, and also recognised that all the inhabitants of South Africa should have equal rights. The ANC was opposed to the apartheid regime rather than any specific groups of people.

KEY FIGURE

Potlako Leballo (1915–86)

Radical Africanist who succeeded Sobukwe as leader of the PAC.

? Explain Sobukwe's arguments as they appear in Source H.

SOURCE H

Extract from Robert Sobukwe's inaugural speech on the formation of the PAC in April 1959 (available at http://v1.sahistory.org.za/pages/governance-projects/organisations/pac/origins.htm).

Against multi-racialism we have this objection, that the history of South Africa has fostered group prejudices and antagonisms, and if we have to maintain the same group exclusiveness, parading under the term of multi-racialism, we shall be transporting to the new Afrika these very antagonisms and conflicts. Further, multi-racialism is in fact a pandering to European bigotry and arrogance. It is a method of safeguarding white interests, implying as it does, proportional representation irrespective of population figures. In that sense it is a complete negation of democracy.

To us the term 'multi-racialism' implies that there are such basic insuperable differences between the various national groups here that the best course is to keep them permanently distinctive in a kind of democratic apartheid. That to us is racialism multiplied, which probably is what the term truly connotes. We aim, politically, at government of the Africans by the Africans, for the Africans, with everybody who owes his only loyalty to Afrika and who is prepared to accept the democratic rule of an African majority being regarded as an African.

We guarantee no minority rights, because we think in terms of individuals, not groups.

Support

The PAC had a simple philosophy, which was easily understood. It gained a great deal of support, especially in the Witwatersrand area where many of its leaders were based, and in more rural areas. Indeed, it has been estimated that by 1959 its membership exceeded the ANC by as many as 25,000.

The PAC regarded itself as a rival to the ANC and sought to pre-empt the ANC in the leadership of anti-apartheid activities. This rivalry was to come to a head in the events which led to the Sharpeville Massacre in March 1961, the events of which are discussed in Chapter 2.

Summary diagram: African nationalism, 1948–59

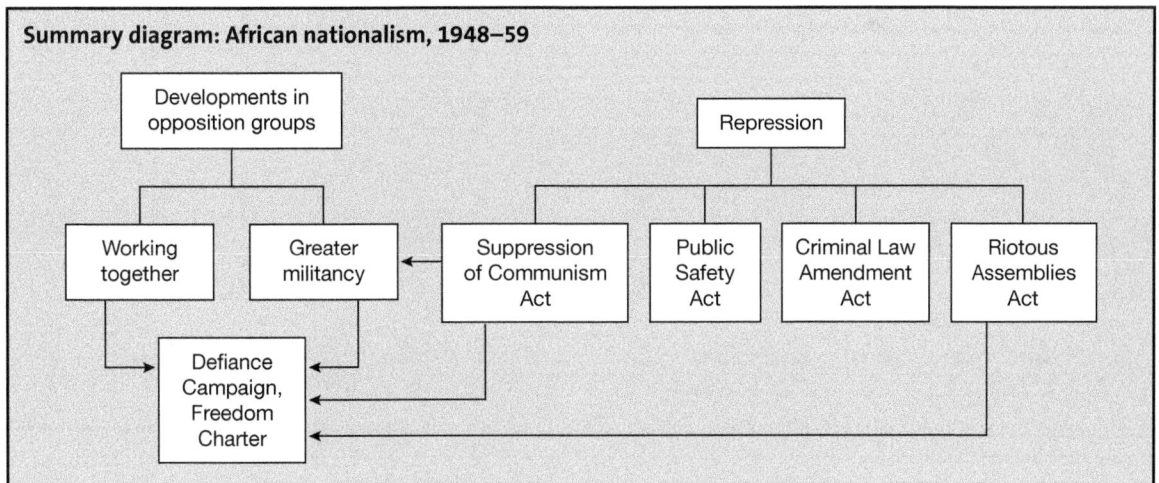

Chapter summary

South Africa had been colonised by white settlers who subdued the indigenous populations. The National Party, supported mainly by Afrikaners, won the 1948 election. This was mainly due to its better organisation, campaigning, weighting of constituencies, which favoured its own candidates, and the weaknesses of the rival United Party. The new government went on to implement a policy of apartheid or strict racial segregation, although, at first, this simply built on existing legislation. The policy of apartheid grew more radical later under the premiership of Hendrik Verwoerd, particularly through the creation of intensified Bantustans, or tribal homelands, where Africans were supposed to reside unless working in white South Africa. The authorities supported this legislation by repressive measures and particularly attacked communism, which they saw at the heart of all dissent. Many non-white Africans protested against apartheid, mainly by peaceful means, such as the Defiance Campaign of 1952, and called for a Freedom Charter, offering a blueprint for a non-racial, democratic, South Africa. However, the authorities fought tenaciously against any attempts at reform. There were several distinct anti-apartheid groups, although the largest was the African National Congress (ANC), which opened its membership to all South Africans. In the mid-1940s, the ANC began to develop a programme of mass protest under the leadership of the Youth League, which advocated direct action; the Defiance Campaign was one example of this. The ANC, however, was urban-based and it often had little influence in rural protests such as the Zeerust uprising against pass laws for women. At the end of the decade a new Africanist force, the Pan-Africanist Congress (PAC), had emerged, many members of which were anti-white people and believed black Africans themselves must control the resistance movements.

Refresher questions

Use these questions to remind yourself of the key material covered in this chapter.

1 How was South Africa divided according to racial groups in 1948?

2 How far was discriminatory legislation already in place before the formal adoption of apartheid?

3 What arguments did white South Africans deploy to justify apartheid?

4 Why did the National Party win the 1948 election?

5 Explain the differences between grand and petty apartheid.

6 Explain the significance of the 1950 Population Registration Act.

7 Why was the Group Areas Act so important in the implementation of apartheid?

8 Why was the 1953 Bantu Education Act so important?

9 How effectively did the government control anti-apartheid protest during the period 1948–59?

10 What was the significance of the 1956 Freedom Charter on the anti-apartheid movement?

11 By what means did the ANC grow more militant during the 1940s?

12 How effective was direct action protest during the 1950s?

Question practice

ESSAY QUESTIONS

1 To what extent was growing African urbanisation the main reason for the implementation of apartheid legislation in the years 1948–59?

2 How accurate is it to say that the growth of Afrikaner nationalism was the most important reason for the victory of the National Party in the elections of 1948?

3 How accurate is it to say that the government's education laws were the most important feature of apartheid in the 1950s?

4 How significant was the leadership of the African National Congress (ANC) and the Pan-Africanist Congress (PAC) in shaping resistance to apartheid in the 1950s?

SOURCE-BASED QUESTIONS

1 How far could a historian make use of Source B (page 13) and Source E (page 22) together to investigate the reasons why apartheid was implemented in the years 1948–59? Explain your answer using the sources, the information given about them and your own knowledge of the historical context

2 How far could a historian make use Source F (page 33) and Source H (pages 36–7) together to investigate the different approaches to anti-apartheid activities in the years 1948–59?

Radicalisation of resistance and the consolidation of National Party power, 1960–68

Peaceful resistance to apartheid continued but its effectiveness was increasingly questioned, particularly after the Sharpeville Massacre of March 1960. The government responded with a state of emergency, which resulted in the banning of most anti-apartheid groups. This, in turn, led them to go underground and also to begin an armed struggle. South Africa meanwhile became a republic and left the Commonwealth. The majority of the African National Congress leadership were captured and put on trial at Rivonia. This saw Nelson Mandela, among others, being imprisoned for life. While the economy grew and most white people enjoyed prosperous lifestyles, the government increased its apartheid programme with the creation of Bantustans. It also extended the role of the security forces. By the end of the decade, South Africa was effectively a police state. These developments are described in the following sections:

★ Resistance to apartheid and government reaction, 1960–61

★ Creating a republic, 1960–61

★ African nationalist radicalisation, 1961–68

★ Strengthening 'separate development', 1961–68

Key dates

1960	'Wind of change' speech	**1963**	Transkei made an 'independent' Bantustan
	Sharpeville Massacre		Rivonia Trial and imprisonment of Mandela
	State of emergency, banning of African		and other ANC leaders
	National Congress (ANC) and Pan-Africanist		UN resolution 1761 calling for voluntary
	Congress		sanctions on South Africa
1961	Suppression of the East Pondoland rebellion		Formation of Organisation of African Unity
	South Africa left the Commonwealth and	**1967**	ANC alliance with Zimbabwean African
	became a republic		People's Union
	Formation of *Umkhonto we Sizwe*	**1969**	Morogoro Conference
1962	Poqo attack on white settlement of Paarl		
	Arrest of Nelson Mandela		

① Resistance to apartheid and government reaction, 1960–61

▶ *How effective was resistance to apartheid in the period 1960–61?*
▶ *To what extent did government reaction stifle protest?*

Protest against apartheid continued throughout the 1950s and early 1960s. By 1961, however, the Sharpeville Massacre had changed the largely peaceful, non-violent nature of protests to a willingness to use violence.

Peaceful protest

Peaceful protest had taken various forms such as strikes, boycotts and demonstrations, but had achieved little:

- The government usually responded with repressive legislation. In 1956, for example, when women protested about the extension of pass laws, the government passed the Native Administration Act which made it easier to remove Africans to their native reserves.
- Many anti-apartheid campaigners were too preoccupied with the Treason Trial (see page 28) to organise ambitious protests.

Nevertheless, the African National Congress (ANC) called for a series of nationwide anti-pass protests to begin on 31 March 1960. The Pan-Africanist Congress (PAC) decided to pre-empt this in its first show of strength.

The PAC and anti-pass law protests

The ANC had called for a series of protests (anti-pass protests – against being forced to carry passes, see page 20) for 31 March 1960; the PAC announced one for 21 March. The campaign was poorly organised. Robert Sobukwe himself had said, 'All we are required to do is to show the light and the masses will find the way', but this was never going to be enough to gather enough people to make an impact. On the day, the protests were disappointing. Sobukwe and his supporters in Orlando protested against carrying passes and demanded the police arrest them; the authorities agreed – because there so few of them, it was manageable to do so. Elsewhere, most Africans went to work as normal with their passes in their pockets either because the official ANC protest was not to start until 31 March, or else because they simply did not want to get involved. The often dire consequences of participating in any protest, such as arrest, imprisonment or deportation back to the homelands, should also not be forgotten.

The Sharpeville Massacre and its significance

Sharpeville was a township in Vereeniging, an industrial centre in the Transvaal, home of 37,000 Africans. Over 40 per cent of the population were under the age of eighteen. Officially, it was a model township with modern facilities including a library. In reality, life there was difficult and it could be a dangerous place with a great deal of crime and street gangs. In 1959, it received a new police station, and the officers were energetic in checking passes, deporting illegal residents and conducting raids against illegal **shebeens** – often at night, when more people might be found in them. It was, therefore, a place where resentment seethed and its people were prime for **radicalisation**.

ANC and PAC in Sharpeville

The local ANC leaders were eminently respectable and moderate in their goals and the organisation had not really penetrated the township. The PAC, however, was active, particularly through the influence of the charismatic Tsolo brothers, Nyakane and Job; the former already had experience of illegal union activities. They worked tirelessly to increase PAC membership, often by focusing on issues associated with women, such as the illicit distilling and selling of alcohol. They were also prepared to manipulate youth gangs to add muscle to persuade residents to cooperate in their activities. Although the PAC membership may have been as little as 100 at the time of the pass protest, its leaders felt confident they could galvanise the local community into participating.

The events of Sharpeville

On Monday 21 March 1960, a crowd estimated at between 5000 and 20,000 gathered outside the police station at Sharpeville. They were peacefully protesting about having to carry passes and demanding to be arrested for not carrying them. The police on duty refused to arrest so many because it was impractical to do so, which was, of course, the point the protesters were making. The standoff continued all morning. The police were reinforced by colleagues from other areas and senior officers arrived to try to take control of the situation. There were 400 police, 200 white officers armed with .303 rifles, and 200 African officers carrying clubs called **knobkerries**.

The killings

Many accounts suggest that a drunken demonstrator, Geelbooi Mofokeng, fired his pistol in the air at the same time as one of the senior officers, Colonel 'Att' Spengler, accidentally stumbled, leading his colleagues to think the colonel had been shot. The policemen began to shoot into the crowd; they fired two volleys, one directly into the centre, killing the demonstrators at the head of the crowd, including most of the organisers, and a second, hitting those who were fleeing. As the dust settled, it was found that 69 demonstrators had been killed and almost 200 injured; many of these would later die of their wounds. It was subsequently discovered that 70 per cent of those killed were shot in the back.

Who was to blame for the Sharpeville Massacre?

Many critics of the South African regime have argued that the Sharpeville Massacre was a premeditated attack on peaceful protesters, while others support the security forces, saying that they were only trying to maintain order and protect themselves in the face of excessive provocation. The truth lies somewhere along this spectrum of deliberate murder and self-defence. Several factors contributed to the tragic events on that particular day in Sharpeville:

- The police were on edge. There had been disturbances at Sharpeville over the weekend, and nine of their colleagues had recently been killed riots in **Cato Manor**.
- The senior police officers under Lieutenant Colonel Pienaar appeared indecisive, not giving firm instructions or leadership.
- It was a hot day and the standoff had been taking place for upwards of five hours. People were getting impatient and tense.
- While the police were reluctant to make arrests, they had arrested the PAC leader Nyakane Tsolo just before the shooting began. The charismatic Tsolo had, it seemed, been able to control the crowd. It was the struggle to arrest other leaders which had prompted Spengler's stumble, which had led to the first shots being fired.
- The police had earlier requested the demonstrators to adjourn to the nearby football field. They may have suggested this simply to manage the crowd more efficiently and safely – the press of thousands in a relatively confined space was dangerous in itself, particularly for the children present – but many of the demonstrators feared the police were attempting to marshal them into a killing field.

KEY TERM

Cato Manor A township near Durban where serious riots took place in 1959 as a result of police trying to close down shebeens.

SOURCE A

Photograph of the aftermath of the Sharpeville Massacre, 1960.

What does the photograph in Source A suggest about reactions to the massacre among a) the police and b) the African onlookers?

The banning of political parties and the state of emergency

The lack of trust between the police and the people was exacerbated even further in the aftermath of the shootings. Police rampaged through Sharpeville, seeking out leaders, arresting the wounded in hospital, aggressively policing pass laws and arresting anyone breaking the curfew. Those leaders arrested were savagely beaten up in detention cells. Police officers were accused of putting rocks and weapons in the hands of the dead to frame them. They built two mounds of rocks, stones and weapons for the benefit of press photographers; these, they asserted, were carried by the demonstrators. In the two-month period following the Sharpeville Massacre a raft of repressive measures was passed, including two hugely significant acts.

A state of emergency was declared on 30 March 1960, which saw the arrest of over 10,000 people, 2000 within the first few days. This number included Nelson Mandela and others who were still enmeshed in the Treason Trial (see page 28).

Additionally on 8 April, the two main African parties, PAC and ANC, were declared illegal under the Unlawful Organisations Act. This was undoubtedly a blow for the ANC which had not been involved in the PAC campaign, although it was already preparing for an armed struggle (see page 53). However, the banning removed the principle legitimate voices for Africans, so that protesting against apartheid became effectively an illegal activity.

The forceful response by the government may have been because they were rattled or because they sought to assert their authority and reassure investors and white citizens that they were fully in control. In the short term after Sharpeville there were indications of uncertainty among the white community which they needed to address:

- There was an increasing demand for firearms.
- On 9 April, Prime Minister Hendrik Verwoerd was subject to an assassination attempt.
- The military wings of the ANC, PAC and the **Liberal Party** (the African Resistance Movement or ARM, comprised mainly of radical young white people) embarked on campaigns of bombing and violence which clearly worried law-abiding citizens.
- In the years between 1960 and 1963, emigration figures exceeded those of immigration. The numbers leaving for Britain, for example, stood at 2000 in 1959 and rose to 5000 by 1962. The mainly white emigrants, moreover, tended to be members of the professional classes whose skills would be missed.
- There were economic upsets, with falling share prices and a net outflow of currency (the **rand**, R) – R194 million in 1960. The amount of foreign reserves fell from R312 million to R153 million between June 1960 and May 1961.

KEY TERMS

Liberal Party Political party made up mainly of white people who opposed apartheid.

Rand In 1960, South Africa decimalised its currency, moving from British sterling (pounds, shillings and pence) to rands and cents.

Continuing government repression

The new Minister of Justice **John Vorster**, appointed in July 1961, instituted a new part-time Police Reserve Unit. This was to develop into the feared Security Police. He also set up secret, quasi-legal bodies to co-ordinate security matters and undertake 'dirty tricks' such as assassinations of opposition figures. These bodies were to integrate in 1969 into the Bureau for State Security (BOSS), but their activities remained state secrets.

Other measures followed:

- The Sabotage Act 1962 not only carried the death penalty for acts of sabotage but also placed the onus on the accused to prove themselves innocent; guilt was implied.
- The General Laws Amendment Act of 1963 allowed the authorities to arrest anyone for 90 days without having to bring charges against them or even giving them access to a lawyer. Once the initial 90-day period was up it could be extended for a further 90 days *ad infinitum*.
- The so-called Sobukwe Clause allowed the security forces to keep people in prison beyond the end of their sentence. Sobukwe was the first victim of it: he was imprisoned until May 1969 and then kept under house arrest.
- Now that there was no effective check on their activities, the security forces increasingly resorted to torture to extract confessions, particularly through the use of electric shocks. This was allowed under the Sabotage Act of 1962.
- The authorities set up a network of spies and informers to infiltrate opposition groups and if necessary to act as *agents provocateurs*. These people were sometimes motivated by money, but more often because they feared that resistance to apartheid was useless and that all Africans suffered for the actions of a few.
- In 1963, a new radio network was set up offering direct communication between over 1000 police stations and the police headquarters in Pretoria to facilitate rapid response to incidents.
- The Bantu Laws Amendment Act 1964 came into effect on 1 January 1965. This empowered the authorities to deport any African from any urban or white farming areas for any reason whatsoever. It also allowed the minister for native affairs to establish quotas in particular areas or industries and deport unemployed Africans back to their homelands. This was a **draconian** measure which gave the authorities complete power over Africans in 'white' South Africa. Anyone who caused problems, or it was felt had the potential to do so, could be removed.

The Wessels Commission of Enquiry

The government appointed the Wessels Commission of Enquiry into the Sharpeville Massacre in March 1960. Inevitably it would be accused by critics as being a **whitewash**. The report made it clear at the outset that the brief was to ascertain what actually happened, not to apportion blame. However, the commission appeared reluctant to interview Africans and ignored any suggestions that the police had tampered with evidence. It was said that Africans either were too intimidated to testify, or were told what to say by the PAC. It was, to a certain extent, critical of the police leadership, which it thought was indecisive, but did suggest that the police felt intimidated and in danger. In the overall conclusion, the police were exonerated from blame. According to the report, they had acted in self-defence against a hostile crowd.

SOURCE B

Extract from the Wessels Report into the events at Sharpeville, 21 March 1960 (available at http://idep.library.ucla.edu/sharpeville-massacre).

There was protracted examination about the steps which Lt Col Pienaar ought to have taken to disperse the crowd before the police fired on them. In my opinion this is not the issue. The police justify their conduct by reference to the conduct of the demonstrators which was regarded by them as an attack. They say they fired because their lives were in danger. That, at any rate is the trend of the evidence of all the police who testified before me. Naturally I did not call all the police who fired as witnesses but there is no reason to believe that any fired simply to disperse the crowd. The police and especially the officers were aware of the steps which should have been taken before force was used to disperse the crowd. Their conduct elsewhere that day is evidence of this. Nor does it fall within the scope of this report to determine whether the actions of Lt Col Pienaar during the short period for which he was present at the police station indicate whether he is guilty of any neglect of duty or contravention of any provision of the law.

How far does Source B criticise the actions of the police in the Sharpeville shootings?

The international repercussions of Sharpeville

Much of the world was shocked by the events at Sharpeville. The United Nations (UN) had passed resolutions condemning apartheid every year since 1952, but **Security Council Resolution 134** was particularly damning, blaming the shootings on the system of apartheid and asserting that violence would continue until apartheid was ended. Because of the economic turbulence that would follow, countries which did business with South Africa were reluctant to antagonise it by imposing sanctions. For example, Britain, along with France, abstained from the UN resolution.

KEY TERM

Security Council Resolution 134
UN resolution condemning the South African government for the Sharpeville Massacre.

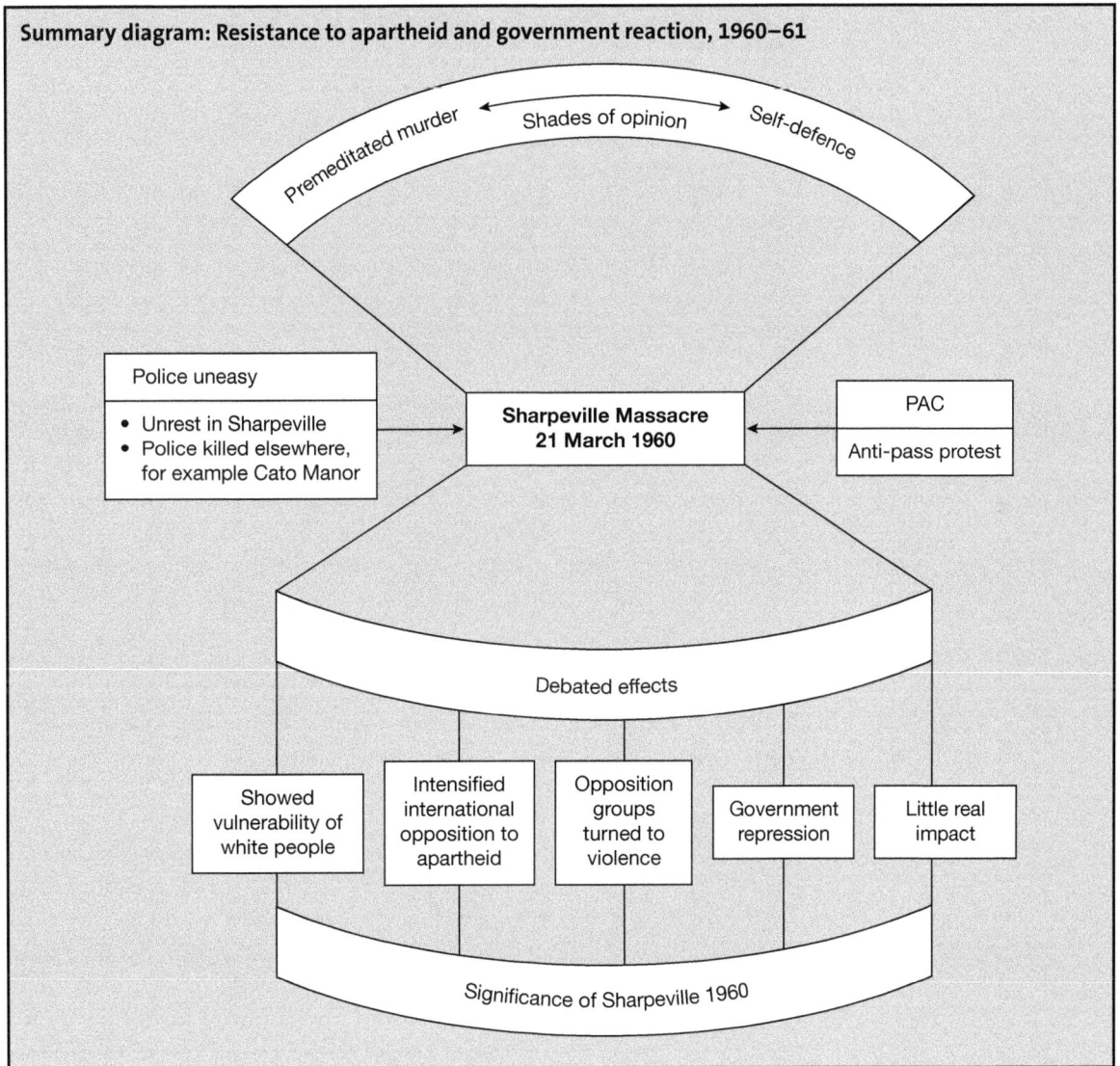

Summary diagram: Resistance to apartheid and government reaction, 1960–61

Premeditated murder ← Shades of opinion → Self-defence

Police uneasy
- Unrest in Sharpeville
- Police killed elsewhere, for example Cato Manor

→ **Sharpeville Massacre 21 March 1960** ←

PAC
Anti-pass protest

Debated effects

| Showed vulnerability of white people | Intensified international opposition to apartheid | Opposition groups turned to violence | Government repression | Little real impact |

Significance of Sharpeville 1960

② Creating a republic, 1960–61

▶ *Why was the Republic of South Africa formed?*
▶ *To what did extent did the creation of the republic change South African foreign relations?*

As prime minister, Verwoerd sought the creation of a South African republic as a totally apartheid state: he was opposed to the influence of Britain and did not want South Africa to remain in the Commonwealth, which he saw as increasingly dominated by newly independent African nations such as Ghana and Nigeria. The South African government had always argued that South Africa was unique: an African country run not by European colonists but by white Africans. It was, moreover, wealthy and efficient because it was run by this group. The white government, they asserted, operated for the benefit of all – and they gave evidence not only of the numbers of migrant workers from other African countries but of the fact that Africans in South Africa had more access to education and a higher standard of living than elsewhere on the continent. While this may have been true, critics replied that it still was not anywhere near high enough and that the wealth should be shared out more fairly and political and civic rights extended.

The significance of Macmillan's 'wind of change' speech, 1960

In February 1960, British Premier Harold Macmillan was touring southern Africa and had been invited to address the South African Parliament in Cape Town. As his audience looked on stony faced, Macmillan made his famous 'wind of change' speech in which he argued that Western governments must accept the independence of African nations and offer them their support lest they turn to communism.

SOURCE C

Extract from the 'wind of change' speech by Harold Macmillan to the South African Parliament, 3 February 1960. Macmillan was the British prime minister.

... the most striking of all the impressions I have formed since I left London a month ago is of the strength of this African national consciousness. In different places it takes different forms, but it is happening everywhere.

The wind of change is blowing through this continent, and whether we like it or not, this growth of national consciousness is a political fact. We must all accept it as a fact, and our national policies must take account of it.

Well you understand this better than anyone, you are sprung from Europe, the home of nationalism, here in Africa you have yourselves created a free nation. A new nation. Indeed in the history of our times yours will be recorded as the first of the African nationalists. This tide of national consciousness which is

What might have been the reaction to Source C among those listening in the South African Parliament? Explain your answer.

now rising in Africa, is a fact, for which both you and we, and the other nations of the western world are ultimately responsible … .

As I see it the great issue in this second half of the twentieth century is whether the uncommitted peoples of Asia and Africa will swing to the East or to the West. Will they be drawn into the Communist camp? Or will the great experiments in self-government that are now being made in Asia and Africa, especially within the Commonwealth, prove so successful, and by their example so compelling, that the balance will come down in favour of freedom and order and justice? The struggle is joined, and it is a struggle for the minds of men. What is now on trial is much more than our military strength or our diplomatic and administrative skill. It is our way of life. The uncommitted nations want to see before they choose.

Anti-apartheid groups and leaders were encouraged by Macmillan's speech. It both acknowledged the reality of what was happening elsewhere in Africa, and pointed the way to the inevitable future of countries whose governments were currently fighting against change.

SOURCE D

Extract from a response to Macmillan's 'wind of change' speech by Chief Luthuli, president of the ANC, dated 1 March 1960 (available at www.anc.org.za/content/what-i-think-macmillans-speech-article-albert-luthuli).

The eminent British statesman, Mr. Harold Macmillan, Prime Minister of Britain turned to Africa, including the Union, 'to see'. But, in the end, he did more than 'see'. He gave us oppressed people some inspiration and hope – and to all in the Union something to think about.

Some of us, fearing that he might be manoeuvred by his host, the Union Government, to act and speak in support of apartheid, advised him that neutrality might be his best policy in the circumstances. But great man that he is, he spoke his mind without let or favour and gave a lie to our fears.

Most of what he said brought to truly progressive non-racial South Africans a refreshing breeze in a land already befogged by apartheid with its stress on sectionalism and racialism. Most of what he said could pass as a re-affirmation of the aspirations of the oppressed people in Africa, particularly those in Southern Africa.

It was heartening to hear him categorically reject discrimination: 'We reject the idea of any inherent superiority of one race over another … our policy, therefore, is non-racial.'

He entertained no fears of the rising African consciousness, but rather saw it as a natural development which, as in Europe, will give rise to separate nations of Africa, some of them multi-racial. In the multi-racial nations democracy, with its rule of majority, would prevail.

According to Source D, how far was **Chief Luthuli** 'heartened' by Macmillan's speech?

KEY FIGURE

Chief Luthuli (1898–1967)

Luthuli was a teacher who became president of the ANC in 1952. His effectiveness during his period of office was reduced, however, by his constant house arrest at his home at Groutville. He won the Nobel Peace Prize in 1961.

South African response to the 'wind of change' speech

The South African government was disturbed by Macmillan's speech and indeed the **decolonisation** going on throughout the continent. However, these developments would not deflect them from apartheid. Indeed, disastrous events – such those taking place in the former Belgian Congo (present-day Democratic Republic of Congo) where a bloodbath and civil war were raging – only served to confirm them in their resolution.

While the 'wind of change' speech may have given encouragement to anti-apartheid groups, the government was firmly committed to the continuation of the system and white control of South Africa; there would be no compromise. The debate, coupled with the increasing condemnation of South Africa within the Commonwealth, led to the creation of a republic independent from Britain.

The establishment of a republic

In October 1960, white South Africans went to the polls to decide whether they wanted to sever political ties with Britain and form a republic. With a 90 per cent turnout, the result was close, with 52 per cent opting for republic status (see page 48). Unsurprisingly, most support for a republic came from the Afrikaner heartlands of Transvaal and the Orange Free State. Natal had voted against the proposal, while voters in the Cape supported it by only 2000. Clearly, there was a split between English and Afrikaans speakers.

Leaving the Commonwealth

After severing its constitutional ties with Britain, it was perhaps inevitable that South Africa would leave the **Commonwealth**. In June 1961, Verwoerd attended his final **Commonwealth Conference**. He withdrew South African membership in the face of criticism over apartheid, although again it was a close-run thing – the withdrawal from the Commonwealth was not an inevitability. One of the main stumbling blocks to continued membership was Verwoerd's refusal to accept diplomats from newly independent African countries; it would, he said, lead to Pretoria being overcrowded with embassies. Privately, he acknowledged that African diplomats in an apartheid state could cause problems.

Relations with white Commonwealth countries

The withdrawal of South Africa from the Commonwealth did nothing to diminish its economic or cultural ties with Britain and the other white dominions such as Australia. One of the arguments of those who wished to retain Commonwealth ties was that trading links would be at risk if South Africa left. This was proved not to be the case: economic and trading links continued to flourish while cultural links were maintained, particularly in terms of sport.

New Zealand and rugby

Of the white dominions, it was New Zealand which presented the most diplomatic problems as South Africa refused to allow **Maoris** to be included in visiting All Blacks rugby teams. The acquiescence in excluding the Maori players for the 1960 tour led to the biggest demonstrations in New Zealand's history. South Africa, however, did not care much, particularly if it meant their side had a greater chance of winning.

South Africa had long retreated into a psychological 'laager mentality' (see page 9) so it was not too concerned with international reactions. The 1960s was to see considerable economic growth, white immigration from Britain and elsewhere in Europe, and the continued support and shelter of neighbouring countries.

KEY TERM

Maoris Indigenous peoples of New Zealand.

Summary diagram: Creating a republic, 1960–61

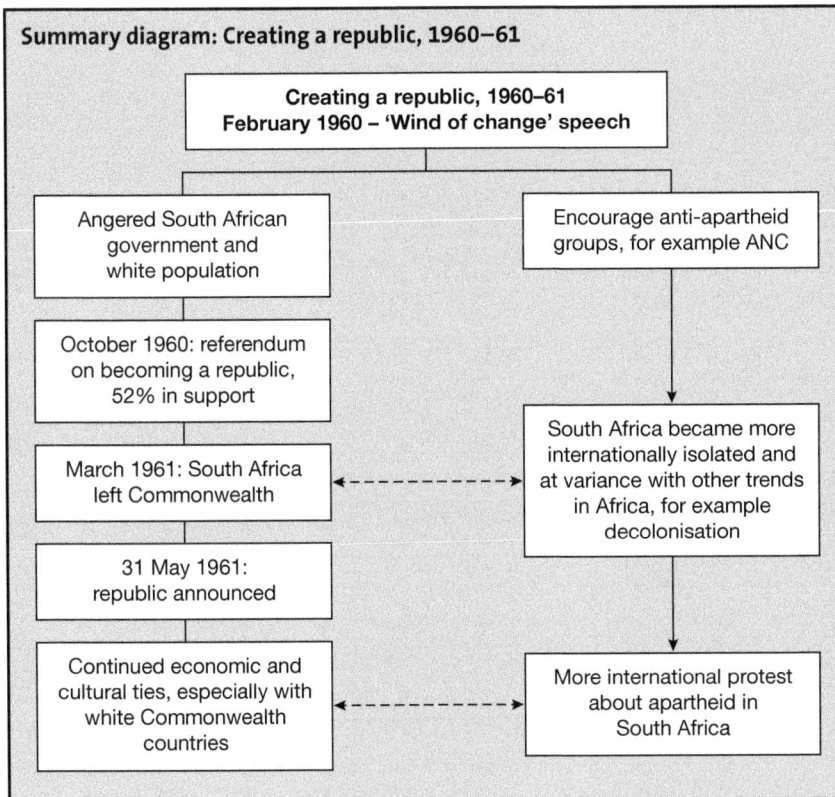

3 African nationalist radicalisation, 1961–68

▶ *Why did anti-apartheid groups turn to armed struggle in the period 1961–68?*

The period 1961–68 saw a greater radicalism in African nationalism exemplified, in particular, by moves to an armed struggle.

Factors in the moves to armed struggle

The Sharpeville Massacre was simply one of a number of factors that led to the creation of **Umkhonto we Sizwe or Spear of the Nation (MK)** in June 1961. Earlier in that year, the PAC had already created **Poqo**; its activities were more militant still.

Government deceit

The government became increasingly devious when dealing with protesters, for example, arresting activists, such as Philip Kgosona, when they attended meetings with government officials, even though their immunity had previously been guaranteed.

Ineffectiveness of non-violent mass demonstrations

Opposition leaders finally realised that peaceful protest had never worked and was never going to work. When burning passes became widespread as an ongoing form of protest, the police commissioner ordered the suspension of arrests for not carrying passes. However, Africans were told they could no longer draw pensions without their passes. Many were forced to queue to reapply for passes while their benefits were suspended.

The final peaceful protest

The ANC's direct action to demand the end of apartheid, planned for 29–31 May 1961, failed. The government mobilised the army and police, ready for insurrection. The PAC, meanwhile, refused to participate because the ANC protest involved both white and black protesters; they told their Africanist (see page 19) supporters to go to work as normal.

In the end, there was poor support for the ANC protest. Few stayed home rather than going to work, fewer still demonstrated. This failure helped convince leaders that peaceful demonstration had finally had its day. This was the final peaceful mass demonstration of the 1960s.

Greater militancy among activists

The security forces had always been prepared to use violence. Anti-apartheid protesters were becoming increasingly militant and frustrated with peaceful tactics, especially in rural areas, for example in East Pondoland where the rebellion led by the Intaba movement (see page 35) had been defeated by government forces in 1961 armed with superior military technology. The decision to begin an armed struggle was to some degree a case of leaders catching up with the demands of their supporters. The ANC remained conscious that they had not been effective in rural areas and had not given any military support to Intaba; the formation of an armed wing could eventually provide this sort of assistance in future conflicts.

The ANC and *Umkhonto we Sizwe*

Nelson Mandela co-founded the military branch of the ANC, *Umkhonto we Sizwe* (MK), in June 1961. Clearly, it could not wage all-out war. It was decided that initially it would commit acts of sabotage on property such as government instillations; the intention was to avoid loss of life. However, a second phase would involve volunteers training for **guerrilla warfare**. The overall aim, according to Mandela, was to make it impossible for the apartheid government to govern effectively.

> 🔑 **KEY TERM**
>
> **Guerrilla warfare** Fighting using techniques such as ambush and bombings, avoiding direct large-scale conflict.

Much stress was laid on MK as being independent from the ANC. Members from the outlawed Communist Party (SACP and SAIC, see page 30) also joined. MK began its campaign on 16 December 1961, to coincide with Covenant Day (see page 3). Africans called this Digane Day, after the Zulu king who was defeated at the Battle of Blood River in December 1838. Bombings took place in government buildings in Durban and Port Elizabeth, including an electricity substation. In the next eighteen months, 200 attacks by MK took place.

Ultimately, the decision to adopt the armed struggle was made because the leaders saw no alternative: it was as much a response to government brutality and intransigence as a desire to end apartheid by force. Mandela argued that the government set the agenda for the forms of protest; when government authorities responded to peaceful protest with violence which was then not prosecuted in the courts, passive resistance had failed.

MK was not the only group making violent protest: the African Resistance Movement (ARM) was an armed offshoot of the white Liberal Party which was becoming increasing radical in its quest to abolish apartheid. While most of their members had been arrested for sabotage by December 1964, their sentences were more lenient than for non-white groups, except for a white anti-apartheid protester, John Harris, who was executed in April 1965 for a bomb attack at Johannesburg railway station which resulted in the deaths of innocent people.

The PAC and Poqo

Poqo, the military wing of the PAC, was the most violent of the armed movements. It was far more prepared to use terror and intimidation than the other groups. It also targeted white people whom it saw as an enemy; for example, the assault on the white settlement of Paarl on 22 November 1962, when a mob of 250 supporters armed with axes and homemade weapons attacked the police station and brutally hacked two young white people to death.

To enhance security, Poqo was divided into secret cells, with members unaware of anyone outside their own groups. It was limited to Africans and particularly targeted African policemen and local chiefs whom they saw as collaborators. Poqo was especially feared because of its ruthlessness and the fact that it operated in rural, largely unpoliced areas. However, by 1964, members were arguing among themselves about the direction of the movement and among which countries it should canvass for support. The movement had also been successfully infiltrated by security forces. Many members were arrested and executed.

By 1964, the armed struggle was effectively over in the South Africa, owing to the ruthlessness and efficiency of the response by the authorities.

SOURCE E

? According to Source E, how do the ANC justify the movement to an armed struggle?

Extract from the manifesto of the movement to armed struggle, the *Umkhonto we Sizwe*, 16 December 1961.

Units of Umkhonto we Sizwe today carried out planned attacks against government installations, particularly those connected with the policy of apartheid and race discrimination … .

It is, however, well known that the main national liberation organisations in this country have consistently followed a policy of non-violence. They have conducted themselves peaceably at all times, regardless of government attacks and persecutions upon them, and despite all government-inspired attempts to provoke them to violence. They have done so because the people prefer peaceful methods of change to achieve their aspirations without the suffering and bitterness of civil war. But the people's patience is not endless.

The time comes in the life of any nation when there remain only two choices: submit or fight. That time has now come to South Africa. We shall not submit and we have no choice but to hit back by all means within our power in defence of our people, our future and our freedom. The government has interpreted the peacefulness of the movement as weakness; the people's non-violent policies have been taken as a green light for government violence. Refusal to resort to force has been interpreted by the government as an invitation to use armed force against the people without any fear of reprisals. The methods of Umkhonto we Sizwe mark a break with that past.

The Rivonia Trial and significance for Mandela

The authorities reacted resolutely to violent protest, both by the expansion of the security forces (see page 45) and by the Rivonia Trial (see below) at which most ANC leaders were accused of treason and threatened with capital punishment. By 1964, South Africa appeared to be a police state with resistance firmly beaten.

After Nelson Mandela was acquitted following the Treason Trial (see page 28), he went underground, working secretly. He became known as the '**Black Pimpernel**' because the authorities could not trace him. Often he was disguised as a chauffeur because this allowed him to drive unchallenged and often he was accompanied by white sympathisers, usually members of the outlawed Communist Party, who would act as his employers. He spent much time hiding at a farm called Liliesleaf in the Johannesburg district of Rivonia; the farm was secretly owned by the Communist Party. It was here, for example, that he helped plan the formation and activities of MK.

Mandela's capture

Early in 1962, Mandela set out for various countries in Africa, seeking support and funds. He also visited London with the same purpose. It was the first time he had been abroad, and he mentioned how surprised he was to see white and black people mixing together in apparent harmony in Tanzania. Mandela was lionised on his journey; he met political leaders in London and spoke at international conferences. In Addis Ababa, Ethiopia, he explained why the armed struggle was necessary and how he feared South Africa was on the brink of civil war, and received military training himself. On his return to South Africa, however, while travelling around to post-tour briefing meetings, he was finally, in August 1962, arrested at a nondescript place called Howick Falls.

Mandela was charged with incitement to strike and travelling abroad without a passport. Grateful that he was not associated yet with MK, he realised that defence was fruitless as the prosecution brought witnesses who could verify all the accusations. Therefore, he turned his defence instead into a further justification of the struggle. He was sentenced to five years in prison without parole.

The Rivonia Trial

While Mandela was in prison on Robben Island, the security forces raided the Liliesleaf farm on 11 July 1963. Here, they found not only MK operatives and caches of weapons but also over 250 incriminating documents. Some of these related to Mandela's role; he had asked for them to be destroyed but they had been kept as valuable historical documents. Mandela became the prime defendant in the Rivonia Trial. He was accused of many actions, including incitement to cause violent revolution, a capital offence. The trial began in October 1963 and attracted great publicity; it was reported in many countries and attracted large crowds each day, mainly in support of the defendants. These included ANC colleagues such as Walter Sisulu and SACP members such as Lionel 'Rusty' Bernstein (who was later acquitted). However, Mandela's guilt could not be in doubt. He felt it more useful to justify the struggle than attempt to plead his innocence. The highlight of the trial was, therefore, the four-hour speech by Nelson Mandela in which he admitted the charges that he belonged to the ANC and MK and again justified the ANC struggle against apartheid.

SOURCE F

Extract from Nelson Mandela's opening speech at the Rivonia Trial (available at www.anc.org.za/content/nelson-mandelas-statement-dock-rivonia-trial).

The lack of human dignity experienced by Africans is the direct result of the policy of white supremacy. White supremacy implies black inferiority. Legislation designed to preserve white supremacy entrenches this notion. Menial tasks in South Africa are invariably performed by Africans. When anything has to be carried or cleaned the white man will look around for an African to do it for him, whether the African is employed by him or not. Because of this sort of attitude, whites tend to regard Africans as a separate breed. They do not look upon them as people with families of their own; they do not realize that they have emotions – that they fall in love like white people do; that they want to be with their wives and children like white people want to be with theirs; that they want to earn enough money to support their families properly, to feed and clothe them and send them to school. And what 'house-boy' or 'garden-boy' or labourer can ever hope to do this? …

Above all, we want equal political rights, because without them our disabilities will be permanent. I know this sounds revolutionary to the whites in this country, because the majority of voters will be Africans. This makes the white man fear democracy.

> **?** How useful is Source F to a historian studying the reasons for the struggle against apartheid?

All the defendants conducted themselves effectively during the trial, and the judge took three weeks to reach a verdict. It was life imprisonment. Most of the leadership of the ANC and MK had been caught up in the Rivonia Trial. As the prisoners departed for Robben Island, the government may have been convinced that it had defeated the most significant challenge to its regime.

International response to the Rivonia Trial

The Rivonia Trial attracted worldwide attention. The UN called for the defendants to be released, while dockworkers in several countries threatened to refuse to handle South African goods in the ports. The new leader of the Communist Soviet Union, Leonid Brezhnev, joined US Congressmen and British MPs in calling for clemency while 50 of the latter led a protest march in London. South African Premier Verwoerd claimed to have been unmoved by international protest. However, this international criticism informed the context in which the judge had to deliver his verdict – and indeed, the international concerns about the Rivonia Trial were significant reasons for the widespread

SOURCE G

Photograph of the police presence during the Rivonia Trial, December 1963.

What does the photograph in Source G suggest about security during the Rivonia Trial?

protests against apartheid and the imposition of sanctions against South Africa in the years to come.

The impact of exile and imprisonment on the ANC and PAC

By the early 1960s, all the principal ANC and PAC leaders had been arrested. Their activities had been diminished. It seemed that the government had been successful in its efforts to stifle protest and revolt. However, anti-apartheid organisations remained active, and were planning and preparing for future conflict.

The impact on the ANC

Following the Rivonia Trial, the structures of the ANC were all but destroyed. Its president, Chief Luthuli, was under house arrest and increasingly out of contact with colleagues. Many of its other surviving leaders, for example Oliver Tambo (see page 88) and SACP activist **Joe Slovo**, went into exile in sympathetic African countries and London. Here they discussed future tactics while members underwent military training. Although there was a real desire to implement a guerrilla war against South Africa, the country was surrounded by friendly nations such as white-controlled Rhodesia, making it extremely difficult to infiltrate guerrilla fighters within its borders. From 1963 and indeed well into the 1970s, there were no MK attacks within South Africa.

However, the ANC regrouped and reorganised in exile. Bases were set up in countries friendly to the anti-apartheid struggle such as Tanzania and Mozambique, and infiltration routes into South Africa were organised. As a result, the ANC did have an infrastructure to accommodate the thousands of radicalised new activists, called 'cadres', who joined following the 1976 Soweto uprising, fourteen years later (explained in more detail on page 78). The exiled

KEY FIGURE

Joe Slovo (1926–95)

A leading Communist who worked closely with the ANC after their leadership went into exile, and in 1987 became chief of staff of MK.

leadership were under no illusions that the struggle would be a long and protracted process.

Relations with foreign countries

Oliver Tambo, in particular, launched a charm offensive, initially from his base in London, and worked tirelessly as an unofficial ambassador during the years in exile. Clearly, building up good relations with and acquiring support and funding from sympathetic nations were crucial – both if the ANC was to survive and if it was to be seen as a viable government-in-exile.

Communist states

To this end, even before their exile, the leaders had attempted to build relations with Communist and non-aligned nations. Leaders such as Walter Sisulu had, for example, travelled to East Europe in the 1950s to make links. In 1960, delegates met Mao Zedong in China, although little concrete help was forthcoming from that quarter. Meetings with Soviet leaders were more fruitful and grants were awarded, $300,000 in 1963 and $560,000 in 1965. Historian Vladimir Shubin has estimated that these grants may have constituted as much as 85 per cent of ANC revenue at the time. Communist states including the Soviet Union, German Democratic Republic (GDR) and Bulgaria also offered military training. The state intelligence organisation in the GDR also offered training in interrogation which was put to good use in investigating those cadres suspected of being planted by the South African security forces. It imposed harsh discipline, particularly on those frustrated by inactivity in the training camps.

African nations

The ANC was generally disappointed in the help it received from independent African nations, except from Tanzania, which allowed four training camps within its borders by 1969. In 1963, the Organisation of African Unity (OAU) had been set up to encourage the newly independent African states to cooperate: its liberation committee set up camps for ANC recruits and provided military training and equipment, but this did not have a great impact.

Alliance with the Zimbabwean African People's Union

In 1967, the ANC allied itself with the Zimbabwean African People's Union (ZAPU), an organisation fighting to destroy the white supremacist regime in Rhodesia. Although this led to good publicity for the ANC, the military results were limited. At best, ANC fighters received combat experience through involvement in the insurrection in the Wankie game reserve in Rhodesia. South African forces reinforced the Rhodesia military. Their superior firepower, and weaknesses with supplies and communications on the part of the ANC, meant the cadres were lucky to escape. At least twelve were killed. Overall, moreover, the Wankie incursion had little or no impact on the capacity of the ANC to extend its struggle, as exemplified by the 1969 Morogoro Conference.

The Morogoro Conference, 1969

This conference of 70 delegates, held in Morogoro, Tanzania, was intended to draw up a plan for victory and reform the structure of the ANC to facilitate this. The ANC recognised its failures so far and seemed determined to learn from them. The main results of the conference were commitments to:

- re-emphasise the importance of the armed struggle within South Africa itself – at the time the ANC had no military presence there – and to give more voice to rank-and-file members. It was not until the late 1970s, however, that the ANC really began to make its presence felt in South Africa itself
- define the relationship between the ANC and its allies in SACP
- re-examine the role in the membership of Africans and non-Africans
- create a management structure to organise the struggle more successfully in future.

The National Executive and Revolutionary Council

While the conference emphasised the multiracial nature of the ANC, it stated that only blacks could serve on its highest body, the National Executive Committee. A new Revolutionary Council was created, however, which was to oversee the military struggle. Members included white Communists such as Joe Slovo, whose links helped maintain military supplies from Communist countries such as the USSR.

Strategy and tactics document

The conference re-emphasised that, while important, the armed struggle was not the only strategy, and that political tactics were also important – particularly in terms of winning support among the African population. However, this showed how out of touch the exiled leaders were. They displayed little awareness of the growing Black Consciousness movement in South Africa (see page 71) and felt that more research and analysis of conditions in South Africa needed to be undertaken.

SOURCE H

Extract from the text of the 'Strategy and tactics document' adopted by the ANC at the Morogoro Conference, April–May 1969 (available at www.sahistory. org.za/archive/strategy-and-tactics-statement-adopted-anc-morogoro-conference-april-may-1969-abridged).

The Relationship between the Political and Military: When we talk of revolutionary armed struggle, we are talking of political struggle by means which include the use of military force even though once force as a tactic is introduced it has the most far-reaching consequences on every aspect of our

> What points are being made in Source H?

activities. It is important to emphasise this because our movement must reject all manifestations of militarism which separates armed people's struggle from its political context … One of the vital problems connected with this bears on the important question of the relationship between the political and military. From the very beginning our Movement has brooked no ambiguity concerning this. The primacy of the political leadership is unchallenged and supreme and all revolutionary formations and levels (whether armed or not) are subordinate to this leadership. To say this is not just to invoke tradition. This approach is rooted in the very nature of this type of revolutionary struggle and is borne out by the experience of the overwhelming majority of revolutionary movements which have engaged in such struggle. Except in very rare instances, the people's armed challenge against a foe with formidable material strength does not achieve dramatic and swift success. The path is filled with obstacles and we harbour no illusions on this score in the case of South Africa. In the long run it can only succeed if it attracts the active support of the mass of the people. Without this lifeblood it is doomed.

The ANC–SACP relationship

The new structure helped clarify the relationship between the ANC and the SACP. The primacy of the ANC was emphasised. However, the SACP's vital role in providing funding for supplies through its contacts with Communist countries was also recognised. The military expertise of Communist cadres was established by their presence on the Revolutionary Council: Communists such as Joe Slovo and Chris Hani would come to dominate military tactics. They also provided a rhetoric based on Marxist theories of revolution such as guerrilla warfare and the mobilisation of the masses.

The impact on PAC and Poqo

The PAC and Poqo fared even worse than the ANC in the 1960s. After the banning of opposition political parties, most of its leaders were arrested until Potlako Leballo emerged as the new leader from his base in Basutoland (now Lesotho). Leballo planned to organise a mass uprising in South Africa on 8 April 1963, in which white people would be killed indiscriminately. However, this was discovered: searches found the names of the entire membership of Poqo. Over 2000 supporters were arrested, effectively defeating the organisation. PAC was riven with dissent until the resignation of Leballo in 1969. There was a short-lived friendship with Communist China and a rebranding of Poqo as the Azanian People's Liberation Army in 1968, but overall it ceased to be significant in the struggle against apartheid.

Summary diagram: African nationalist radicalisation, 1961–68

```
Decision to take up armed
         struggle
                                    Spear of the          Poqo          African Resistance
                                    Nation (MK)                            Movement
• Government intransigence
• Failure of peaceful protests                        Attacks on non-
• Violence used by security        Bombings          white collaborators      Bombings
  forces
• Power of government                                  Attacks on whites
                                                      Attacks in rural areas

                                                       Defeated by           Defeated by
                                                    government forces      government forces

                                   Government raid
                                      July 1963

                                    Rivonia Trial
                                  Oct. 1963–July 1964

                                   Life imprisonment
                                      for leaders
```

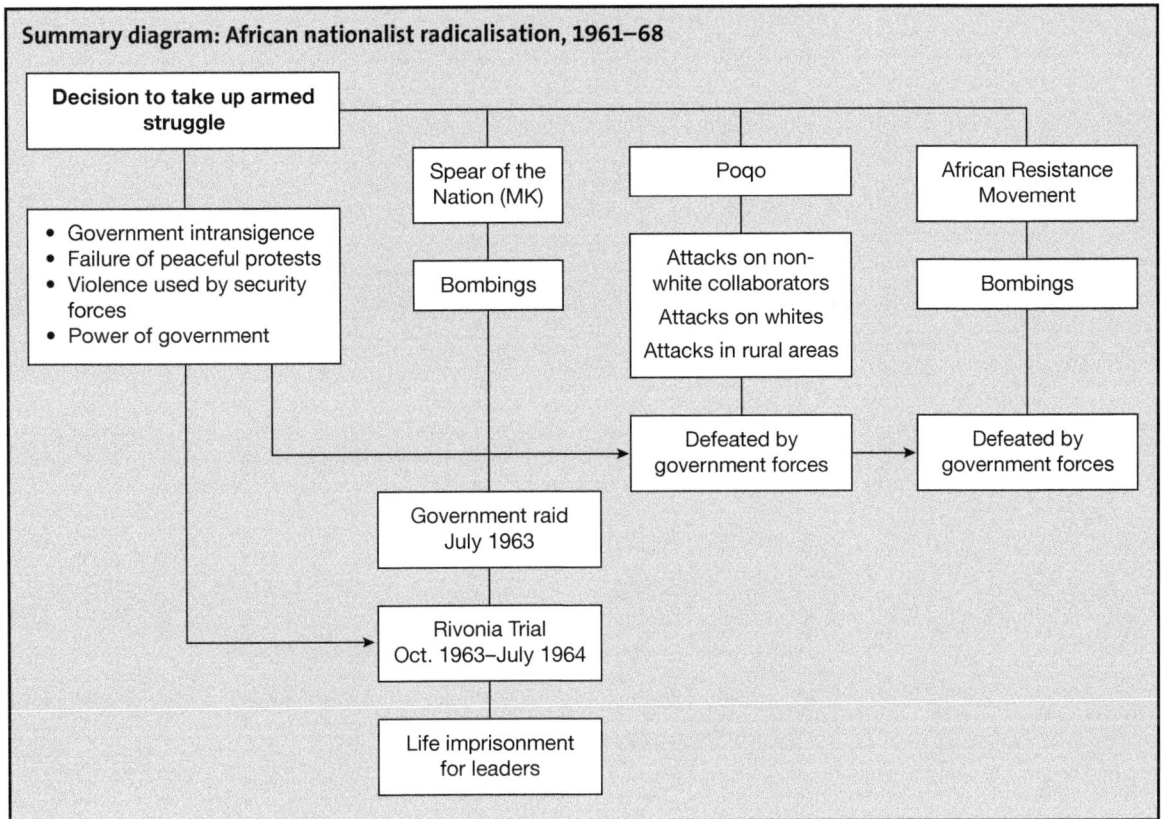

4 Strengthening 'separate development', 1961–68

▶ *How firmly was apartheid entrenched during the period 1961–68?*

The mid to late 1960s probably saw the apartheid regime at its most secure and confident. It was surrounded by friendly countries, opposition was largely defeated and many foreign interests were ready to invest in South Africa.

Economic recovery

While the economy had suffered in the months following Sharpeville, with a reduction in foreign investment and a worrying level of emigration by professional white workers who feared civil war, it was quick to recover in the wake of government repression and control. The 1960s and early 1970s marked the most confident years of the apartheid state.

Growth in Afrikaner prosperity

Traditionally, the English-speaking white population had enjoyed more economic prosperity in South Africa but the 1960s saw a growth in Afrikaner wealth. Afrikaners also took more management posts, for example, from 43.2 per cent of management and technical positions in 1948 to 68.1 per cent in 1960.

Table 2.1 Afrikaner ownership of industrial concerns in 1948 and 1964

Industry	1948	1964
Mining	1%	10%
Manufacturing/construction	6%	10%
Professional	16%	27%
Finance	6%	21%

Source: Frank Welsh, *A History of South Africa*, HarperCollins, 2000, page 463.

International investment

International investment grew, with many investors able to receive a fifteen to twenty per cent return on their outlays. This investment stimulated the economy, with average economic growth six per cent a year:

- The number of white people employed in manufacturing rose from 957,000 to 1,181,000 between 1960 and 1966.
- The white population itself rose from 3.09 million to 3.77 million over the course of the 1960s, largely as a result of immigration.
- Per capita income among white people rose by almost 50 per cent during the 1960s, from R22,389 to R32,779.
- By the end of the 1960s, South African foreign reserves had quadrupled from the 1960 figure of $240 million.
- Overall, during the decade, US trade grew by 79 per cent, UK trade by 88 per cent and that with Japan by a staggering 379 per cent.
- The value of gold, always crucial to the health of the South African economy, grew by 85 per cent during the 1960s.

British investment

Britain maintained close economic ties with South Africa. British banks such as Barclays controlled 60 per cent of South African bank deposits.

Diplomatic ties

South Africa emphasised both its anti-Communist stance and its position of stability in an increasingly unstable African continent. While many Western countries had anti-apartheid movements, their governments tended to value investments and ties more. Few protested against apartheid.

The USA also maintained close ties, not least because it had extensive interests in South African minerals. While its leaders condemned apartheid, particularly during the Civil Rights era, they continued to see South Africa as a bulwark against communism and opposed sanctions; they also sold arms to South Africa to support its stance against communism.

Friendly neighbours

South Africa was surrounded by friendly countries, for example the Portuguese colonies of Angola and Mozambique and white-controlled Rhodesia. Even newly independent African nations such as Zambia relied on South Africa for trade and access to ports.

Potential economic problems

The South African economy had three fundamental problems:

- It required considerable foreign investment.
- It required the importation of heavy machinery and technical innovations, particularly in its mining industry.
- It required the importation of all its oil.

In the 1960s, these problems were all negated by the prevailing economic conditions, which were favourable to the white minority in power. However, should any or all of them change, South Africa would be very vulnerable.

Life in white South Africa, 1961–68

Life for white South Africans was generally good during the 1960s. They had access to plentiful economic opportunities, excellent social services, hospitals and education, and many could afford at least one servant. Relative prosperity for Afrikaners compared to English-speaking white South Africans was growing – from half that of the incomes of English speakers in 1946 to two-thirds by 1970. Statistics on quality of life suggested that white South Africans as a group were among the most comfortably off in the world. All statistics on health, education and life expectancy compared favourably with those in other developed nations. Their homes were generally comfortable, with all the modern conveniences. The English-speaking northern suburbs of Johannesburg were said to have almost as many swimming pools as the wealthiest area of Los Angeles, Beverly Hills. Many could afford leisurely Christmas holidays in coastal resorts. They were united by such things as a love of sport, particularly cricket and rugby, and outdoor activities. They were understandably reluctant to allow such a lifestyle to come under threat from change.

? What reasons does
  Woods give in Source I
  for his frustration with his
  lack of success in changing
  people's minds about
  apartheid?

SOURCE I

Extract from Donald Woods, *Biko*, Paddington Press, 1978, page 40. Woods was an anti-apartheid journalist. Here he is discussing his lack of success in persuading whites to abandon apartheid. The Federal Party was a political party which opposed apartheid.

The Federal party nominated me … for election in a parliamentary constituency, but the white electorate was horrified at the idea of a non-racial franchise, which would lead in time to black majority rule, and I lost the election utterly, polling fewer than a thousand votes. Being twenty-three and resilient, I was undismayed. Concluding that it would be a long time before white voters could be persuaded to scrap apartheid, I quit the white political party and went into journalism. If I couldn't convert my fellow whites with oratory I would try to do so with the pen! That at least was the intention … Today, twenty years later, and having written an estimated million words or more against apartheid, I acknowledge the effort has not been crowned with success. People are reluctant to abandon their prejudices, especially a minority of whites fearful of an overwhelming majority of blacks, and although there has been an increase in the number of whites rejecting apartheid, the majority of South Africans remain committed to it.

White insulation from other groups

White people rarely came into contact with other races outside master–servant relations. They were insulated, through government control of the media, from the outside world. Television, for example, was banned until January 1976: government officials feared it would encourage communism and racial mixing. Indeed, when television was finally introduced, it was initially for only two hours a day, one hour in Afrikaans and one in English. There was strict censorship of the literature allowed into South Africa and the broadcast news had to toe the government line. The state-run radio was reluctant even to broadcast Western pop music: teenagers surreptitiously listened on their transistors under the bedclothes to their favourite records transmitted from Lourenço Marques (present-day Maputo) in Mozambique. They were taught in schools that apartheid was the natural order of things and that people of colour were inferior. Since white people had little access to alternative views, many of them accepted that any protest was orchestrated by Communists. They were effectively living a lifestyle that was unsustainable both economically and politically.

Developing the Bantustans

Life for Africans was challenging. In 1980, one influential survey showed South Africa had one of the most unequal societies in the world: ten per cent enjoyed 58 per cent of the national wealth while the lowest 40 per cent shared only six per cent. The lack of opportunities for Africans was exacerbated by the total apartheid policies pursued by the government, such as developing the Bantustans.

Verwoerd's government had plans to solve the racial problems beyond mere repression. The idea was to develop the policy that Africans should live on tribal reserves and only enter 'white South Africa' as migrant workers, so that the Africans' tribal homelands became Bantustans (see below). In this way, their homelands would be more to their inhabitants than just reservoirs of cheap labour.

The National Government under Verwoerd had three fundamental beliefs:

- That Afrikaners were fulfilling God's divine purpose – confirmed, of course, by the prime minister's recovery after the abortive assassination attempt (see page 23).
- That every group of people had a right to existence.
- That national aspirations should be fulfilled within one's own country.

The last-mentioned belief meant that people could not aspire to belong to a country of which they were not citizens and whose values and customs were alien to them. The idea was based not only on the notion that white people and Africans were different, but also on the idea that non-white people of different ethnic origin were also different, as indeed were Africans of different tribal origins. All African groups then should have their own homelands in which they could achieve their own national identities, adopting a society and culture which suited their own traditions.

The creation of Bantustans

The 1958 Bantu Self-government Act laid the basis for the creation of eight Bantustans. This was not a new idea (see page 20). Afrikaners of extremist views had long suggested total separation of the different races, with Afrikaners themselves doing the unskilled work previously reserved for Africans. D.F. Malan had argued this was impractical; Verwoerd had been one of its proponents, and indeed had once said South Africa should choose 'to be poor and white rather than rich and multi-racial'. He may have tempered his views as South Africa did eventually become wealthy for its white inhabitants (see page 63). He accepted the continuing need for cheap African labour, but he was adamant that there was no place for Africans in white society.

Verwoerd had also been influenced by the decolonisation which was happening in Africa. Ghana had become independent from Britain in March 1957 and Guinea from France in October 1958. It was clear that other countries would shortly follow. The idea of Bantustans was a South African imitation of decolonisation. The African homelands, currently governed as types of colonies with tribal chieftains assisted by white officials, would henceforth be prepared for full independence, to become fully self-governing and self-financing. Apartheid supporters could not understand how South Africa could possibly be accused of racism if this policy was pursued.

Transkei

To investigate how well the policy worked, the creation of Bantustans and how they fared can be considered by the example of Transkei, the first Bantustan to be created in 1963 as a self-governing state. It received full 'independence' in 1976.

Transkei already had a quasi-parliament, the Territorial Assembly dating from 1958, a legislature of 110 members, 65 of whom were appointed chieftains and 45 elected through a democratic franchise. The chiefs were already in the majority but they also controlled the management of elections to ensure, in theory, that compliant delegates were returned to Parliament. However, the three main chieftains were in disagreement, and the Democratic Party, which opposed independence and demanded South African citizenship and an end to apartheid, won 38 out of the 45 elected seats. Nevertheless, the powerful Kaiser Mathanzima could still control Parliament through his authority over sufficient numbers of chieftains. He relied on coercion and declared a state of emergency, which continued for much of the lifespan of Transkei. He attempted to prevent unrest and banned opposition groups through Proclamation R400, which had been issued to address the Pondoland rebellions which ended in 1961 (see page 35).

However, no other government recognised the Transkei, which was condemned by the UN and faced considerable unrest from the activities of Poqo, the military wing of PAC. Mathanzima survived multiple assassination attempts but other chieftains were not so lucky; in October 1962, for example, Poqo assassinated Chief Gwebindala Mabuza of the Tembo tribe.

Transkei never achieved anything like economic independence from South Africa and it continued much as before, as a reservoir for cheap labour. As an independent state, Transkei remained a sham. However, it was made up only of three segments, whereas Bophuthatswana, a later-created Bantustan, comprised nineteen separate segments spread over hundreds of kilometres.

However well intentioned Verwoerd was with the Bantustan policy, it clearly did not achieve its objectives and never won acceptance either outside South Africa or from opponents of apartheid within. Opposition, moreover, became more militant with the beginnings of violent protest and armed struggle.

Vorster's use of police powers and defence forces

Verwoerd's successor, John Vorster, had been a hard-line minister of justice and continued to build up the police and defence forces; indeed, the defence budget rose from R44 million to R255 million during his period as justice minister from 1961 to 1966. The defence forces and police cooperated and were closely linked: sometimes it was difficult to discern which organisation those dealing specifically with counter-insurgency actually belonged to. By 1970, South Africa had all the trappings of a police state, which would be developed and extended in the wake of the Soweto uprising of 1976.

Defence forces

The South African Defence Force (SADF) had been created in 1957 with a dual mission to defend the borders and combat counter-insurgency. During the 1960s, this meant that most focus was on preventing infiltration by anti-apartheid groups. In 1963, the SADF had a strength of 25,000. This was considerably extended after 1967 when conscription was introduced for white men: they had to serve initially for nine months with compulsory camps and further training at regular intervals thereafter. Most conscripts found themselves in locations near the borders. The counter-insurgency role also had a retaliation focus; hence, in 1968, South African paramilitary police units were sent to the Wankie game reserve to help Rhodesian forces combat ZAPU–ANC insurgents.

Faced by international boycotts, the South African government was finding it difficult to legally acquire weapons, although they employed all types of subterfuge to do so. Better, however, to create their own arms industry. To this end, an Armaments Production Board was set up in 1964 to co-ordinate domestic arms production: R33 million was invested here. With the waves of measures of repression by the security forces, South Africa seemed to be on a war footing.

Police forces

Police forces were given ever-greater powers such as Section Six of the 1967 Terrorism Act, which gave them authority to detain indefinitely anyone suspected of terrorist activities or of supporting them. Similarly, the 1965 Police Amendment Act had empowered police to make searches without any need for a warrant within one mile of the borders. The police were to extend these powers in the ensuing decade but already they had quasi-legal authority to do as they wished. In 1969, the Bureau for State Security (BOSS) was created to co-ordinate the work of the defence and police forces. It reported directly to the prime minister; its activities were secret.

Summary diagram: Strengthening 'separate development', 1961–68

```
        ┌──────────────────────┐                    ┌──────────────────────┐
        │  White South Africans │                    │  Black South Africans │
        └──────────────────────┘                    └──────────────────────┘

┌─────────┐ ┌──────────┐ ┌──────────┐      ┌──────────┐ ┌──────────┐ ┌──────────┐
│Growth in│ │ Foreign  │ │ Friendly │      │Bantustans│ │  Strict  │ │  Police  │
│Afrikaner│ │investment│ │neighbour-│      │ in which │ │apartheid │ │ powers   │
│prosperity│ │  and     │ │  ing     │      │Africans  │ └──────────┘ │of control│
└─────────┘ │diplomatic│ │countries,│      │  were    │              │and strong│
            │  ties    │ │for example│     │ citizens │   ┌────────┐ │ defence  │
            └──────────┘ │ Rhodesia,│      └──────────┘   │Africans│ │ policies │
                         │Mozambique│                     │  as    │ └──────────┘
                         └──────────┘                     │'guests'│
                                                          │in white│
                                                          │ South  │
                                                          │ Africa │
                                                          └────────┘
```

High point of apartheid

| White prosperity, whites enjoying high living standards and security | Poverty and repression, poor living standards in Bantustans, no security in South Africa |

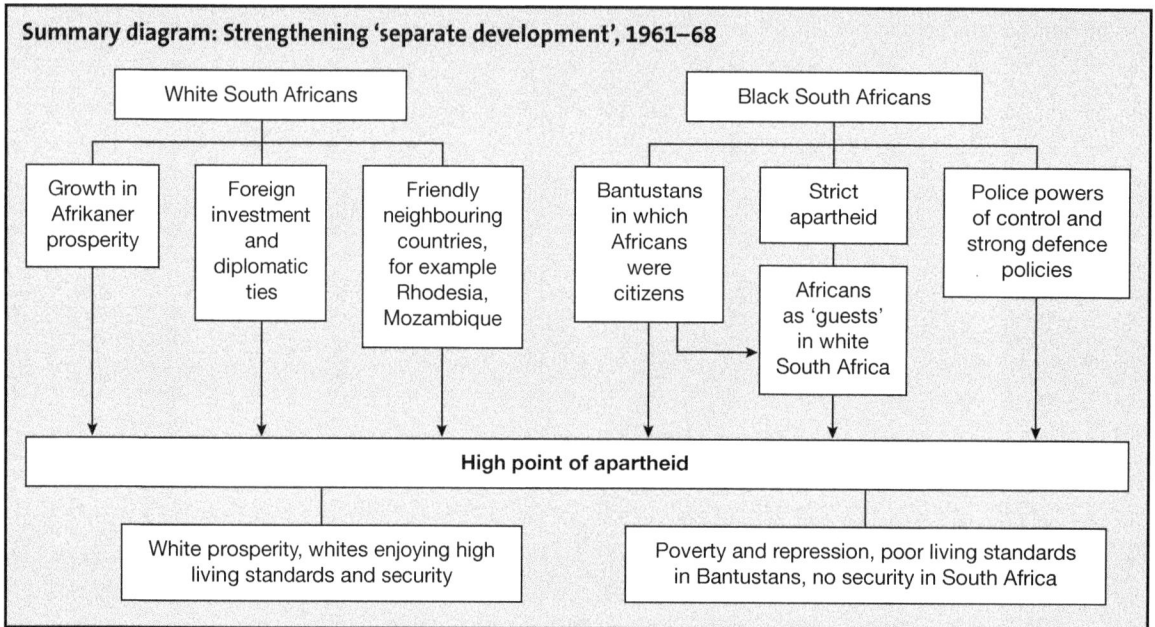

Chapter summary

While peaceful resistance to apartheid continued, its effectiveness was increasingly questioned as the government usually responded with brutality and repression. This was particularly the case in the Sharpeville Massacre of March 1960, where security forces killed 69 peaceful protesters. The government responded with a state of emergency, which resulted in the banning of most anti-apartheid groups, such as the ANC and PAC. This in turn led them to go underground or into exile, and also to begin an armed struggle. The MK focused on sabotage of property but Poqo targeted whites and African 'collaborators'. In the face of worldwide condemnation of apartheid, South Africa meanwhile became a republic and left the Commonwealth.

The majority of the ANC leadership were captured and put on trial at Rivonia. This destroyed the ANC leadership within South Africa and saw Nelson Mandela, among others, being imprisoned for life. The anti-apartheid organisations regrouped abroad but recognised that their struggle would be long and arduous. None could launch any attacks inside South Africa, which was surrounded by friendly countries, such as Rhodesia with its white government. The period marked the most confident period of white rule. While the economy grew substantially and most white South Africans enjoyed prosperous lifestyles, the government extended its apartheid programme with the creation of Bantustans. It also extended the role of the security forces and developed a substantial arms industry, so that by the end of the decade South Africa was effectively a well-defended police state.

⚲ Refresher questions

Use these questions to remind yourself of the key material covered in this chapter.

1 Why had peaceful protest achieved so little by 1960?

2 What conditions led to the PAC becoming more effective in Sharpeville than in other townships?

3 How effective were the measures taken by the government to control unrest in the wake of the Sharpeville shootings?

4 Why did South Africa leave the Commonwealth in June 1961?

5 Why did anti-apartheid organisations such as the PAC and ANC turn to violence?

6 What was the significance of the Rivonia Trial for Nelson Mandela?

7 Why was the 1969 Morogoro Conference so important in the history of the ANC?

8 How far did international investment grow in South Africa during the period 1959–68?

9 How far were Bantustans merely 'repositories of cheap labour'?

10 How effectively did South Africa develop its defence and security forces during the period 1959–68?

⚲ Question practice

ESSAY QUESTIONS

1 'Government measures effectively stifled anti-apartheid protest in the years 1961–68.' How far do you agree with this statement?

2 To what extent did South Africa's becoming a republic change its relationships with other countries during the period 1961–68?

3 How significant was the movement towards an armed struggle on the effectiveness of anti-apartheid organisations in the years 1961–68?

4 'The creation of Bantustans was largely intended as a source of cheap labour when required by South Africa.' How far do you agree with this statement?

SOURCE-BASED QUESTIONS

1 With reference to Source B (page 46) and Source E (page 54), and your understanding of the historical context, assess the value of these sources to a historian studying the reasons for the movement to an armed struggle by anti-apartheid groups in South Africa during the early 1960s.

2 With reference to Source F (page 56) and Source H (pages 59–60), and your understanding of the historical context, assess the value of these sources to a historian studying the problems faced by the anti-apartheid movement in South Africa.

CHAPTER 3

Redefining resistance and challenges to National Party power, 1968–83

The late 1960s saw the development of Black Consciousness, a movement offering pride in their race to Africans. While this influenced the 1976 Soweto uprising, the immediate causes were problems with education for Africans. The uprising had a major impact in that it set the scene for continued unrest. Meanwhile, thousands of young people left to join the exiled African National Congress (ANC). The Soweto uprising and death in police custody of Black Consciousness activist Steve Biko caused worldwide condemnation for South Africa. It became subject to intensified sanctions and boycotts, and the economy began to weaken. This was coupled with greater involvement in military operations in the face of hostile regimes on its borders. Conditions for Africans in the Bantustans continued to remain poor. The National Party itself faced scandal through Muldergate, so the confidence of the apartheid regime began to falter.

These developments are described in the following sections:

★ Black Consciousness and the Soweto uprising

★ The ANC restrengthened

★ Domestic challenges to National Party power, 1974–83

★ External pressures on National Party power, 1974–83

Key dates

1969	Formation of South African Students' Organisation	1978	Visit of ANC leadership to Vietnam, leading to an intensification of its struggle against apartheid
1975	Independence from Portugal of Angola and Mozambique		Kassinga massacre in Namibia
1976	Soweto uprising		UN Resolution 435 calling for a peace settlement in Namibia
1977	Death of Steve Biko in police custody		'Muldergate' scandal undermined government of Vorster
	Transkei given full independence	1980	Rhodesian settlement with formation of Zimbabwe
	United Nations (UN) Resolution 177: arms embargo on South Africa		Venda given 'full independence'
	Gleneagles agreement on severing Commonwealth sporting links with South Africa	1981	Ciskei given 'full independence'
	Announcement of Total Onslaught and Total Strategy to combat it		

1 Black Consciousness and the Soweto uprising

▶ *What were the causes and effects of the 1976 Soweto uprising?*

In the absence of the African National Congress (ANC) and Pan-Africanist Congress (PAC), new movements were taking shape in South Africa which would come into fruition in the 1970s. With existing leaders in prison or exile, a new generation of activists were coming to the fore, many of whom were motivated by the **Black Consciousness** movement.

Black Consciousness

Black Consciousness was an international movement which had originated in the USA. It was concerned with taking pride in black identity, history and culture. Indeed, in South Africa this manifested itself in a realisation among young Africans that the country offered them nothing and the purpose of education was to teach them they were inferior. In 1969, university students formed the South African Students' Organisation (SASO) to fight for better conditions and opportunities. This formed the germ of a wider protest movement in the 1970s, dominated by the charismatic SASO leader and co-founder Steve Biko.

Black Consciousness was tolerated by the government at first because it felt that its emphasis on separate development might tie in with apartheid. Its goals included:

● Non-cooperation with white groups, even those sympathetic to the ending of apartheid.
● Encouraging Indians and coloured people to see themselves as black and equally subject to white oppression.

However, this tolerance was soon eroded as its influence grew, particularly among the young, to whom it gave a new consciousness of their identity and heritage. At the least, it helped develop a pride in being an African.

Black Consciousness and white people

The Black Consciousness movement was not necessarily anti-white, but felt it had to fight apartheid through its own efforts. Many supporters believed they should not accept help from any white sympathisers within South Africa. One popular slogan was 'Black man, you are on your own'. Biko argued in the late 1960s that most white liberals opposed apartheid mainly to assuage their own consciences and would always ultimately side with other white people. He later tempered this view, particularly after his friendship with white activists such as journalist **Donald Woods**, but the emphasis on eschewing white help remained. In 1976, activist Ranwedzi Nengwekhulu articulated a further perspective of Black Consciousness towards white people.

KEY TERM

Black Consciousness
Movement based on Black Power in the USA in which African people took increasing pride in their culture and identity. This was particularly associated in South Africa with Steve Biko and the South African Students' Organisation (SASO).

KEY FIGURE

Donald Woods (1933–2001)
A white journalist and anti-apartheid activist whose biography of Steve Biko was important in bringing the latter to international attention.

? How does the author of
Source A explain the
relationship between
Black Consciousness and
white people?

SOURCE A

Extract from a speech by Ranwedzi Nengwekhulu to the International University Exchange Fund, an organisation which supported Black Consciousness, in Geneva, 22 November 1976.

We do not doubt that there are sincere Whites in the White community who want to see change brought about by peaceful or any other means in South Africa but we doubt it would be possible for us to try to seek out all those sincere Whites and to bring them into the fold. Our point of departure has been that we go it alone and we do not negotiate with anyone. We fight for liberation … and we do not expect to receive our liberation 'on a silver plate'. The new kind of perspective of politicised Blacks in South Africa is that we have nothing to do with the people who think they are a master race, who hold the monopoly on truth, who can decide on our future and our direction to the extent of deciding with whom we shall stay, with whom we shall have sex and how many children we shall have. We have decided to go it alone, to forget about them.

Steve Biko and the South African Students' Organisation

In 1972, the SASO organised strikes on university campuses in protest over inferior facilities. In 1975, it celebrated the overthrow of the Portuguese colonial regimes in Mozambique and Angola (see page 99), clearly seeing the struggle against the apartheid regime in South Africa in the same terms. In 1972, moreover, the Black Consciousness movement began to inspire schoolchildren to feel pride in their ethnicity and protest about their conditions. It encouraged rather than controlled their activities.

The South African Students' Movement

There is some controversy over the precise date of the formation of SASM, as it emerged out of previous organisations such as the African Students' Movement (ASM). It moved on from the fundamentally educational aims of the ASM, such as having more say in the governance of schools through the formation of student representative councils, to more general protest. It organised disruption of local meetings of the South African Bureau of Racial Affairs (SABRA), for example, and heckled members of the Dutch Reformed Church when they came to speak in African schools. Importantly, SASM was independent of Black Consciousness and SASO. However, the government saw all protest as part of the same movement and so conflated SASM activities with those of Black Consciousness. Hence, although Steve Biko and SASO may not have been directly involved in SASM activities, the government acted firmly in response to the general protest of the early 1970s. In 1973, Steve Biko was arrested and charged with fomenting terrorism. The SASO itself was banned in 1975. However, it continued as an underground organisation. SASM, meanwhile, remained legal and continued its activities.

Steve Biko

1946	Born
1950	Father died
1962	Expelled from Lovedale High School
1968	Co-founded SASO
1972	Co-founded Black People's Convention to spread ideas of Black Consciousness through the wider community
1973	Banned from speaking publicly
1977	Arrested and died in police custody

Early life and political involvement

Steve Biko was born in 1946 in the King William's Town area. His father, a clerk in the local Native Affairs Department, died suddenly in 1950, leaving his mother to raise the family while working as a cook in the local hospital. Steve was quickly noted for his intelligence and he jumped school grades. However, his association with supporters of Poqo led to his arrest and subsequent expulsion from Lovedale High School in 1962. Biko felt this injustice deeply; his brother felt that it radicalised him.

Steve's brother found him a place at St Francis College in Kwazulu, where he graduated in 1966. He enrolled in the University of Natal as a medical student and became involved in the multiracial National Union of South African Students (NUSAS). Biko increasingly felt frustrated because this was dominated by whites and followed apartheid procedures, for example in housing delegates during conventions: he walked out of a 1967 national conference in protest.

Black Consciousness and SASO

Biko became increasingly interested in the ideas of Black Consciousness and in particular that non-white people could overcome apartheid by their own efforts. To this end he co-founded SASO, a black African students' group, in 1968. At first, he hoped to work with NUSAS but increasingly SASO operated independently, both inspiring and being inspired by other wholly black organisations such as the South African Students' Movement (SASM).

In 1972, Biko became involved with the Black People's Convention, which promoted Black Consciousness within the wider community. In 1975, he co-founded the Zimele Trust to provide aid to political prisoners and their families. As Black Consciousness organisations were banned, Biko himself came to the notice of the security forces, and in 1973 he was barred from speaking in public and confined to King William's Town. However, he went underground to circumvent the ban and was arrested four times, often being held without trial. In 1975, he had been called as a defence witness for arrested Black Consciousness activists: the eloquence of his testimony made the authorities reluctant to give him a similar stage in the future.

Arrest and death

Biko was caught defying his ban in August 1977. He was arrested at Port Elizabeth, and died mysteriously in police custody 700 miles way in Pretoria. No one was prosecuted for his death, but he did remain an important figure in the anti-apartheid movement. His inspiration in the fight against apartheid survived him; he became the subject of a major film in 1982 and countless protests against apartheid.

The mobilisation of schoolchildren

By the mid-1970s, the education of black schoolchildren in South Africa had reached a critical pitch owing to various government policies and ineffectiveness. School students were increasingly frustrated by the lack of educational opportunities and, indeed, by the 1970s an increasing awareness that the purpose of school was largely to keep them in servitude rather than to offer opportunities for advancement.

African education from 1948

Education for African children was not compulsory. The deputy minister for Bantu education, Punt Jackson, estimated in May 1977 that compulsory education would require the employment of 970,000 teachers at a cost of R126 million, with a further R130 million to provide the necessary classrooms. African children already had to provide their own equipment. Schools lacked the resources to teach pupils the skills necessary to access any but the most menial jobs.

However, economic recession from the late 1960s made many realise the need for more skilled African workers. As a result, more schools were built – between 1972 and 1974, 40 new schools appeared in Soweto alone – but nowhere near enough to meet the demand. Most African youth valued education highly as a means to escape crime and poverty. The numbers in secondary schools, for example, increased from 178,959 in 1974 to 389,066 by 1976. Nevertheless, the **oil crisis of 1973**, which saw the price of oil rise considerably, and a fall in the price of gold in 1975 meant that the government spent only 0.53 per cent of gross national product on African education – R102 million out of a total of R19,000 million. For every R42 spent on a black African child's education, his or her white counterpart received R644.

In part, the government's response to increased demand was to cut the number of years for schooling for Africans from thirteen to twelve years, essentially to save money. This was achieved in 1975 by cutting the final year at primary school, adding to the numbers attending secondary schools, with no extra facilities to accommodate the increase. The essential point is that while the numbers of schoolchildren were growing, the amount spent on them was in decline. This clearly impacted adversely on the quality of African education.

Overcrowding

During the early 1970s, government spending on African education per pupil slipped to ten per cent of that spent on white children, because of the growth in numbers. This effective reduction in government spending, compounded by dramatic increases in the numbers of schoolchildren, led to massive overcrowding: high school enrolment among Africans increased by 150 per cent between 1970 and 1975, and class sizes, for example in Soweto, could be as high as 70–100. In Soweto in 1975, three-quarters of households accommodated children of school age.

Enforcement of Afrikaans in African schools

In 1974, the minister for Bantu education and development, M.C. Botha, introduced the Afrikaans Medium Decree, which made the use of Afrikaans compulsory in schools from Standard Five, the last year of primary school, upwards. In 1976, his hard-line successor **Andries Treurnicht** insisted that half the lessons in African schools including Maths be taught in Afrikaans,

KEY TERM

Oil crisis of 1973 A massive increase in the price of oil, threatening the prosperity of many developed nations.

KEY FIGURE

Andries Treurnicht (1921–93)

Deputy director of Bantu education in 1976. He was later to form the Conservative Party, which was opposed to any reform of apartheid.

a language that not all African children spoke and which was regarded as the language of repression. The government supposed it reasonable that Africans speak Afrikaans – their employers could well be Afrikaans speakers – but they severely underestimated the resentment this decision occasioned. In a sense, the teaching in Afrikaans was the final straw: children resented being taught through the language of their oppressors, in which many were not fluent enough to learn the content of the lessons. Schoolchildren and their parents had protested about educational provision in Soweto before 1976, but the protests were generally peaceful. It was the decrees on teaching in Afrikaans which provoked the uprising of 1976.

South African Students' Movement in Soweto

Soweto had seen the creation of the school-based SASM to campaign specifically against poor-quality education: it organised the Soweto protests in 1976. Observers, such as activist Ranwedzi Nengwekhulu, suggested that it was not that Soweto was any worse off than other townships, but the presence of this organisation there led to the uprising. Many of its members were over normal school age, having often been forced to defer their schooling due to cost. They had already organised boycotts about the teaching in Afrikaans which they knew would depress their grades. SASM was also independent of control from other groups; although its membership overlapped, for example, with the ANC and PAC, it tended to be more anti-white than the former and openly supported foreign revolutionary movements such as FRELIMO in Mozambique and the People's Movement for the Liberation of Angola (MPLA) in Angola.

> What might be the impact of the photograph in Source B on people's attitudes to the South African authorities in 1976?

SOURCE B

Black students protesting against the compulsory teaching of Afrikaans in black schools charge during a riot in Soweto in 1976.

Although the mobilisation of schoolchildren was key to the uprising in Soweto in 1976, other long-term factors also contributed towards it:

- The conditions in overcrowded townships such as Soweto. Religious leader **Desmond Tutu** had warned the government three weeks earlier that anger was at crisis point. In Soweto, for example, it was common for as many as twenty people to share a four-roomed house with minimal sanitation.
- The influence of movements such as Black Consciousness had given Africans more pride in themselves and their culture. One sociologist compared his 1971 research, which showed increasing African confidence particularly among the young, with his earlier work which suggested that Africans felt inferior and indeed often believed white people were genetically superior. One particular issue here was the growth of African popular culture in terms of soccer and ethnic music such as *mbaqanga*, which whites tended not to share.
- The increasing urbanisation of Africans had significant effects. They were, for example, much more likely to be literate – two-thirds of them by 1970. Over 75 per cent read newspapers: the tabloid *World* increased its circulation six times between 1962 and 1975. This made them more aware of events both within South Africa and elsewhere. Urban Africans were becoming more sophisticated and less patient with the ways they were treated.
- The absence of recognised leaders who could possibly have marshalled their frustrations. ANC leader Oliver Tambo was later to recognise, for example, that the ANC had few active units and no military presence inside Soweto, and communication between the exiled leadership and townships was poor. He did, however, assert that links were made wherever possible, citing activist Joe Gqabi, recently released from Robben Island, who worked with SASM, and was later assassinated by the security forces. However, other commentators have revealed that many of the organisers had no concept of previous protests such as the Defiance Campaign or boycotts (see pages 31–2 and 35). They thought they were the first Africans to defy the government.

The Soweto uprising

Soweto was one of the biggest of the townships, with all the problems of overcrowding, squalor and crime. While 50,000 new homes had built in Soweto during the 1950s, resources in the ensuing decade had been diverted into subsidies for the homelands, despite the fact that the population was rising dramatically. By 1976, it was home to as many as 1 million people. Problems in Soweto, as elsewhere, by the mid-1970s, were exacerbated by the government's cutting subsidies on maize and corn at a time of economic downturn. There was also resentment at the large numbers of shebeens or drinking dens – one at each of Soweto's twenty railway stations for example – where parents sometimes found temptation too strong after their long working hours, and spent money on alcohol rather than food for their families.

The events of the Soweto massacre, 16 June 1976

On 16 June 1976, there was a massive demonstration against the medium of Afrikaans in teaching in Soweto, organised by SASM three days earlier. SASM went on to create the Soweto Student Representative Council (SSRC), which co-ordinated the activities on 16 June and subsequent protests. Thousands of children took part in marches from their schools to a rally in the soccer stadium in Orlando, a central part of Soweto. The security forces tried to disperse the marchers as they converged on the stadium, initially with tear gas and warning shots and eventually with live bullets from machine pistols. At least twenty students died, notably thirteen-year-old Hector Pieterson, whose image with that of his horrified sister was caught in an iconic photograph. The protests spread to other areas in the Transvaal, Natal and the Cape; at least 100 places were affected.

Following the outbreak in Soweto, the uprising continued throughout South Africa until at least the end of the year. By October there had been at least 80 protests. Children went on strike and schools were burnt down, as were shebeens. The demonstrations and protest were the biggest seen so far in South Africa. The security forces may have killed as many as 1000 people as a result of the protests.

The suppression of the Soweto uprising

The authorities were taken by surprise at the strength of the initial demonstrations in Soweto. Nevertheless, they held firm. Minister of Justice Jimmy Kruger blamed the demonstrators for fomenting trouble and justified the killings: 'Natives,' he said, 'had to be made tame to the gun.' Government officials accused them of seeking Communist revolution while the official line remained that, as the government provided the resources for African education, it had the right to choose the form it would take. Although the directive to teach in Afrikaans was later rescinded, clearly the uprising had moved way beyond one specific issue. It was almost as though it escalated under its own momentum.

Banning orders, imprisonment and the suppression of eighteen organisations, including the Christian Institute, a religious organisation which had never been involved in violent protest, followed. As many as 52,000 arrests were made, 90 banning orders were imposed, and the security forces were routinely using at least eighteen different forms of torture, including electric-shock treatment to extract confessions and implicate others in the unrest.

Importantly, the Soweto uprising appeared to have crossed a line: despite the ruthlessness of the security forces and the increasing deployment of troops in the townships, the protests would not go away. Essentially, protest in its various forms was to continue from this period until the demise of the apartheid state in 1994.

SOURCE C

What impression does the photograph in Source C give of security in Soweto after the 1976 uprising?

Photograph of protesters surrendering to the security forces in Soweto in 1976.

Significance of the Soweto uprising

As the demonstrations continued, it became apparent that no central organisation was directing them: not ANC, PAC or even the Black Consciousness movement. Most were localised, spontaneous and organised by schoolchildren themselves. This was a new feature of anti-apartheid protests, more dangerous because of its unpredictability.

The armed struggle

Thousands of young people slipped away, to join armed groups preparing for guerrilla warfare. With sympathetic regimes in power in Mozambique and Angola, the time was propitious for the return to armed struggle. Both ANC and PAC actively recruited new cadres and advised them on how to illegally cross borders, where they headed for military training camps. The intention was to infiltrate them back into South Africa. The first incidents took place in autumn 1976, at Dikgale, where a train was sabotaged, and Bordergate, where there was a firefight between guerrillas and security forces, which left two of the latter injured. Although the ANC, in particular, had been surprised by the Soweto uprising, which may have taken place in part because of the absence of an effective ANC presence in Soweto, the ANC and PAC were nevertheless the beneficiaries. The main concrete effects of the Soweto uprising were:

- the supply of cadres to allow the armed struggle to resume
- enhanced sympathy for the armed struggle as a result of the revulsion at the brutal response of the security forces.

Total Strategy

In 1978, while still defence minister, P.W. Botha stated that South Africa was facing a **Total Onslaught**, a concerted attack by Communist forces supported by the USSR. He believed this could only be combated by a **Total Strategy**. One important effect of the uprising, therefore, was the development of this Total Strategy and reforms to the apartheid system.

Botha's Total Strategy was explained by the chief of the South African Defence Force (SADF), General M.A. Malan, in 1977, who argued that every aspect of society should be deployed against the perceived enemy. This involved, among other things, diplomatic, economic and psychological factors. In fact, the military role was not the only concern in the Total Strategy, although security was vital.

The Total Strategy involved the restructuring of government with the emphasis on security. Botha was helped in this by having been minister of defence for many years and having had especially good relations with the chief of the SADF, General Malan.

In 1979, Botha established a National Management System to oversee government. There were four cabinet committees in charge of policy: economic affairs, social affairs, constitutional affairs and security, with the last the most important.

Botha set up the State Security Council, comprised of army generals and police chiefs, to oversee security. It was supported at local levels by joint management committees. The police and armed forces therefore worked together, sharing information, planning joint operations and so on. The security forces were also involved in clandestine operations; for example, the assassination of activist Ruth First in 1982 and the bombing of the ANC headquarters in London in the same year.

In addition, joint local management centres were set up and tasked with gaining two types of intelligence:

- Hard intelligence: knowledge of plots and insurrections.
- Soft intelligence: ascertaining local grievances.

Armaments Corporation of South Africa

The Armaments Corporation of South Africa (ARMSCOR) was set up to bypass the world boycott on arms sales to South Africa. It developed the country's own arms industries. By the 1970s, South Africa was producing its own helicopters, armed vehicles and artillery. Despite the 1977 arms embargo, it acquired French help in building Mirage fighter bombers, and British help in training South African military personnel in radar air-surveillance equipment. One report in 1979 suggested no army in southern Africa could have lasted more than an afternoon against the SADF.

KEY TERMS

Total Onslaught The fear that there was a total co-ordinated attack orchestrated by Communists to destroy apartheid.

Total Strategy Botha's response to Total Onslaught. This involved the deployment of every possible means, for example political, economic and military to protect the apartheid regime.

P.W. Botha

1916	Born in Orange Free State
1934	Began to study law at Grey University College
1938	Left university for a political career
1946	Head of National Party Youth
1948	Elected to House of Assembly as National Party MP for George, Cape Province
1958	First government office as deputy minister of internal affairs
1966	Became minister of defence
1978	Became prime minister
1984	Became first executive president after constitutional reforms
1989	Resigned over ill health
2006	Died

Early life and career

In 1916, Pieter Willem Botha was born on a farm in the Orange Free State to staunchly Afrikaner parents. Although he entered university to study law in 1934, he left after four years for a career in politics. During the early part of the Second World War he became a leading figure in the pro-Nazi Oxwagon Sentinel, but subsequently disagreed with its policies and ordered National Party members not to join it. By 1946, Botha was head of National Party Youth. He had excellent organisational skills; his political work in Cape Province is credited for the support his party won there in the 1948 elections, with Botha being elected for the constituency of George. He could, however, also be extremely abrasive: he earned the nickname 'Crocodile' for his explosive temper.

Government career

Botha valued loyalty to party and gained the reputation as someone whom the leaders could rely on. In 1958, he was appointed to his first government office, as deputy minister of internal affairs, and in 1961 promoted to minister for coloured affairs: here, he oversaw many deportations under the terms of the Group Areas Act and was responsible for the removals in District Six in Cape Town. He was minister of public works in 1964 and in 1966 minister of defence. Here, he was responsible for the huge expansion of the security forces and developed good rapport with senior military and security figures.

Prime minister and president

Botha became prime minister in 1978, when he developed the policies of Total Strategy against what he saw as Total Onslaught facing South Africa. He also reformed apartheid with the aim of giving more non-white Africans a stake in society. In 1984, he became first executive president, having overseen a new constitution which gave coloured and Indian South Africans their own parliaments (see page 114). While his regime was more liberal in some ways, it also enforced remaining laws rigorously and embarked on extensive military engagements to secure the apartheid state. However, his reforms were too little, too late, and issues such as the continued violence and foreign disinvestment meant that the end of apartheid was inevitable. Botha retired through ill health in 1989, leaving his successor to dismantle the state he had ultimately tried to maintain. Botha lived until 2006: shortly before his death he maintained he had done nothing to be ashamed of.

The minister of law and order, Adriaan Vlok, summarised the overall aim of security policy as removing the activists while addressing the genuine grievances which increased their support. It was, therefore, recognised that the two aspects were closely connected and knowledge was passed on to organisations which could address grievances. The police force meanwhile numbered 50,000.

International reaction

Government reaction to the Soweto uprising led to widespread international condemnation of the police brutality. The United Nations (UN) responded with Resolution 392 only three days after the initial killings; it condemned the government response and apartheid generally. Many multinational companies with subsidiaries in South Africa were pressurised by anti-apartheid groups to withdraw. On university campuses in the USA and elsewhere, there were movements to encourage companies to withdraw their South African investments; many companies, indeed, supported the Campaign to Oppose Bank Loans to South Africa, which saw many funds withdrawn. In November 1977, Polaroid (a global photography company) withdrew completely from South Africa.

Key debate: what was the significance of the Soweto uprising?

No one doubts the importance of the Soweto uprising and many see it as a key event in the fight against apartheid. Certainly, it unleashed new forces, and it escalated into wider protests, which effectively continued in different forms until the demise of the apartheid state in 1994. Historians, however, have emphasised different effects of the Soweto uprising.

The ANC as beneficiary

Some historians have stressed how the ANC was the ultimate beneficiary of the uprising because it welcomed the thousands of young cadres who were to form the basis of its escalating armed struggle. In his history of the movement, Francis Meli, for example, suggested that it brought into the ranks young people who previously had no contact with the ANC and were ripe to be radicalised according to ANC beliefs. It also led to an uninterrupted armed struggle between the masses and the regime – implying that the mass of Africans supported the ANC.

EXTRACT I

Extract from Francis Meli, *A History of the ANC: South Africa Belongs to Us*, James Currey, 1989, page 190.

The heroic struggles of Soweto had a profound impact on the ANC. They resulted in the accelerated expansion of the movement both inside and outside the country, increasing the relative proportion of youth and students within the ANC ranks … Young, militant cadres who were ready and yearning to carry out even the most difficult missions the ANC wished to give them, were put at the immediate disposal of the movement and this was particularly important since the resumption of the armed struggle was an extremely important matter.

In his 2000 history of the ANC, Saul Dubow was inclined to agree. He argued that the ANC was well placed to benefit. Organisations affiliated to the Black Consciousness movement were destroyed and PAC, which may have been closer to the ideas of radicalised young people, was relatively ineffective at the time. Although the ANC may have been out of touch with the radicalism of movements such as SASM, it was quick to embrace the energies of their adherents and also to educate them in ANC philosophy.

EXTRACT 2

Extract from Saul Dubow, *The African National Congress*, Sutton Pocket Histories, 2000, page 83.

… it proved receptive to the energies of this youthful generation and showed sufficient flexibility to adapt to and draw strength from, their evolutionary enthusiasms. The arrival on Robben Island of numbers of Black Consciousness [BC] activists provided a unique opportunity for veteran ANC leadership to promote **Charterist ideals** *and to inculcate theories of class struggle and organisational discipline … many, though by no means all, BC leaders were gradually persuaded by the principles of non-racialism …*

> **🔑 KEY TERM**
>
> **Charterist ideals** Refers to the Freedom Charter of 1955. The ANC still adhered to these goals.

Writing in 2011, Tom Lodge emphasised the wider issue of generational conflict. It was young people who had taken the initiative in Soweto and driven the protests. They were less prepared in future to listen to their elders.

EXTRACT 3

Extract from Tom Lodge, 'Resistance and Reform 1973–1994', in the *Cambridge History of South Africa, Vol. 2 1885–1994*, Cambridge University Press, 2011, pages 442–3.

Continuing assertion and strengthening awareness of their generational identity by so-called youth leadership was one important consequence of the revolt. During the rebellion, youngsters often spoke contemptuously about the political disposition of their elders … The revolt accelerated the erosion of elder authority, a process that was a consequence of teenagers often better educated than their parents and an effect of their growing up in a more urbanised cultural context in which patriarchal forms of socialisation no longer functioned effectively.

Missed opportunity

Historian Dale McKinley agrees that the Soweto uprising was important. However, he feels that the insurrection was quickly suppressed and suffered from a lack of local structures to direct the protests.

EXTRACT 4

Extract from Dale T. McKinley, *The ANC and the Liberation Struggle: A Critical Political Biography*, Pluto Press, 1997, page 47.

The uprising had thus clearly revealed both the potential power and the severe limitations of black consciousness 'ideology': at one level it had succeeded in mitigating the subservient attitude it was so concerned to combat; but on the other, it had no theoretical or strategic base from which to organise and direct the resistance that followed.

The government perspective

We have seen that the immediate government response was repression. However, there was wider and often conflicting reaction. Afrikaner historian Hermann Giliomee argued that the uprising ended government thinking about the relaxation of apartheid, and Vorster in particular felt it best to avoid any new initiatives.

EXTRACT 5

Extract from Hermann Giliomee, *The Afrikaners: Biography of a People*, Hurst & Company, 2003, pages 584–5.

Vorster probably briefly toyed with the idea of a change of course, but after Soweto erupted he dropped all such plans … He understood that reforms introduced by a repressive government did not necessarily enhance stability. Since the racial problem was intractable it was better to play for time than embark on rash action.

How far do Extracts 1–5 disagree on the significance of the Soweto uprising for the ANC?

Vorster, however, retired two years later and his successor, Defence Minister P.W. Botha, was more amenable to change – particularly as he had been informed by the security forces that they could not successfully fight insurgents outside South Africa's borders and deal with insurrection within the country.

It will be seen, then, that while the uprising intensified the opposition and provided the cadres to engage in armed struggle, the government in the longer term learnt it could not control events simply by repression. In this sense, the Soweto uprising sparked a period of continuous conflict until settlement was eventually reached.

The impact of the death of Steve Biko in 1977

Steve Biko had been given a banning order in 1973; however, he often broke it by working in community projects. He was subject to harsh surveillance by the security forces; it is estimated that he was arrested 29 times during a three-year period. In 1976, Biko was called as a defence witness in the trial of nine young SASO activists accused of inciting hatred against white people. Like Nelson Mandela at the Rivonia Trial, he used the opportunity to explain African grievances and why apartheid was doomed to failure. In so doing, he attracted wide publicity and became an international figure.

SOURCE D

Extract from Steve Biko's testimony at the 1976 trial of SASO activists, quoted in Donald Woods, *Biko*, Paddington Press, 1977, page 142.

We believe that history moves in a particular logical direction, and in this instance, the logical direction is that eventually any white society in this country is going to have to accommodate black thinking. We are mere agents in that history. There are alternatives. On the one hand we have groups that are known in this country, who have opted for another way of operation, they have

What does Source D reveal about Steve Biko in 1976?

opted for violence. We know that the ANC and PAC have done this, but we don't believe it is the only alternative. We believe that there is a way of getting to where we want to go, through peaceful means. And the very fact that we decided to actually form an above-board movement implies that we accepted certain legal limitations to our operations … Some of us get banned, like I am. Others get arrested, like these men who are here, but inevitably the process drives towards what we believe history also drives to, an attainment of a situation where whites have to listen.

I don't believe that whites will be deaf all the time. … This government is not necessarily set on a Hitlerised course. I think it is buying time. From their interpretation of the situation at the moment, … Mr Vorster can postpone some problems, … but I believe that as the voice which says 'no' grows, he is going to listen, he is going to begin to accommodate the feelings of black people.

Steve Biko died in police custody in September 1977. He was arrested on 19 August at a police roadblock outside Grahamstown for defying his banning order. The circumstances of his death both illustrate the uncontrolled powers of the security forces and explain the worldwide opprobrium which the news of his demise engendered. Biko spent twenty days in solitary confinement, naked and denied exercise and hygiene. He was then taken to police headquarters in Port Elizabeth, where he was savagely beaten until collapsing with head injuries. He spent the next two days still naked and chained to a metal grille. A doctor eventually was summoned but he reported no injuries. With Biko increasingly incoherent, he was finally taken, covered in only a blanket, on a 700-mile trip to a prison hospital in Pretoria. Here, on 12 September, he finally died.

Biko was initially accused of attacking police officers during interrogation and falling against a wall during a violent struggle. A subsequent inquiry found he had in fact died of brain damage worsened by the journey to hospital. No one was condemned or even prosecuted over his death. The inquiry found that 'on the available evidence the death cannot be attributed to any act or omission amounting to a criminal offence on the part of any person'.

The death of Steve Biko had great significance. It was not that Biko was the only victim of police brutality: the ANC recorded fourteen deaths in police custody in 1977 alone. He was, however, both widely known and respected abroad. He had, in a sense, become the face of African protest. His death in such horrific circumstances shocked many not only in South Africa but all over the world:

- Both the UN and USA protested over his death.
- There was widespread worldwide condemnation. He was to be the subject of a very popular movie, *Cry Freedom*, in the following decade, which led to further international condemnation of the apartheid regime.
- The authorities remained impassive and without compassion, as exemplified by Minister of Justice Jimmy Kruger, who said of Biko's death, *'dit laat my koud'* ('it leaves me cold').

- The inquest reported improbably that Biko had gone berserk before fatally hitting his head against the wall. Few believed it.

The Soweto uprising and death of Biko were hugely significant. Many people now feared that the chance of any peaceful solution to the problems caused by apartheid was impossible. The government had spoken vaguely in August 1977 about giving coloured people and Indians more political rights but this had no impact at the time. It seemed a battle between an intractable and determined government and increasingly militant opponents of apartheid.

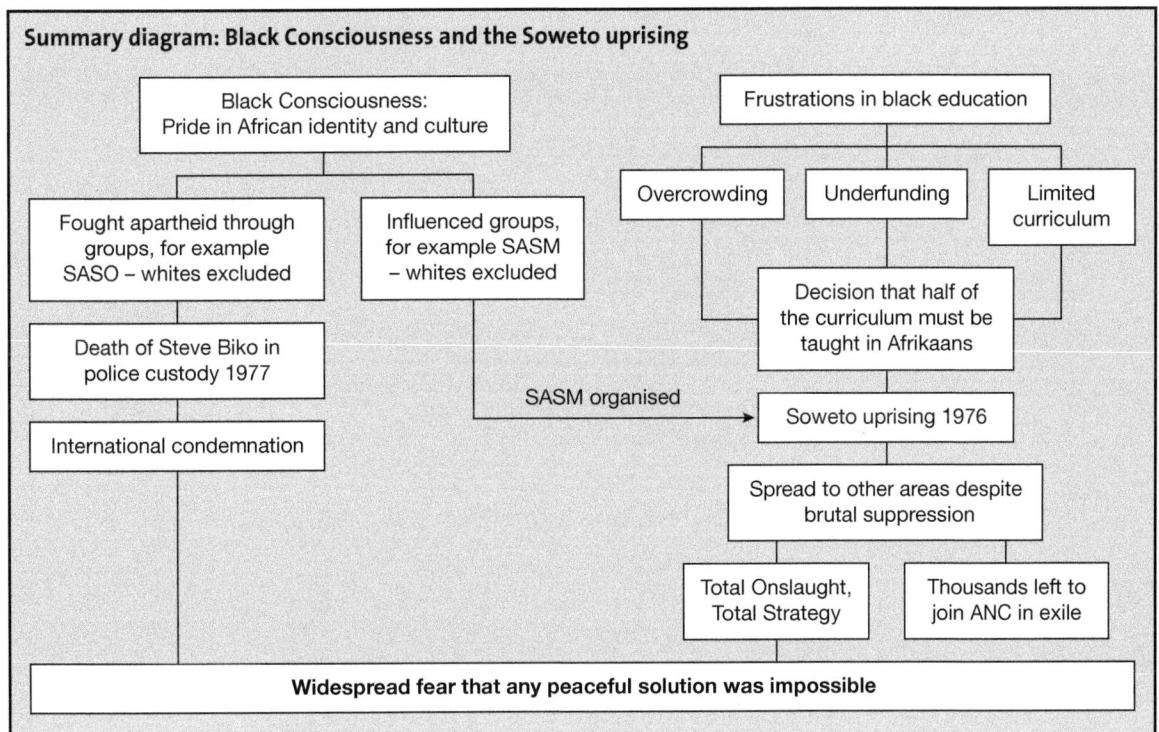

Summary diagram: Black Consciousness and the Soweto uprising

```
Black Consciousness:                          Frustrations in black education
Pride in African identity and culture

                                    Overcrowding   Underfunding   Limited
Fought apartheid through   Influenced groups,                     curriculum
groups, for example        for example SASM
SASO – whites excluded     – whites excluded      Decision that half of
                                                  the curriculum must be
Death of Steve Biko in                            taught in Afrikaans
police custody 1977
                              SASM organised      Soweto uprising 1976
International condemnation
                                                  Spread to other areas despite
                                                  brutal suppression

                              Total Onslaught,          Thousands left to
                              Total Strategy            join ANC in exile
```

Widespread fear that any peaceful solution was impossible

2 The ANC restrengthened

▶ *How far was the ANC strengthened during the period 1968–83?*

As the Soweto uprising was organised locally, and spread, largely unplanned, to other parts of South Africa, it was felt that the traditional leaders of opposition to apartheid were becoming more irrelevant. However, the ANC was reorganising itself and preparing for a new phase of struggle, taking advantage of the thousands of cadres who joined following the Soweto uprising in 1976.

Decline of the ANC in the early 1970s

On the surface, the ANC declined in importance in the 1970s. Its former leaders were still in prison, and the organisation itself was in exile since its banning in 1960 (see page 44). Many of those arrested after the Soweto uprising in 1976 initially treated people like Nelson Mandela with some degree of contempt when they met them in prison. The older activists seemed relics of a previous age. Those who had taken the initiative in the protest movement in the absence of the ANC or PAC were both more militant and ready to deploy violence. Many distrusted the integrationist policies of the ANC and were more prepared to see all white people as enemies. However, Mandela and other long-term prisoners opened up a dialogue in which they both learnt about the new waves of protest and activity, and educated their young fellow prisoners in the aims of the ANC and hopes for a unified South Africa (see page 56).

The ANC had not been involved in a military campaign since the unsuccessful Wankie uprising in 1967 (see page 58). The Soweto uprising rejuvenated the ANC and provided it with new cadres to engage in its campaigns.

Internal reorganisation

Under the leadership of Oliver Tambo, the ANC was planning for a new phase of struggle. It was reorganised abroad to co-ordinate the following key activities:

- Oversee the growing number of exiles.
- Co-ordinate the activities of *Umkhonto we Sizwe* (MK).
- Raise funds.
- Set up ANC offices throughout the world.

There were frustrations, particularly among those who had left South Africa to be trained to fight. While the ANC maintained a growing number of military camps, it faced mutinies on at least two occasions when recruits grew angry about the lack of activities. It also expelled eight dissidents in 1975 for their Africanist views and criticism of the ANC's relations with SACP.

The ANC had headquarters in London, where its strategies for gaining international support were mainly co-ordinated. It maintained forward bases in friendly African countries from where it could launch raids into South Africa.

Visit to Vietnam

In 1978, the ANC visited Vietnam to study what it saw as the North Vietnamese victory over the USA (regarding the **Vietnam War**) and success in uniting the country. As a result, it changed tactics from attacks in rural areas to guerrilla warfare in urban areas, which it felt would carry more publicity. It saw its role as both military in terms of armed attacks and political in building up a mass organisation.

KEY TERM

Vietnam War Civil war between Communist North and non-Communist South Vietnam. The war escalated after the Communist Vietcong rebelled against the government in the South in the mid to late 1950s, and the North supported them. The USA supported the South, becoming involved full time in their support after 1965. In 1975, the North Vietnamese invaded the South and united the country under communism.

The biggest task for the ANC, however, was to make itself the clear leader of the opposition against apartheid. To do this, it needed to win international legitimacy – to be seen not as a terrorist group but effectively as a government in exile.

External legitimacy

The ANC spent much of the 1970s winning external legitimacy, both in Africa and in the wider world.

In 1963, the Organisation of African Unity (OAU) and ANC were working together to gain power in African countries. However, these countries were not strong enough to give more substantial support to the ANC; most traded with South Africa and some were dependent on it. Zambia, for example, was reliant on South African railways and ports to export its copper, which comprised 95 per cent of its income. South Africa also placed pressure on these countries to expel the ANC, for example, on Tanzania in 1969.

ANC leaders also visited non-Communist countries to try to win support and legitimacy. They were, however, disadvantaged by being seen by many as pro-Communist. This was particularly so within the context of the Cold War when many countries opposed the Communist regimes who offered support for the ANC. This was, of course, exacerbated by their close ties with the SACP.

Many groups and individuals in Western countries disliked the ANC's stance on violence, typically asking them to stop the armed struggle: right-wing leaders and organisations in Britain and the USA, for example, often regarded the ANC as a terrorist organisation. This limited its overall support.

The role of Oliver Tambo

Oliver Tambo had been Nelson Mandela's law partner and a fellow leader in the ANC. During the state of emergency on March 1961, he managed to escape and set up ANC headquarters in Dar Es Salaam, Tanzania. Tambo effectively became the international 'face' of the ANC, its global ambassador. He remained its acting president until the death of Chief Luthuli in 1967, when he finally assumed the ANC presidency.

Tambo's strategy

Tambo developed the two-pronged strategy of military conflict and the development of a mass political organisation, but progress was slow and the organisation could be riven with discontent. In an attempt to prove its military credentials, it launched a joint offensive with the MPLA government forces against the National Union for the Total Independence of Angola (UNITA) in Angola in 1983; the lack of success caused more frustrations and open conflict with the organisation.

Oliver Tambo

1917	Born in the eastern Cape to a farming family
1938	Enrolled at Fort Hare University
1941	Expelled for protests as secretary of Students' Representative Council
1943	Co-founded ANC Youth League
1951	Qualified as a lawyer
1957	Elected deputy president of ANC
1960	Left to head ANC in exile
1962	Given the role of leading ANC's diplomatic mission
1967	Became president of ANC
1985	Exhorted support in South Africa to make it ungovernable
1990	Returned to South Africa; relinquished presidency to Nelson Mandela
1993	Died

Early life and career

Tambo was born to a farming family who valued education and made sacrifices to send him to school. He originally wanted to become a doctor but opportunities for Africans to study medicine were very limited. In 1938, he opted to study sciences at Fort Hare University where he involved himself in student politics, and in 1941 was expelled for protests about not being able to use the tennis courts on Sundays. He worked thereafter as a teacher and became involved in the ANC. In 1943, frustrated with its lack of progress, he co-founded the ANC Youth League with friends such as Nelson Mandela, calling for direct action. In 1951, Tambo qualified as a lawyer and went into partnership with Mandela.

Work in the ANC

During the course of the 1950s, Tambo was involved in all the major protests and campaigns such as the Defiance Campaign and the signing of the Freedom Charter. In 1957, he was elected deputy president. However, in 1960, in the face of the banning of the ANC and subsequent arrests, it was decided he should go abroad to lead the organisation in exile. After his success on foreign visits in Africa, Europe and the USA, where he addressed the UN, Tambo was given the role of leading ANC ambassador. He spent the next 25 years campaigning for international support as well as leading the organisation and trying to keep it focused and united. In 1967, Tambo became ANC president. As the 1980s saw more and more unrest, he exhorted supporters in 1985 to render South Africa ungovernable.

Return and death

Tambo suffered a stroke in 1989. After returning to South Africa in 1990 after the unbanning of the ANC, he relinquished the presidency to Nelson Mandela. He continued on diplomatic missions until his death in 1993. Tambo's contribution to the demise of apartheid has often been underestimated. His greatest achievements were keeping the movement together during the long years of exile and acting as ambassador to maintain its international credibility.

Tambo faced various mutinies in which frustrated recruits sought to return to South Africa (see page 86) and complained about lack of resources and poor conditions in the camps. He visited dissidents in camps in Angola in 1983 and Mozambique in 1984 after the Nkomati Accords (see page 99) meant their expulsion. In 1985, after the Kabwe conference in Zambia addressing their grievances, he issued a code of conduct concerning procedures and punishments in the cadres' camps. Nevertheless, problems in the camps continued. The security department of the ANC, Mbokodo, could be ruthless in quelling dissent: members were quick to apply interrogation techniques in East European countries such as the German Democratic Republic, and leaders such as Tambo were powerless to rein them in. However, he did keep the organisation intact and provided a unifying figure.

Need for international support

Tambo saw the need to build up international support and counter the accusations emanating from South Africa about the ANC's relationship with communism. To this end, he would meet regularly with influential figures to explain the ANC position and assure them, where necessary, that the ANC supported capitalist development. He met, for example, representatives of US multinational companies in the early 1980s in the face of US President Reagan's aggressive stance against communism, and indeed belief that South Africa was making real progress towards racial equality. In October 1985, he gave evidence to a British House of Commons Committee, justifying the armed struggle. It was this meeting which led to the Commonwealth Eminent Persons Group visit which subsequently supported the use of sanctions against South Africa (see page 115).

Making South Africa ungovernable

One of Tambo's biggest challenges was to keep the ANC unified while appealing to foreign supporters and indeed reassuring white people that they would having nothing to fear from an ANC victory. In January 1985, in the face of President Botha's state of emergency (see page 117), he advocated making the country ungovernable through military and non-cooperative actions.

Beginnings of guerrilla warfare

The ANC had begun to infiltrate guerrilla fighters into South Africa from the early 1970s (see page 78). This was made easier after its neighbours won their independence and could be used as a springboard for attacks. However, one should not overemphasise this point. The ANC was never strong enough militarily to threaten the apartheid regime, although the persistence of conflict could weaken the latter in tandem with other factors, and did lead to a huge military commitment which drained the economy (see page 116).

Umkhonto we Sizwe or Spear of the Nation attacks

MK attacks from the mid-1970s included sabotage on railways and industrial plants, attacks on government offices and assassinations, particularly of those accused of collaborating. Often they were planned to tie in with local concerns, such as an attack on a police station at Soekmekaar at a time when local people were angry about forced removals. Their strength was in their persistence rather than large-scale effects.

The global anti-apartheid movement

The global anti-apartheid movement covered many countries where people organised rallies and public events to show their opposition to the regime in South Africa. Governments themselves were often lukewarm, reluctant to offend South Africa, and wary of the ANC ties with communism and its military activities. There were exceptions: India, for example, maintained close ties with the ANC, and there was anti-apartheid encouragement from organisations in the Netherlands and Canada. Scandinavian countries, particularly Sweden, provided aid and support. Sweden had maintained close ties with the ANC throughout the 1960s, although it was reluctant to give official support until 1969 because of the links with communism. Nevertheless, when official recognition was forthcoming, other Scandinavian nations followed suit, and all gave substantial help such as welfare, education and healthcare facilities. One reason for their support was so the Communist bloc should not be seen as the only developed countries to offer aid to anti-apartheid groups, but they did insist that none of it found its way into the coffers of MK. ANC accountants apparently were conscientious in ensuring that this was not the case.

Other examples included the anti-apartheid movement in Britain in the 1960s, which promoted sanctions and boycotts. In 1970, there were significant protests against the South African rugby team's tour and several games were abandoned owing to disruption. British people were encouraged not to buy fruit from South Africa. Demonstrations took place outside banks such as Barclays which had close ties with South Africa. In addition, anti-apartheid support in the USA led to Congress in October 1986 overriding President Reagan's veto, to impose sanctions on South Africa.

Summary diagram: The ANC restrengthened

Problems		Solutions
Leaders in exile or prison	→	Role of Oliver Tambo in reorganisation and international diplomacy
Sense of irrelevance to development of Black Consciousness and struggles of 1970s	→	1 Nelson Mandela and ANC prisoners recruited young cadres in prison 2 Thousands left South Africa to join ANC in exile
Failures in armed struggle, for example no operations in South Africa in 1970s	→	1 Visit to Vietnam in 1978 to learn about successful guerrilla warfare 2 Attacks within South Africa on government instillations
Associations with communism	→	1 Diplomacy by Oliver Tambo 2 Winning support of ordinary black South Africans 3 Trying to be seen as a government in exile

3 Domestic challenges to National Party power, 1974–83

▶ *How significant were the domestic challenges to National Party power in terms of the survival of apartheid?*

Political unrest

The National Party continued to win elections and be the governing party. However, as the 1970s progressed it faced more political challenges. As South Africans became more aware of the wider world, there were two conflicting responses:

- A growth in liberalism, particularly among the young. This manifested itself in the rise of the Progressive Party from one MP to seven MPs in the 1974 elections. This party advocated a federal structure for a non-racial South Africa. It renamed itself the Progressive Federalist Party when the old United Party collapsed in 1974, and became the official opposition in Parliament. However, with seventeen seats in 1977 as opposed to the National Party's 134, its impact was limited.
- Other white people became more entrenched, opposing any reform. They became associated in particular with Education Minister Andries Treurnicht (see page 74), although they did not yet break away from the National Party.

Prime Minister Vorster advocated reform in giving Indian and coloured people their own parliaments (see page 114). The aim was to isolate black Africans further by bringing these two groups into limited power sharing. It was, however, too much too soon for white hard-liners who opposed the scheme. The government successes in the 1977 elections emboldened it to attempt limited constitutional reform. Although the Muldergate scandal and leadership change interrupted the process, by February 1981, a separate President's Council made up of white, Indian and coloured South Africans was formed to advise the government, replacing the Senate. A separate black African Council had also been proposed but was shelved as no black Africans were prepared to join it.

Problems in the Bantustans

The Bantustans meanwhile continued to fail. Four were granted full independence: Transkei in 1976, Boputhatswana in 1977, Venda in 1979 and Ciskei in 1981. None, however, was recognised by any country other than South Africa. All were dependent on South Africa for subsidies; neither were they economically viable. By 1985, Transkei received 85 per cent of its income directly from South Africa.

Economic problems

Economic statistics show the stark poverty of the Bantustans:

- In 1970, only 25 per cent of those Africans in employment actually lived in the Bantustans, and many of these commuted into South Africa on a daily basis.
- Of those actually employed in the Bantustans, 60 per cent worked in subsistence agriculture.
- Less than ten per cent of the manufacturing and mining in the area of South Africa employed workers in Bantustans.
- In 1973, only three per cent of South African **gross domestic product (GDP)** came from the Bantustans.

KEY TERM

Gross domestic product (GDP) The value of goods and services produced within the country; one criterion commonly used for determining national wealth.

Table 3.1 GDP of Bantustans in 1970

Source	Percentage of GDP
Migrant workers in South Africa	70%
Generated within Bantustans	13%
South African government subsidies	17%

Boputhatswana

Boputhatswana comprised nineteen separate areas of land, hundreds of kilometres away from each other. It became the closest to attaining a degree of economic independence. This was largely because it contained an entertainment and casino complex, Sun City, which became a leisure centre for wealthy, mainly white, South Africans as such venues were banned in their homeland. However, one should not exaggerate the economic impact of South African tourism. As many as 65 per cent of the population worked outside Boputhatswana.

Bantustans could not begin to support their official populations. In 1986, almost 250,000 Africans were arrested for pass offences. Most were classed as illegal aliens. One issue was that with developments in technology and indeed problems in the economy (see page 116), less unskilled labour was needed. Even some white South Africans were being forced to take relatively unskilled jobs as a result of the downturn. As a result, more Africans found themselves being deported. The Bantustans found their roles shifting from a repository for cheap labour to one where those no longer needed could be deported.

Bantustan leaders

Bantustan leaders were largely unpopular and seen as collaborators by both their own citizens and anti-apartheid groups. Typically, Bantustans remained dictatorships protected by South African forces. Hence, in 1988, the South African authorities intervened to restore 'president for life' Mangope after an attempted coup. Nevertheless, the authorities did not always oppose change, particularly when, in Transkei in 1987 and Ciskei in 1990, the coups opposed corrupt and venal leaders.

National Party division and scandals

As the 1970s progressed, the problems facing the National Party were compounded by scandals and economic challenges.

The National Party was dividing into opposing wings, one of which favoured limited reform and a more conservative one which opposed all change. In the early 1980s, the latter grouping was to split away to become the Conservative Party, while others formed even more extreme groups prepared to use extra-parliamentary violence to maintain apartheid.

Initially, there were cosmetic name changes to suggest reform, which aimed mainly to satisfy the rival groups within the National Party. The name of the Department of Bantu Affairs, for example, was changed to that of 'collective development', while pejorative words in official government parlance were altered to cause less offence to non-white groups. 'Discrimination', for example, became 'differentiation'.

It seemed, however, that having survived the Soweto uprising and death in custody of Steve Biko, the biggest threats to the National Party came from within its own ranks. In 1978, the National Party faced the so-called 'Muldergate' scandal in which large sums of money were discovered to have siphoned off to pay for propaganda purposes in a covert programme called 'Operation Senekal'. Activities included:

- The purchase of an English language newspaper, *The Citizen*, to support the regime. The perpetrators ploughed R30 million into this venture alone. According to journalist Donald Woods, the government attempted at least three attempts to neutralise newspapers hostile to the regime.
- Bribes were distributed in countries such as the USA and Britain to promote the regime and justify apartheid.
- Some funds were simply appropriated for the perpetrators' own uses.

In the event, the auditor general's investigation of April 1977 found two government ministers had worked with the head of the Bureau for State Security (BOSS) to appropriate a secret fund of R64 million to pay for the activities listed above, most of which were illegal. The scandal was focused around the minister of information and the interior, **Connie Mulder**, who had been a potential candidate for prime minister when Vorster had suddenly resigned from that post in 1977, citing ill health. It was subsequently discovered that Vorster himself had been implicated, hence the prescient resignation. Mulder was associated with other senior government figures, thus threatening the very position of the government.

KEY FIGURE

Connie Mulder (1925–88)

Hard-line politician who was implicated in the 1978 scandal named after him, and subsequently helped form the Conservative Party.

Impact on government

Mulder reluctantly resigned from the National Party. He went on to form the Conservative Party with other intransigents within the National Party. This was itself to become absorbed into the Conservative Party of South Africa, formed by opponents of Botha's constitutional reforms.

The state president, Nico Diederichs, died in August 1978, and Vorster replaced him. Judge Erasmus's report into Operation Senekal (see page 93) was published in two stages: the first, in December 1978, implicated Mulder but exonerated Vorster; the second, in June 1979, recognised Vorster's involvement. Vorster chose to retire as president, and the scandal died away with the demise of Vorster and Mulder from government. This paved the way for P.W. Botha, defence minister, who was not implicated in the scandal, to become prime minister in September.

Botha's reforms

As well as the Total Strategy (explained on page 79), Botha introduced constitutional reforms (discussed on page 116) and structural reforms aimed at gaining the support of non-white groups. The abolition of many petty apartheid measures would follow later in the 1980s (see page 116).

P.W. Botha, prime minister from 1978, was a former defence minister who maintained strong relations with the security forces. Experts such as General Malan had told him that the security forces could not deal simultaneously with external threats and internal unrest. The only solution was to give some non-white South Africans more of a stake in society by a policy that would extend the non-white middle class.

There were, moreover, other reasons for reform:

- The security forces needed more recruits. Indians, coloured people and black Africans had been recruited since 1968, but the late 1970s saw increases in numbers and more active involvement in combat. When conscription had been extended to two years and the requirement to attend annual camps had been imposed with greater rigour, many employers had complained. The answer was to recruit more non-white people into the security forces. This would also have the added advantage of negating the idea that South Africa was fighting a war on racial lines, since the military campaigns would involve a mix of ethnicities.
- Most African military recruits came from rural areas. While they were allocated housing and other benefits, comparatively few had Section Ten residential rights (see page 96). This was an incentive to perform well and avoid trouble: as they had no formal residential rights malcontents could be deported back to the Bantustans.

- There were increasing shortages of skilled workers: a shortfall of approximately 100,000 by the beginning of the 1970s. Clearly, the answer was to recruit and train more Africans. However, this was also predicated on improving housing and living conditions. Efforts were increasingly made to provide electricity and other services to those parts of the townships which could afford them and also to offer security of home tenure. In 1976, Africans could obtain 30-year leases on homes in the townships, and in 1983 they were allowed to purchase them. It has been estimated that in 1970, 86 per cent of the African workforce was comprised of migrants; by 1979, 68 per cent was classed as stable permanent residents.

Botha's policy was to reform the political situation and ease conditions for non-white people but without sacrificing white supremacy. He did this by offering enough to non-white South Africans to ensure they worked with white South Africans to maintain the system and National Party control. Botha was prepared to compromise on apartheid, particularly in terms of relaxations in petty apartheid, but not to share power as such. He saw reform as a key part of the Total Strategy. Nonetheless, he did not want to fundamentally change the system. Historian David Harrison wrote in 1981 that, 'In truth, although Botha had tried to give apartheid a new image, the edifice remained intact.'

Structural reform

Structural reforms included the legalisation of African trade unions and relaxation of influx control. Following the recommendations of the 1979 Wiehann Report, black trade unions were recognised and given limited powers under the 1981 Industrial Conciliation Amendment Act. The Wiehann Report was produced in response to shortages of skilled workers and the need to recognise African trade unions, in order to both control them and to have clear contacts with whom employers could negotiate:

- During severe strikes in Durban in 1973, there had been no obvious African leaders with whom to negotiate, making settlements far more difficult.
- Many people recognised that more jobs had to be opened up to Africans if the economy was to grow.

Wiehann advocated that African trade unions should have the same rights as white ones. He proposed the following:

- African unions should be registered with the government and have their accounts audited.
- Unions should have access to the industrial court to settle disputes on the same basis as white unions.
- They should have the right to strike after a 30-day notification.

Problems for African unions

The government reserved the right to refuse to register any unions it considered subversive or overtly political. Characteristically, it feared Communist influence. White trade unions meanwhile began to set up African unions alongside them. These often became the ones which were registered, leaving genuinely independent African unions outside the system. The authorities meanwhile continued to behave ruthlessly. One African union official at the Ford plant in Port Elizabeth was banned for five years for leading an unofficial strike, while the Johannesburg City Council deported 1000 municipal workers back to their homelands after they went on strike in July 1980.

Riekert Commission and influx control

The Riekert Commission in 1979 advocated that those Africans qualified to live in white areas, because of their skills, should receive various types of preferential treatment; for example, more freedom to look for better jobs and the right to bring families to live with them, the so-called 'Section Ten' after the relevant section of the Bantu (Urban Areas) Consolidation Act of 1945. It was estimated that about half a million Africans, plus their dependants, would qualify out of a total population of 18 million in South Africa as a whole. The aim was to build a more stable, skilled African workforce. However, the corollary was that existing restrictions were more rigorously enforced and even extended: Riekert recommended that Africans would have to register for employment in their homelands. In 1978, 273,000 Africans were deported for pass offences, 5000 more than in the previous year. For the first time, white employers were fined for employing 'illegal' workers; they could also have their cars impounded if found guilty of transporting them into South Africa.

Despite the restrictions, 'illegals' continued to arrive: in 1980 it was estimated that there were half a million living in Soweto alone. Riekert failed to appreciate that the paucity of opportunities in the homelands meant it was economically profitable to work illegally in South Africa, even if this meant prison. One university study of October 1979 worked out that a worker from Bophuthatswana who worked illegally in Pretoria for nine months, before spending three months in jail, could be 85 per cent better off than if he had stayed at home. The corresponding figure for Ciskei, after just three months' work and nine months' jail, was 234 per cent. Ultimately, the reforms failed, partly as a result of their limitations but also because of a faltering economy.

Economic pressures

South Africa faced increasing economic pressures. The costs of maintaining and subsidising the Bantustans were costly in themselves, but with the cost of defence added, the economy was struggling. This was in part due to the fluctuating price of gold in international markets, and South Africa, like most developed countries, suffered from huge increases in oil prices as a result of the 1973 oil crisis (see page 74).

Part of the problem was that throughout the 1970s, GDP increased less than population, so people – including white South Africans – were becoming poorer. Inflation was never less than ten per cent. Although it was most difficult for black Africans, it nevertheless hit whites hard. By 1977, more were migrating from South Africa than coming in, and many of those who left were the most skilled. The white population fell from 21 per cent of the whole at its peak in 1936 to sixteen per cent by 1980.

The cost of defence commitments

South Africa spent one per cent of its GDP on defence in 1960; by the mid-1980s this had risen to four per cent, or thirteen per cent of total government expenditure. The SADF had doubled in size between 1960 and 1965, and continued to grow as its foreign commitments became more complex and widespread.

The SADF increased in numbers as its commitments grew during the 1970s. In 1977, conscription was extended to two years, with a requirement of 90 days' attendance at annual camps for eight years after demobilisation. The first cohort affected by this extension, that of 1979, was 1000 recruits short. Non-attendees were to be punished more severely. Military expenditure meanwhile grew exponentially.

Table 3.2 Growth in military expenditure and personnel, 1961–81

Force	1961	1974	1977	1981
Police	27,000	59,000	72,000	77,000
SADF (including reservists)	79,000	269,000	367,000	51,500
Total armed forces	106,000	328,000	439,000	592,000
Estimated total under arms at any one time	39,000	90,000	150,000	255,000
Military expenditure excluding police	R72 million	R707 million	R194 million	R3000 million

Source: International Defence and Aid Fund for South Africa in cooperation with the UN Centre Against Apartheid, *Apartheid: The Facts*, London, 1983.

As South Africa's neighbours won their independence and turned from support into hostility, its military commitments grew (see page 99). In August 1975, South Africa invaded Angola to try to impose its client organisation, UNITA, on that newly independent country. By 1977, military spending peaked at five per cent of GDP, with forces being deployed both externally and internally as a result of the Soweto uprising.

Summary diagram: Domestic challenges to National Party power, 1974–83

```
                          ┌─────────────────────┐
                          │ Domestic challenges │
                          └─────────────────────┘
```

| Growth of liberal ideas vs growth of conservatism | Political scandal, for example Muldergate | Failure of Bantustans | Failure to reform constitution | Standards of living among white people falling |

Growth of conservatism

'Cosmetic' changes

Growth in white migration

Corruption among leaders

Continuing poverty

Challenges to National Party power, 1974–83:

• Pressure to reform vs opposition to reform
• Greater costs of defence vs weakening economy
• Need for greater security vs increasing loss of confidence

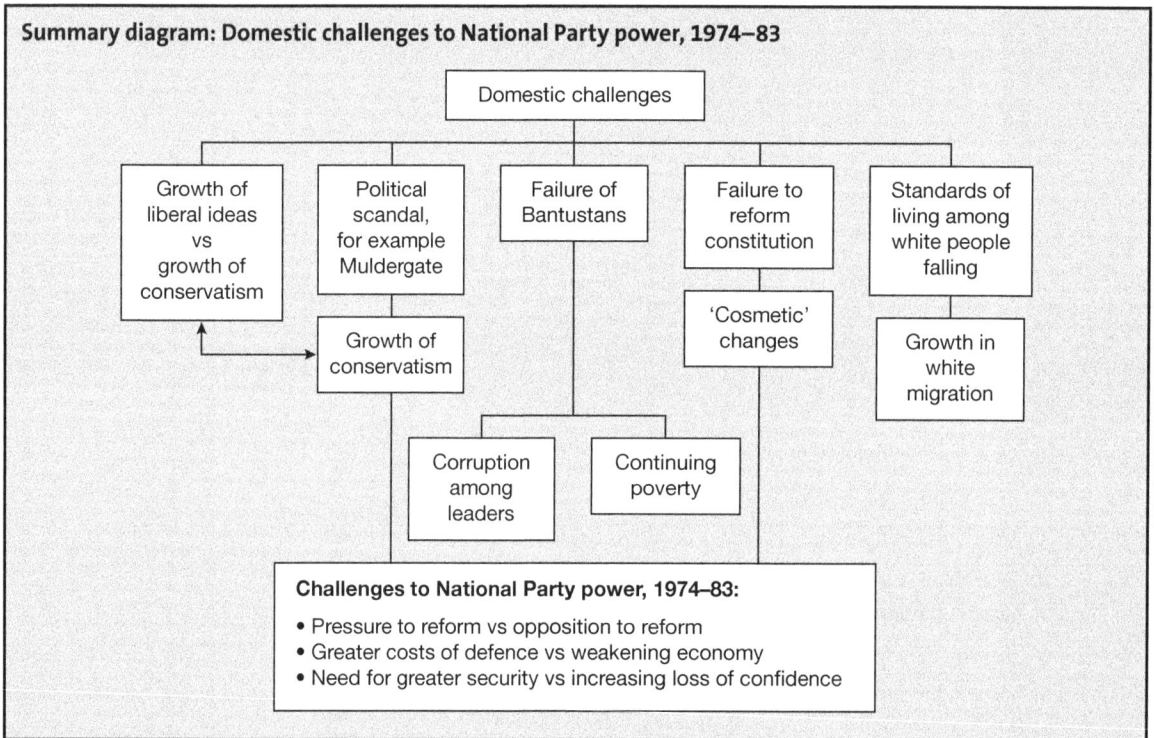

4 External pressures on National Party power, 1974–83

▶ *How effectively did the National Party government deal with the external threats to its power during the period 1974–83?*

Political change in southern Africa

By the mid-1970s, South Africa's control of its borders had become far more tenuous as former allies, in the form of Portuguese colonies, gained their independence and Rhodesia was gripped by a vicious war in which the black population was fighting to end white governance. The entire **polity** of southern Africa changed. However, South Africa maintained its economic influence.

Economic dependence

Longer established states in southern Africa may have protested about apartheid but maintained ties with South Africa through economic necessity. Zambia, Malawi, Botswana and Swaziland, for example, all relied on South Africa for trade and egress to ports. South Africa controlled oil and electricity supplies to these neighbours and employed their surplus workers: 280,000 in 1984.

KEY TERM

Polity Used to refer to an organised society.

Efforts by these countries to cooperate to reduce their dependence on South Africa failed.

The impact of decolonisation

South Africa had relied on the Portuguese, in particular, for helping to control its borders with Angola and Mozambique. However, in 1975 the dictatorial regime in Portugal was overthrown and a new democratic government gave these countries their independence. South Africa became involved in their post-independence history in order to maintain this control. This was exacerbated in 1980 when a settlement in Rhodesia saw the creation of black majority rule in the renamed Zimbabwe. The success of the radical Zimbabwe African People's Union (ZAPU) shocked many in the South Africa: they had expected the more moderate Zimbabwe African National Union (ZANU), with whom they hoped to negotiate agreements, to win. They saw the new regime as Communist leaning and backed by the USSR and Cuba, which sent thousands of troops to support the Marxist groups, for example, in Angola. In this context, South Africa genuinely saw the developments both as a Communist plot to ensnare all of southern Africa, and as an opportunity to act as a reliable anti-Communist ally of the USA.

Mozambique

In Mozambique, the Marxist FRELIMO group took power in 1975, although South Africa joined with Rhodesia in offering support to its rival RENAMO, to little avail. However, while Mozambique remained a threat and, indeed, one of the leaders of MK, Joe Slovo, had his headquarters there, South Africa seemed to accept its existence and, in 1984, came to the Nkomati Accords, which ended the ANC presence there (see page 88).

Angola

South Africa's most significant involvement during the 1970s was in Angola, where a civil war followed independence from Portugal. Here it sided with the USA in supporting the pro-Western organisations UNITA and the National Liberation Front of Angola (FNLA) against the Communist-leaning MPLA, which was backed by the Soviet Union and Cuba. To that end, on 14 October 1975, the SADF launched Operation Savannah – a partial invasion. It also gave $14 million in arms to the organisations it supported. By December 1975, 3000 South African troops were fighting in Angola, often against the 4000 Cubans who had arrived in support of the MPLA. Three South African columns aimed to capture the capital Luanda, but were thwarted largely by the Cubans. However, in the face of the extended conflict and the weaknesses of both UNITA and FNLA, US support shrank. In December, the US Congress refused any further funds for the conflict, and South Africa was left isolated. It withdrew from Angola in July 1976, although continuing to offer more covert assistance to UNITA and FNLA.

> **KEY TERM**

Mandate Former colony of the defeated powers after the First World War, given to the victorious powers to prepare for independence. Most powers were reluctant to relinquish control.

Namibia

South Africa had taken the former German South West Africa as a **mandate** after the First World War and effectively governed it as a colony. We have already seen how it was used to give the National Party a greater majority in government (see page 16). In 1967, the UN formally ended the mandate and in 1973 declared continuing South African occupancy illegal. South Africa was given until 30 May to leave. It ignored the UN.

South Africa's motivation to keep control was largely for Namibia to act as a buffer zone between it and Angola, to counter what it saw as the Communist threat from Angola; not surprisingly, the MPLA supported the South West African People's Organisation (SWAPO) guerrillas. South Africa was, in any event, embroiled in a full-scale war with the independence movement SWAPO. This continued until peace negotiations took place in 1989 following UN Resolution 435. South Africa was accused of atrocities in Namibia, notably the attack on Kassinga refugee camp in May 1978.

Rhodesia

South Africa gave aid to Rhodesian forces fighting against independence groups. However, when Mozambique and Angola gained their independence, the South African government increasingly felt the Rhodesian regime was unsustainable, and began to concentrate its efforts, with little success, on convincing the white supremacist government to negotiate with more moderate black groups. In 1980, Zimbabwe became officially independent.

South Africa's political isolation: international condemnation and calls for economic sanctions

By the end of the 1970s, South Africa was increasingly politically isolated internationally. While many governments opposed sanctions, they were aware that apartheid was unpopular with many in their populations. Officially, they encouraged South Africa to reform and suggested that continued links were the best way to do this; privately, they were more critical of the apartheid regime.

South Africa maintained close ties with two countries which also felt isolated: Taiwan and Israel, both of which continued to supply arms to South Africa despite the UN embargo of 1977.

The United Nations

The UN condemned apartheid routinely and regularly advocated sanctions: an attempt to expel South Africa from membership in 1974 had been defeated only by the veto of Britain, France and the USA in the Security Council. However, South Africa's economic influence helped mitigate any effects political isolation might have.

South Africa had been condemned internationally since the National Party victory of 1948. However, it was after Sharpeville, and the decolonisation process in Africa, that protest grew more vehement. The regime did little to assuage this condemnation through its refusal to substantially reform apartheid.

Calls for economic sanctions

The call for economic sanctions was widespread. In Britain, for example, the anti-apartheid movement originally focused on economic boycotts. It called, for example, for a month-long boycott of South African goods in March 1960, and advocated an international committee on sanctions to be held in Britain in April 1964. The UN had passed Resolution 1761 in November 1962, setting up a Special Committee against apartheid and supporting economic sanctions.

However, many Western counties refused to join this committee and, as members of the Security Council, Britain, France and the USA had the power of veto which they used to prevent sanctions becoming mandatory. The UN had called for an oil embargo as early as 1960, but this was not mandatory.

Western opposition to sanctions

We have seen that Western countries saw South Africa as a useful ally in the global struggle against communism. However, governments also argued that the regime might be more susceptible to reform if it remained part of the international community; if isolated, it might become even more intransigent. Leaders also argued that sanctions would hurt the African population, as the poorest group, the most. This view was often shared by South African opponents to sanctions themselves.

SOURCE E

Extract from a talk by Helen Suzman to members of the European Democratic Group in Luxemburg, 10 July 1985. Suzman was a veteran South African MP opposed to apartheid.

Not only do I not believe these campaigns [calls for sanctions and disinvestment] would be effective – I believe they would be counter-productive. ...

The vacuum left by the withdrawal of US and European firms will be filled – if it is filled at all – by companies with less interest in the welfare of their black employees. Moreover, if it is fondly imagined that the South African Government will buckle under such pressures and abandon apartheid faster than it intends to do, this illusion should be immediately dispelled. Far more likely, far more in keeping with the temperament of the Government and of the majority of the white inhabitants, would be the development of a siege mentality. ...

How could Source E be used to explain how far sanctions and boycotts would be effective against South Africa?

That disinvestment, lack of foreign capital and imposition of sanctions would be effective as a punitive measure is, of course, undeniable. But it would not be selective of its victims.

Indeed, although white South Africans would be affected, the major sufferers would be black – South African Blacks and also Blacks from neighbouring states in Southern Africa which are heavily dependent on South Africa for financial aid, grants, markets and jobs …

Arms embargo

The one area where sanctions became mandatory was arms sales. The UN had called for a voluntary arms embargo as early as 1963. However, it did not become mandatory until 1977, with Resolution 418, after widespread condemnation of the brutality with which the regime dealt with the Soweto uprising. However, other groups had made their own embargoes. The 1971 Commonwealth Conference, for example, saw a resolution against arms sales and a projected deal by which Britain would supply helicopters and frigates was abandoned.

The impact of economic sanctions

Until the mid-1980s, economic sanctions, such as they were, had only a limited impact on South Africa, although they did add to the sense of hostility and isolation:

- As mentioned on page 87, countries in southern Africa needed to maintain trade links with South Africa.
- Countries that wished to continue trading, notably Israel, could always get round them.

During the 1980s, significant opposition to apartheid grew in the USA, particularly as the fear over the USSR and communism diminished. Congress overrode the president's veto over sanctions (see page 102). As a result, more companies withdrew investment – 50 in 1986 and 40 in the following year. Particularly seriously, US banks such as Chase Manhattan began to refuse to renew loans, for example $10 million of short-term loans maturing in 1987. This created a severe financial crisis which was an important factor in obliging the South African government to begin negotiations to end apartheid. Overall, one 1989 report estimated that economic sanctions had reduced the potential growth rate in South Africa by ten per cent and cost 5 million potential jobs.

Cultural and sporting boycotts

Cultural and sporting boycotts had begun in the 1960s with South Africa's being suspended from the 1964 Olympic Games and formally excluded in 1970. As a sporting nation, these boycotts were keenly felt. Overseas South African tours often attracted disruption (see pages 50–1). The South African government itself had banned tours if they included non-white players: in 1968 it banned the English cricket team because it included Basil D'Olivera, originally a coloured South African. The government had banned a New Zealand rugby tour in 1967 on the grounds that it included Maoris; this was rescinded in 1970 when Maori players were declared honorary whites. The acclaimed white South African runner Zola Budd had to take out British citizenship in order to compete in international competitions. The Commonwealth passed the Gleneagles Agreement in June 1977, which forbade members competing against South Africa in any sporting activity. New Zealand faced considerable criticism when it invited the South African rugby team, known as the Springboks, to tour in 1981. Generally, South Africa was isolated in terms of sporting and cultural links. Many called for a worldwide boycott of South Africa as well as economic sanctions.

SOURCE F

Extract from Donald Woods, *Biko*, Paddington Press, 1978, pages 281–2. Anti-apartheid journalist Woods wrote this biography secretly while under house arrest. The final section of the book was a scathing indictment of apartheid and called for an international boycott of South Africa.

> In Source F, why does Woods believe a sporting boycott would be effective?

There are many pressures that can be applied in many fields, economic, diplomatic, strategic, financial and social. And they all add up to one word – ostracism. There has been a belief for many years that ostracism is a negative and destructive process, and this may well have been so in certain contexts, but not where the nationalist government is concerned.

Indeed, for many years I myself opposed the breaking of international links with South African associations – especially in the sphere of sport – until I was proved wrong by a young fellow-South African named Peter Hain, who organised anti-apartheid demonstrations in Britain … I argued, if South African sports people were ostracized this would drive them further away from reason and would confirm them in their prejudices in isolation.

Such links were preserved for many years, and the result was that apartheid persisted in South African sport. The white South Africans regarded the continuing tours as evidence that their approach was still acceptable in the world, that they were still approved of in spite of apartheid.

Summary diagram: External pressures on National Party power, 1974–83

```
                        ┌─────────────────────┐
                        │  External pressures  │
                        └─────────────────────┘
        ┌───────────────────────┼───────────────────────┐
┌───────────────┐      ┌──────────────────┐      ┌───────────────┐
│   Impact of   │      │    Growth of     │      │ Sanctions and │
│ decolonisation│      │ involvement in   │      │   boycotts    │
│  in southern  │      │ external conflict│      └───────────────┘
│    Africa     │      └──────────────────┘              │
└───────────────┘               │               ┌───────────────┐
        │               ┌──────────────┐         │     Arms      │
┌───────────────┐       │   Angola,    │         │   embargoes   │
│  Hostility of │       │   Namibia,   │         └───────────────┘
│  Angola and   │       │   Rhodesia   │
│  Mozambique   │       └──────────────┘
└───────────────┘
```

Challenges to National Party power, 1974–83:

- Pressure to reform vs opposition to reform
- Greater costs of defence vs weakening economy
- Need for greater security vs increasing loss of confidence

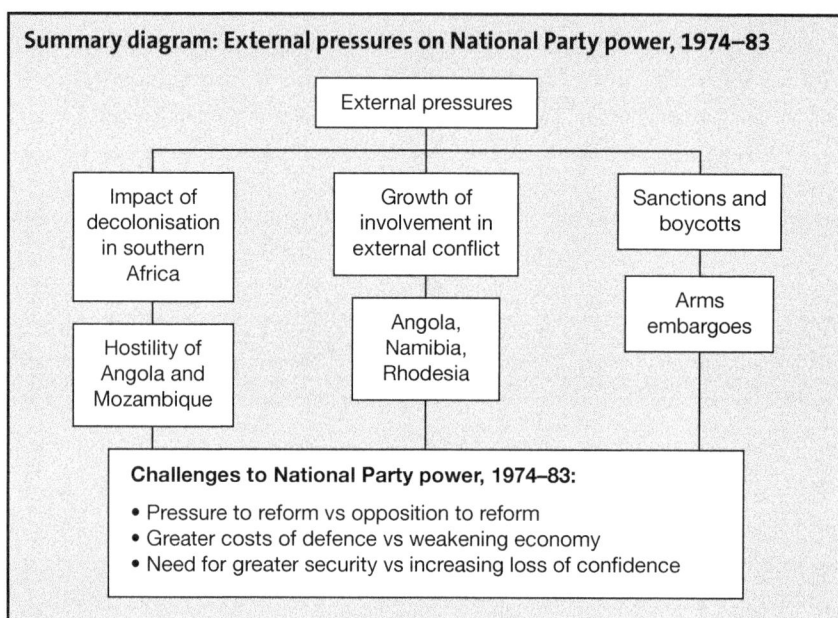

Chapter summary

The late 1960s saw the void filled by the apparent demise of the ANC and PAC with the development of Black Consciousness. This was a movement offering pride in their race to Africans, which resonated particularly with the young. It created SASO, which campaigned for improvements in higher education for Africans. It influenced the creation of SASM, which organised the protests that were to lead to the 1976 Soweto uprising. The immediate causes were problems with education for Africans, but it reflected wider discontent and the protests it sparked were to remain and intensify throughout the apartheid period. Meanwhile, thousands of young people left to join the exiled ANC, which was rejuvenated by their presence. In exile, it continued the armed struggle and diplomatic activities to gain international support. The Soweto uprising and death in police custody of Black Consciousness activist Steve Biko caused worldwide condemnation for South Africa. It became subject to intensified sanctions and boycotts, and the economy began to weaken, partly as a result of the 1973 oil crisis. This was coupled with greater involvement in military operations in the face of hostile regimes on its borders.

The need for defence led to huge rises in military costs and South Africa was increasingly drawn into warfare against neighbouring states. Meanwhile, conditions for Africans in the Bantustans remained poor. The National Party itself faced scandal through Muldergate and was increasingly divided. Hard-liners eventually left to form the Conservative Party, which threatened National Party domination. Anti-apartheid groups increasingly called for heightened sanctions. Although there was considerable debate about the efficacy of these, international opinion appeared to be turning more in their favour. South Africa appeared increasingly isolated in the world although hostile neighbours, such as Zambia, still needed to maintain economic links. Overall, however, in the period 1968–83 the confidence of the apartheid regime began to falter.

Refresher questions

Use these questions to remind yourself of the key material covered in this chapter.

1. What were the beliefs of Black Consciousness?

2. How significant were the June 1976 Soweto protests to the progress of the anti-apartheid movement?

3. What are the meanings of Total Onslaught and Total Strategy?

4. Why did the death of Steve Biko in 1977 attract so much international attention?

5. How was the ANC reorganised in the 1970s under the presidency of Oliver Tambo?

6. How effective was the global anti-apartheid movement in protesting against apartheid?

7. What political challenges did the National Party face in the years 1968–84?

8. What problems did Bantustans face?

9. How far did political changes affect South Africa in the 1970s?

10. How far was South Africa internationally isolated by the end of the 1970s?

Question practice

ESSAY QUESTIONS

1. To what extent was the Soweto uprising of 1976 a result of disaffection with African education?

2. 'The ANC was the main beneficiary of the Soweto uprising of 1976.' How far do you agree with this statement?

3. 'The government of South Africa in the years 1968–83 was dominated by the need for security against internal opponents.' How far do you agree with this statement?

4. How significant were external pressures on National Party rule in the years 1974–83?

SOURCE-BASED QUESTIONS

1. With reference to Source A (page 72) and Source D (page 83), and your understanding of the historical context, assess the value of these sources to a historian studying the beliefs and activities of Black Consciousness in the years 1968–78.

2. With reference to Source E (page 101) and Source F (page 103), and your understanding of the historical context, assess the value of these sources to a historian studying the arguments for imposition of sanctions and boycotts on South Africa in the years 1968–83.

CHAPTER 4

The end of apartheid and the creation of the 'rainbow nation', 1984–94

By 1984, the townships were in a state of permanent unrest. The United Democratic Front was created to coordinate protests and develop community awareness in the fight against apartheid. This had a close relationship with the exiled African National Congress (ANC). However, it embraced over 500 separate organisations, some more militant than others, and was criticised for not being able to control the more volatile elements. Meanwhile, government repression continued. Prime Minister P.W. Botha sought to reform apartheid in order to win the support of more black South Africans without compromising white supremacy. To this end, a new constitution was created in 1983. Meanwhile, economic sanctions and international criticisms continued and South Africa became increasingly isolated. Botha's successor, F.W. de Klerk, realised apartheid could not continue. After four years of protracted negotiations, a new constitution was created and the first fully democratic elections took place in April 1994. These developments are described in the following sections:

★ Revolt in the townships, 1984–87

★ Reasons for Botha's decision to negotiate, 1985–89

★ Negotiation and compromise, 1989–91

★ A new political settlement, 1992–94

Key dates

1984	New constitution with P.W. Botha becoming executive president	1990	Mandela and other anti-apartheid leaders released
1985	Botha's 'Rubicon' speech	1991	CODESA I
1986	US Congress overrode President Reagan's veto on sanctions	1992	Referendum among white voters accepted the need for change
	Abolition of pass laws		Creation of CODESA 2
	Severe financial crisis	1993	Creation of Transitional Executive Council to prepare for democracy
	State of emergency		
1988	Nelson Mandela's seventieth birthday concert at Wembley arena in London		Murder of Chris Hani, *Umkhonto we Sizwe* leader
1989	F.W. de Klerk became president	1994	First elections under new non-racial constitution: creation of Government of National Unity with Mandela as president
1990	De Klerk's 'New Course' announced		

1 Revolt in the townships, 1984–87

▶ What was the impact on the apartheid state of the revolt in the townships, 1984–87?

By the mid-1980s, South Africa was in ferment with increasing violence and protest often from the grass-roots level, uncontrolled by any central organisations.

The United Democratic Front and grass-roots organisation

In August 1983, 575 organisations in South Africa founded the **United Democratic Front (UDF)**, whose aim was to co-ordinate internal opposition, specifically against Botha's constitutional reforms (see page 116). Its wider goal was the creation of a new South African government based on the tenets of the Freedom Charter (see page 33). Initially, the UDF was heavily influenced by Christian principles. Influential activists in its creation included senior Christian figures such as Allan Boesak and Frank Chicane, who condemned apartheid and, indeed, in the absence of secular leaders (who were either imprisoned or in exile) became leading voices for change in the 1980s. The UDF came to be seen as the internal wing of the African National Congress (ANC), although it eschewed violence. However, because it was a loose organisation, many affiliated groups were militant, and some turned to violent demonstrations and intimidation within their communities. Critics argued that the UDF had no control over such groups.

Protest strategies

Support for the UDF may have been as high as 2 million people. Many responded to Oliver Tambo's exhortation to make South Africa ungovernable:

- The UDF was particularly supported by the Indian Congresses and Congress of South African Trade Unions (COSATU). The number of strikes proliferated – and the number of days lost grew from 1 million in 1986 to 6 million in 1987.
- The UDF organised marches, protests and demonstrations throughout South Africa. Local groups, such as the Port Elizabeth Black Civic Organisation, were affiliated and organised protests against, for example, poor housing and lack of electric supplies under its banner.
- The Congress of South African Students (COSAS), created in 1979 in the aftermath of the Soweto uprising, organised frequent school strikes and boycotts. The problem with this, of course, was that students were at risk of missing out on such education as was available in schools.
- The National Education Crisis Committee (NECC), formed in March 1986, tried both to provide alternative educational facilities and to encourage students to return to school. It felt they required education even if it was

🔑 **KEY TERM**

United Democratic Front (UDF) Organisation created in 1983 within South Africa to co-ordinate the struggle against apartheid.

substandard. Students needed to be educated as far as possible to understand the issues facing them and be able to function effectively in a post-apartheid society.

- In 1983 and 1984, UDF groups campaigned to collect a million signatures for a mass petition against the proposed new constitution and African local government. Less than twelve per cent of Africans voted in the elections for the new community councils.

Township government

The Community Council Act of 1977 established elected township councils. The intention was to give Africans more of a say in the running of their communities and so defuse some of the antagonisms towards the largely white officials, who had hitherto been solely responsible. The powers of these African councillors were augmented and extended until, in 1982, the councils became solely responsible for running the townships. In fact, this led to huge problems because those choosing to participate were seen as collaborators and were targeted by mobs. They also had to raise their own revenues. The most obvious way to do this was by rent increases, which led to more unrest and rent strikes. Sometimes councillors were themselves corrupt. As violence intensified during the 1980s, they often became the target of assassination attempts. Not surprisingly, very few Black Africans took part in the local councils.

SOURCE A

What does Source A suggest about the UDF protest in the 1980s?

Grass-roots organisation

The UDF began a programme of 'People's Organs, People's Power' using local organisations to plan such activities as rent strikes and local courts to oversee communities. By 1989, rent arrears had grown to half a billion rand. In 1983–84, Ciskei workers boycotted the buses taking them to work in the city of East London.

Rallies

The 1980s saw more mass rallies and protests. Increasingly, these became more nationalist in tone, with flags and banners of banned organisation such as the ANC, incendiary speeches and the widespread use of the ANC anthem *Nkosi Sikelel' iAfrika* ('God Bless Africa'). Often the funerals of victims of the violence became foci for protest: the victims themselves, especially if they had been activists, were seen as martyrs to the struggle and celebrated as heroes.

The advantage of these activities for the UDF was that there were no obvious national figures to arrest or ban; although in 1987 the UDF was banned, and many members were arrested, its activities continued because there was no central organisation for the security forces to target. The problem was that UDF-sponsored organisations were unable to stem a growing rate of violence.

Communal violence

Violence was getting beyond anyone's control. In 1984, in violent demonstrations against rent increases in the Pretoria–Witwatersrand–Vereeniging area, 175 people were killed. Many of the local courts descended into violence, with alleged malefactors being lynched or '**necklaced**'. In 1985 alone, over 800 people were killed as a result of political activity. Many leaders spoke out against 'kangaroo courts' which seemed to dole out punishments as a result of personal vendettas more than evidence against any malfeasance. If anything, the punishments intensified and helped create an atmosphere of fear and distrust in the areas in which the courts operated.

One concern was that different groups of Africans were turning on each other. In particular, the Zulu group **Inkhata** emerged, claiming to be a national liberation group but increasingly responsible for black-on-black violence.

Chief Buthelezi and Inkhata

Chief **Mangosuthu Buthelezi** was the powerful chief of the Zulu nation. He had earned respect as a moderate, who, though he opposed apartheid, was prepared to work with the regime for reform. He supported capitalism, rejected communism, decried the use of violence and opposed economic sanctions except for arms sales. Buthelezi had won the admiration of foreign leaders such as US President Ronald Reagan and British Prime Minister Margaret Thatcher. Buthelezi's main policy was the consolidation of the Zulu nation within a

> **KEY TERMS**
>
> **Necklaced** Vigilante punishment by setting victims on fire by enveloping them in petrol-soaked tyres.
>
> **Inkhata** Zulu nationalist organisation which developed into the Inkhata Freedom Party in 1990: it opposed the ANC in the 1980s and sought an independent Zulu homeland.

> **KEY FIGURE**
>
> **Mangosuthu Buthelezi (1928–)**
> Hereditary Zulu chief who headed the Inkhata Freedom Party.

federated South Africa, almost like the USA, where all the different states were on an equal footing. To this end, he opposed independence for KwaZulu as a Bantustan.

Although Buthelezi had originally supported the ANC, he grew distant from it while it was in exile. Many Africans, moreover, saw him as a collaborator: it is said he never forgot having been stoned during the funeral of Robert Sobukwe in 1978. A conference held in London in 1979 failed to settle the differences between Inkhata and the ANC and from this time relations between the two organisations became overtly hostile.

When the government began to talk to other African leaders in the late 1980s, Buthelezi may have feared a loss of influence. He had already revived the Zulu nationalist movement Inkhata and said all Zulus were members. For all the rhetoric, neither Buthelezi nor Inkhata favoured democracy, and the movement effectively led to KwaZulu becoming a one-party state. It was the largest and most powerful political group within South Africa.

Inkhata opposed the creation of the UDF as a front for the ANC. Buthelezi himself took on the role of police chief within KwaZulu, where the authorities turned a blind eye to increasing violence against ANC supporters.

Hostel residents

There had long been hostility between migrant workers who lived without their families in barrack-hostels and residents of the townships who favoured the ANC. In the 1980s, this enmity escalated, particularly in Natal between supporters of the ANC and Inkhata. Because the latter tended to support the government more, they often had covert assistance from the security forces in their attacks on alleged supporters of the ANC.

Many feared that South Africa was descending into civil war. The townships, in particular, seemed uncontrolled. The government itself added to the violence with its often brutal responses.

Government violence

The government was accused of brutal, often covert, activities within South Africa. In 1984, for example, the State Security Council authorised the assassination of the 'Cradock Four' anti-apartheid activists. In 1987, they were accused of bombing the headquarters of COSATU on the basis that it was used by members of *Umkhonto we Sizwe* (MK). In 1987, the Civilian Co-operation Bureau was established to identify 'enemies of the state', after which the security forces would act, for example, assassinating anti-apartheid critic David Webster in May 1989.

Many of the operations in which security forces were involved were covert:

- Crowbar was a special-forces group, founded in 1979, and trained to fight the South West African People's Organisation (SWAPO) in Namibia.
- Government forces also infiltrated cells within South Africa, using spies and collaborators.

At other times, the authorities simply reacted to demonstrations with brutality. For example, in 1986 alone as many as 500 black Africans were shot dead by police. The security forces became almost a state within a state. They carried out as many as 40 political assassinations. They made raids in neighbouring countries including Angola, Lesotho, Mozambique and Zimbabwe. In 1982, they bombed the ANC headquarters in London. However, they were also operating within South Africa itself.

A 'third force'

A 'third force' was operated by members of government security forces. This worked with vigilante groups to undertake covert operations in order to undermine any attempt at negotiations. However, it is also important to say that many commentators eschew any suggestion of official government involvement in the 'third force'. Many now believe it was made up of rogue groups operating clandestinely and without the knowledge of the most senior officers and government officials.

Inkhatagate

In 1991, the scandal of 'Inkhatagate' broke when it was discovered certain members of the security forces were giving covert assistance to Inkhata cadres and, indeed, sometimes accompanying them on operations. It was discovered, for example, that the so-called 'third force' had cooperated with Inkhata in the murder of thirteen members of the family of ANC activist Victor Ntuli. Nelson Mandela was to report that the security forces themselves were destabilising the Vaal Triangle area. There were stories that weapons confiscated by the authorities from ANC cadres mysteriously found themselves in the hands of Inkhata members shortly afterwards. Similarly, the ANC had discovered that Inkhata members were going to attack ANC supporters in Sebokeng township in the Vaal Triangle on 22 July. Although they informed the authorities, busloads of Inkhata members arrived in Sebokeng on the allotted day, accompanied by members of the security forces, who did nothing to prevent subsequent attacks.

Vigilantes

The security forces often gave help to vigilante groups who, later in the 1980s, were accused of responsibility for 90 per cent of deaths related to unrest. In 1985, one gang, the Phakatis, terrorised those supporting a schools boycott in the Orange Free State. In 1988, vigilante groups were blamed for the deaths of 1200 people in the Edendale Valley, a centre of unrest and ANC support in Natal.

Government suppression

The government became increasingly effective at suppressing protest:

- More people were arrested and died in custody.
- It passed an Internal Security Act in 1982 by which anyone could be investigated and people banned without the need to give a reason.
- Censorship was extended: the Inquest Act of 1982 outlawed the reportage of deaths in custody and criticism of the security forces was banned under the Police Act.

The principal military policy was to destroy ANC and other anti-apartheid group bases both at home and in the frontline states. This involved attacks on bases and indeed suspected perpetrators, as we have seen (see page 111), but also continued army operations in neighbouring states. Here, the hope was to destabilise radical regimes such as the People's Movement for the Liberation of Angola (MPLA) in Angola and replace them with more amenable moderate regimes such as the National Union for the Total Independence of Angola (UNITA), or at the very least to stop them supporting the ANC and other anti-apartheid groups.

Angola

The South African Defence Force (SADF) faced military reverses in Angola. In late 1986, MPLA and its Cuban allies launched a major offensive to destroy UNITA. The SADF came to UNITA's aid and laid siege to the key Angolan military base at Cuito Cuanavale in 1988. While this incursion failed, enemy troops also managed to gain control of the border with Namibia, thus cutting off the SADF escape route. To break out would have been unacceptable in terms of white casualties. Therefore, the South African government negotiated a truce under which the SADF would withdraw from Angola so long as the MPLA closed the SWAPO bases there. This would prevent SWAPO guerrillas from attacking targets in Namibia.

Mozambique

The FRELIMO regime in Mozambique came to an agreement with South Africa in March 1984. The Nkomati Accords committed FRELIMO to closing ANC bases in Mozambique in return for South Africa's ceasing to support opposition groups there. While these agreements were precarious and both sides broke them from time to time, they had two effects:

- They gave the SADF a respite from full-scale military activity.
- They closed down ANC bases in a neighbouring frontline state which could have been used to launch attacks on South Africa, and made it more difficult for SWAPO to operate effectively in Namibia.

Summary diagram: Revolt in the townships, 1984–87

Revolt of the UDF:
- Co-ordinate internal opposition
- Organise marches, petitions
- Support community action

↓

People's organs, people's power

Failures of township government:
- Community councillors seen as collaborators, faced violence
- Had to increase rents to raise revenue

↓

Faced non-cooperation, strikes, increasing violence, for example 'necklacing'

Violence

'Black on black'

Inkhata vs ANC

Government violence

Covert activities:
- Assassinations
- Support for 'third force'
- Support for vigilante groups

'Make South Africa ungovernable': ANC President Oliver Tambo, 1985

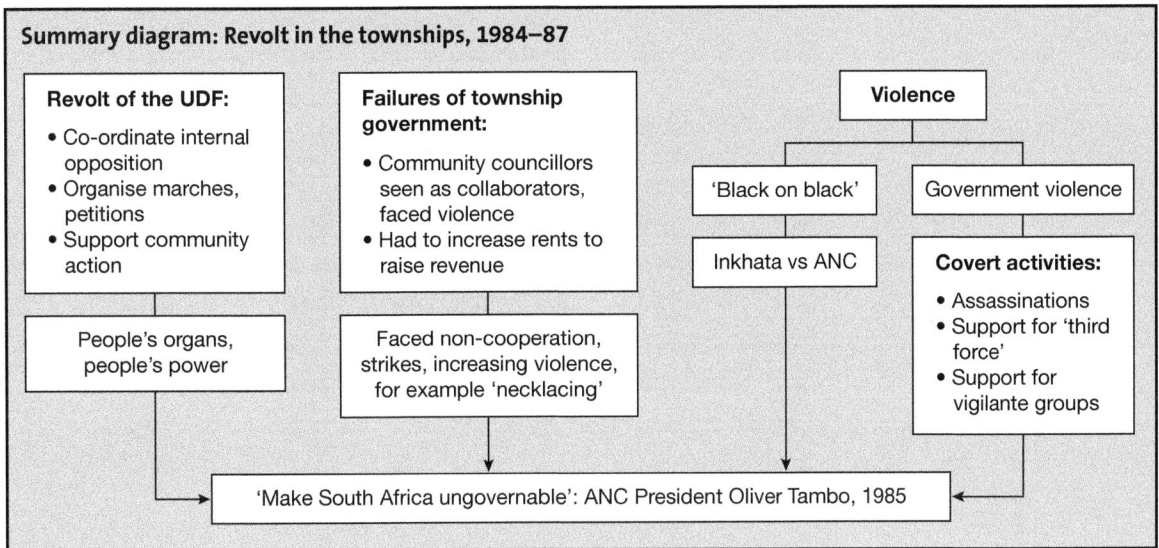

2 Reasons for Botha's decision to negotiate, 1985–89

▶ *To what extent did Botha offer genuine reform of apartheid?*

By the later 1980s, Botha realised that the policy of Total Strategy had failed. South Africa was becoming more violent, protests were increasing both in number and intensity, and the effectiveness of economic sanctions, for example in the financial sector, threatened the stability of the entire state. He saw no alternative but to negotiate reform with anti-government groups, most of which were banned at the time.

Reasons for the failure of Total Strategy

The aim of Total Strategy was to defeat the ANC and bring order back to South Africa. It failed for a variety of reasons:

- South Africa's economy was struggling. Partly as a result of economic sanctions, inflation rose from eleven per cent in 1983 to eighteen per cent by 1986.
- News of government operations served only to harden world opinion against South Africa and give support to opposition groups.
- There was no end to the violence in the townships.
- The security forces seemed unable to prevent the ANC and other groups committing acts of terror within South Africa, for example, attacking bars popular with members of the security forces. The number of incidents rose from 45 in 1984 to 281 by 1988.

- There was dissent within Botha's government: some wanted to maintain the military pressure, but it became apparent that this was not succeeding.

Reasons for change

Botha knew the apartheid regime needed to be reformed to survive. As mentioned, he instituted several structural reforms (see page 96). However, the nature of apartheid also came under review. He recognised that black Africans were a permanent factor in townships and their hostility had to be assuaged. To this end, many examples of petty apartheid were abandoned:

- The Mixed Marriages Act of 1949 was repealed in 1985.
- Local authorities were encouraged to desegregate parks and public amenities.
- Pass laws were abolished in 1986.

Botha's reforms

The reform policy has variously been called 'WHAM' – 'Winning of Hearts And Minds' – and 'Adapt or Die'. Botha's main aim was still, however, to maintain white supremacy. He felt this could best be achieved by 'divide and rule'; in other words, by including the Indian and coloured South Africans in the political process, they could be separated from black Africans. Some historians, for example Hermann Giliomee, felt Botha's reforms have been underestimated. The abandonment of influx control, the assertion of the rights of African trade unions and the abolition of much of petty apartheid were significant changes, whatever the motivation.

As mentioned on page 94, the armed forces were recruiting more non-white South Africans: by the late 1970s, they comprised fourteen per cent of the forces. In 1978, black South Africans were given 99-year leases on properties in the townships – previously they had only been accepted as temporary residents. However, the most significant reform was that of the constitution, since it widened the right of parliamentary entry to include coloured and Indian South Africans.

Constitutional reform

In 1984, Botha introduced a new constitution after a referendum of white voters accepted it by a two-to-one majority. There was to be a new **tricameral** Parliament:

- House of Assembly, comprising 178 white members
- House of Representatives, comprising 85 coloured members
- House of Delegates, comprising 45 Indian members.

In any joint sessions, white members could outvote the other two groups. It should be noted, too, that Africans were not represented at all.

KEY TERM

Tricameral A Parliament comprised of three houses, in this case assembly, representatives and delegates.

Governance

There would be a multiracial cabinet responsible for 'general affairs', by which was meant issues such as taxation, defence, business and foreign affairs. Uniracial ministerial councils were to be responsible for 'their own affairs', for example in education, health and local government, in so far as these applied to the separate racial groups.

Role of the prime minister

The prime minister became a president with executive powers, thereby increasing a role that had formerly been largely ceremonial. Now, the prime minister was:

- elected by a college of 50 voters, including 50 white, 25 coloured and 13 Indian MPs
- given the power to dissolve Parliament at any time
- responsible for African affairs
- given the power to appoint a cabinet from members of all three houses.

In addition, the multiracial President's Council (see page 91) was given the power to settle any disputes between the three houses. The new system faced fierce criticism and the backlash from intransigent white politicians led to the formation of the Conservative Party of South Africa (see pages 93–4).

Botha's 'Rubicon' speech

In August 1985, many in South Africa and around the world were expecting to see real change announced at the National Party Congress in Durban. In previous meetings to discuss the changes – such as freeing Mandela and accepting that the South African government needed to truly represent all South Africans – Botha had remained silent, and government officials took this silence to mean agreement. However, a few days before the Congress, Botha declared he would write his own speech rather than the one drafted for him. On 15 August, Botha's speech was broadcast live to a global audience of over 200 million people. It was a long, rambling, insular speech: 'South Africa's problems will be solved by South Africans and not by foreigners … My Government and I are determined to press ahead with our reform programme, and to those who prefer revolution to reform, I say they will not succeed.' It became known as the '**Rubicon**' speech but Botha had failed to cross the 'river' into introducing real reform. The speech was a disaster.

Botha did welcome an 'Eminent Persons Group' of various Commonwealth heads of state to South Africa. He allowed them to meet with the imprisoned Nelson Mandela in March and initiated government contacts with Mandela. The government had been meeting Mandela for some time to try to resolve the

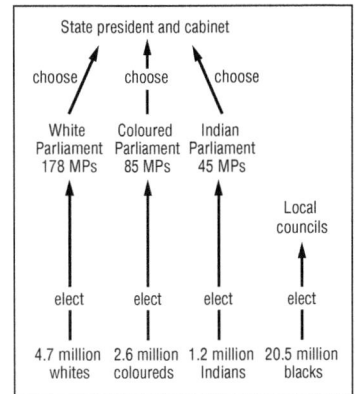

The structure of the new tricameral Parliament.

> **🔑 KEY TERM**
>
> **Rubicon** 'Crossing the Rubicon' is a term used to describe the taking of a critical decision that cannot be reversed.

impasse over the future of South Africa. He had been offered his freedom by P.W. Botha as early as 1985, for example, if he would renounce violence. While no agreement had been made between Mandela and government officials, by meeting regularly they had learnt to trust each other. Yet, Botha would not take the final step of releasing Mandela. At the same time, government oppression continued and Botha intensified military activities against ANC and Pan-Africanist Congress (PAC) bases abroad. In May 1986, the security forces bombed the capital cities of three neighbouring states.

Many still felt that Botha's reforms were largely cosmetic:

- The principal planks of apartheid such as the Population Registration Act remained in force.
- While much petty apartheid had been repealed much still remained, for example while buses had been desegregated, trains had not.
- More significantly, the townships where most lived still faced the same problems of overcrowding and squalor. It was in attempting to improve these that the new black councils faced insurrection as a result of having to raise rents.

Economic problems and the impact of international isolation

The South African government faced increasing pressures in the mid-1980s, resulting in the declaration of a new state of emergency in 1986. Nevertheless, Botha had come to the decision to secretly begin talks with outlawed and imprisoned leaders such as Nelson Mandela (see above). Indeed, one can discern the contradictions which characterised a government loss of confidence. On the one hand, apartheid was being reformed and yet what remained was being enforced ever more rigorously. Botha was prepared to talk to anti-apartheid campaigners, yet the security forces oppressed them more severely. His 'Rubicon' speech let down many expectations (of outlawing discrimination and freeing Mandela) and caused the rand to fall dramatically against other currencies. The later 1980s saw a government in turmoil with its problems exacerbated by economic crisis.

The economic problems facing the state grew particularly as a result of US sanctions and the boycott by banks:

- In 1985 and 1986, over 90 US firms, including photographic giant Kodak, closed down their South African operations.
- In 1985, the international value of the rand fell by 35 per cent and the stock exchange was in crisis. The foreign exchange temporarily closed on 30 August 1985 to uphold the value of the rand by stifling the amount of money leaving the country.
- The cost of imports rose by 60 per cent between 1986 and 1987.

- Sally Tollin, a diarist who worked with disadvantaged youngsters, often mentioned price rises and their impact on the economy and everyday life. On 1 April 1984, for example, electricity prices rose 100 per cent, while on 22 January 1985, petrol rose 31 per cent, which 'will have a disastrous effect upon the economy and the unemployed, as all goods will increase in price'.
- In 1987, World Bank figures suggested that South African growth rates were among the lowest in the developed world, while inflation was the third highest among the industrial nations.
- Afrikaner businessmen were very pessimistic, fearing that investment would never return without meaningful reform. The white population was in decline while that of the Africans rose exponentially, particularly in the cities. It was estimated that black Africans would outnumber whites by five to one by 2000.
- Ironically, non-white South Africans as a whole were growing more wealthy, with the emergence of the new middle class. It was estimated that the national percentage of disposable income for white people would fall from 55 to 42.5 per cent between 1985 and 2000.

The effect of the state of emergency

Botha declared a state of emergency in 1986. Its aim was to re-establish internal control, particularly over the townships. However, it sought also a lasting settlement within South Africa and continued domination over its neighbours. These ideas were no longer feasible unless the fundamentals of the regime were changed. Ultimately:

- The state of emergency did not remove underlying problems, which were now too great to control through coercion.
- The SADF deployed almost 8000 troops in the townships and committed acts of barbarism which, by 1987, saw 43 admitted deaths in police custody, and as many as 29,000 arrests – but still the violence continued.
- Over 30 organisations including the UDF were banned. Media restrictions meant that comparatively little went reported.

The main effect of the state of emergency was to turn South Africa into a dictatorship governed by coercion and suppression of information, but this had little impact on the problems it faced.

Internationally, many countries saw Botha's reforms as, at best, window dressing. The continuing violence and brutality on the part of both the authorities and increasingly lawless groups added to the concerns. In particular, his constitutional reforms in 1984 were criticised because:

- White South Africans dominated.
- Racial separation was maintained.
- The president was too powerful, for example being able to dissolve Parliament at any time.

- Reforms were costly and over-bureaucratic.
- Africans were isolated with no input. They were granted powers in local government (see page 108) but this created more problems than it solved. Indeed, Indian and coloured South Africans were at best apathetic, and at worst hostile, for example only 30 per cent of coloured voters and 20 per cent of Indian voters participated in the elections. The constitutional reform was generally seen as too little, too late, as a last-ditch attempt to maintain white supremacy.

Botha's 'Rubicon' speech in 1985, preceding the state of emergency in 1986, saw yet more international isolation.

? What point is being made in Source B?

SOURCE B

Declaration of the 'Seminar on the Legal Status of the Apartheid Regime and Other Legal Aspects of the Struggle Against Apartheid'. This was a declaration emanating from an international seminar on apartheid held in Lagos, Nigeria, between 13 and 16 August 1984 (available at https://omalley.nelsonmandela.org/omalley/index.php/site/q/03lv01538/04lv01600/05lv01636/06lv01637.htm).

In South Africa itself, a massive militarisation drive coupled with a complex series of adjustments to the apartheid system – mistakenly referred to as reforms by some of South Africa's allies – have centralised and consolidated white state power. In this process, nearly 8 million Africans have been denationalised in pursuit of the South African regime's policy of establishing 'independent' homelands for Africans, and nearly 3.5 million Africans have been deported from their residences. A new constitution is about to be inaugurated establishing a tricameral parliament for whites, so-called Coloureds and South Africans of Indian descent.

The Seminar recognised that the international community had already condemned the total illegitimacy of the new constitutional arrangements in South Africa. These represented a step in the direction of consolidating rather than eliminating apartheid. The principles of white domination, ethnic division and African exclusion run right through the constitution. Apartheid in the form of racial group areas was brought right into parliament. The white chamber has a permanent majority. The African people are totally excluded. White domination is legally protected under the constitutional phrase 'own affairs' which excludes the competence of the other chambers to consider the whole legislative scheme of apartheid which is thus constitutionally protected.

The only acceptable constitution is one based on non-racial and democratic principles in which all the people have the vote on a basis of full equality in an undivided country.

Mission to South Africa: the Commonwealth Report, June 1986

This report, produced by the 'eminent persons' who toured South Africa on behalf of the Commonwealth (see page 89), was deeply pessimistic in tone. It feared South Africa was on the verge of civil war if it did not dismantle apartheid. There appeared no present prospect of meaningful dialogue between the government and anti-apartheid groups. By the time of the state of emergency, South Africa was more isolated than at any time in its history.

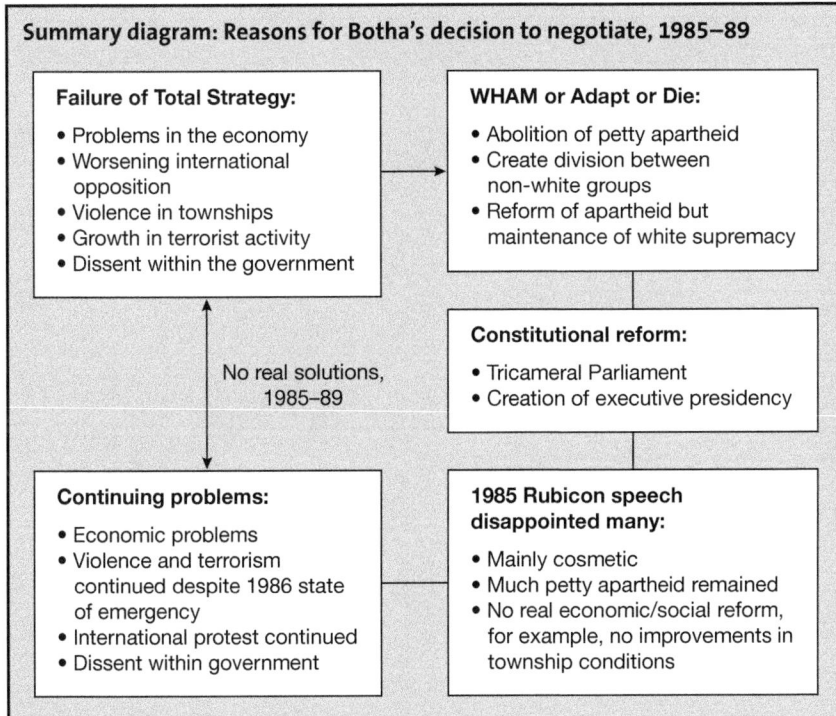

Summary diagram: Reasons for Botha's decision to negotiate, 1985–89

Failure of Total Strategy:

- Problems in the economy
- Worsening international opposition
- Violence in townships
- Growth in terrorist activity
- Dissent within the government

WHAM or Adapt or Die:

- Abolition of petty apartheid
- Create division between non-white groups
- Reform of apartheid but maintenance of white supremacy

No real solutions, 1985–89

Constitutional reform:

- Tricameral Parliament
- Creation of executive presidency

Continuing problems:

- Economic problems
- Violence and terrorism continued despite 1986 state of emergency
- International protest continued
- Dissent within government

1985 Rubicon speech disappointed many:

- Mainly cosmetic
- Much petty apartheid remained
- No real economic/social reform, for example, no improvements in township conditions

---

③ Negotiation and compromise, 1989–91

▶ *In what ways was apartheid finally dismantled?*

P.W. Botha was incapacitated by a stroke in February 1989. In his first speech as president, his successor, F.W. de Klerk, outlined a 'New Course' which promised a real end to apartheid and power sharing between the different racial groups, but not integration as such. However, de Klerk realised that the only alternative was increased repression. He was not prepared to accept this, as he had come to believe that fundamental change was inevitable and to deny it now would only be to delay matters. He seems to have accepted that long-term factors had determined this:

- The continuation of apartheid was hurting Afrikaners as a whole. Their original motivations for applying it had largely gone. They were no longer rivals with English speakers for hegemony – their relative wealth had increased and their party had been in power for 40 years. Nevertheless, the threat of economic weakness as a result of international boycotts threatened their status. They largely recognised, moreover, that they needed an educated, skilled African middle class to maintain economic prosperity. However, these views were not shared by many conservative and poorer Afrikaners (see page 93).
- There was always a fear that unrest in the townships, which was intensifying, could spill over into white areas. White South Africans could no longer be confident that their security forces could contain the violence.

Figure 4.1 South Africa and its independent republics and self-governing territories post-1948.

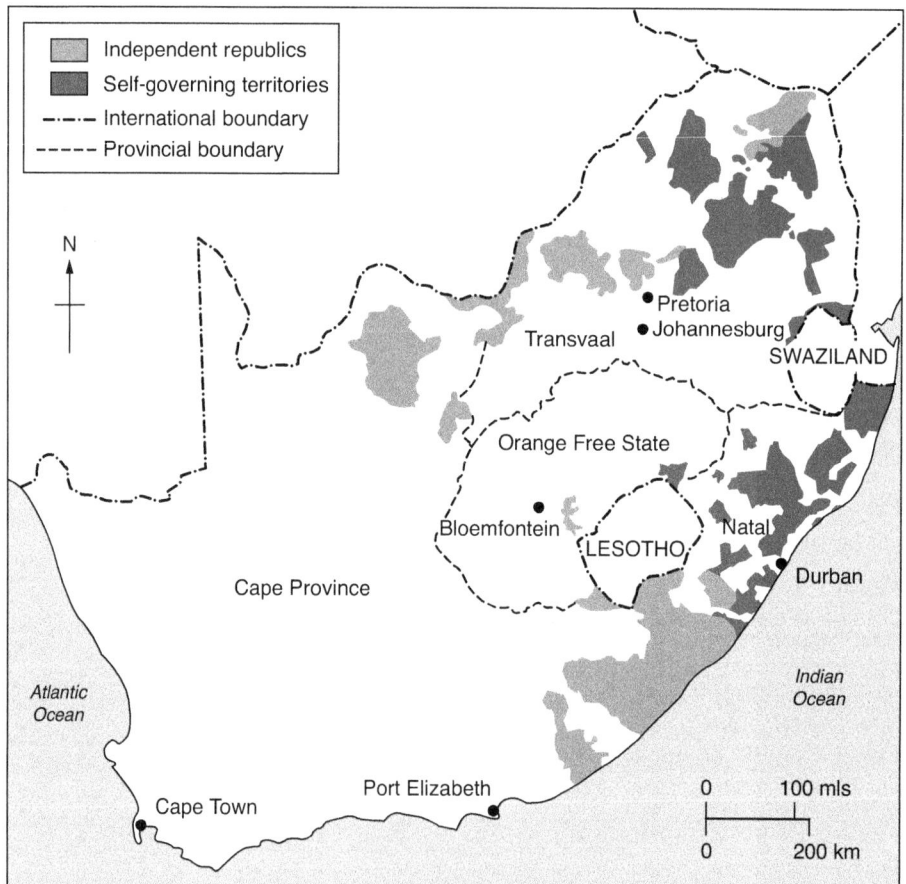

F.W. de Klerk

1936	Born in Johannesburg
1958	Graduated in law from Potchefstroom University
1972	Elected to Parliament as a National Party MP
1978	First government post as minister of sports and telecommunications
1989	Became leader of National Party and state president
1990	Presidential inaugural address proposing release of political prisoners and significant reform
1993	Awarded Nobel Peace Prize jointly with Nelson Mandela
1994	Became deputy president after first fully democratic elections
1996	Resigned as deputy president
1997	Retired from politics

Early life and career

Frederik Willem de Klerk was born in Johannesburg in 1936, the son of a leading Afrikaner politician with links to influential political families. He graduated from the University of Potchefstroom in 1958 with a law degree and began a successful practice in Vereeniging. He became involved in civic affairs and in 1972 entered Parliament as National Party MP for Vereeniging.

Political career

De Klerk gained a political reputation for efficiency and reliability, someone who would not support change. His legal expertise helped him rise quickly in government. He held his first government post in 1978 as minister of sport and telecommunications. He served constantly as a minister thereafter. In 1986, he was appointed leader of the House of Assembly. He was minister for education and planning from 1984 to 1989, in which role he supported segregated universities and never questioned the merits of apartheid.

President and the transition to democracy

Following the retirement of P.W. Botha, de Klerk became leader of the National Party in January 1989 and state president in September. He had, however, come to the realisation that apartheid could not continue, and used his inaugural address in February 1990 to announce the release of political prisoners and a commitment to political reform. To this end, he initiated four years of often tortuous negotiations to see South Africa move to democracy.

De Klerk was awarded the Nobel Peace Prize jointly with Nelson Mandela in 1993. After the first fully democratic elections in April 1994 he became deputy president, a position he resigned in 1996. De Klerk retired from politics in 1997.

The ANC position

The ANC realised it was not strong enough to take power anytime soon by a policy of insurrection. It could not win a war against the apartheid regime. Although there had been difficult debates throughout the 1980s, most of the leadership was by now reconciled to negotiation as the only realistic means of ending apartheid. It would have to talk to the government – as the government now recognised it would have to talk to the ANC.

De Klerk's 'New Course'

De Klerk's New Course reflected the realities of the late 1980s:

- South Africa seemed on the verge of, if not already involved in, civil war.
- Economic decline continued.

- The National Party was losing support. Although it won the 1989 election, it was with a reduced majority.
- Support from the USA and other Western countries diminished as communism was no longer seen as a threat.
- Influential business groups had pre-empted the New Course by already seeking dialogue with the ANC. In Senegal, for example, in July 1987, three days of talks ended with a call for a negotiated settlement.

Table 4.1 Elections to the House of Assembly: the three largest parties

Party	May 1987	September 1990
National Party	124	94
Conservative Party	22	39
Progressive Federal Party 1987/Democratic Party 1990	19	33

The New Course was effectively a statement that the government would work towards equal rights for all South Africans. It recognised the need to talk to opposition groups; to this end, the ANC, PAC and South African Communist Party (SACP) were legalised, and long-term political prisoners such as Nelson Mandela were to be released.

The significance of Mandela's release

Nelson Mandela was released on 11 February 1990 after 27 years in captivity. While other anti-apartheid activists were also freed, his particular release was significant because of his fame and symbolism as the victim of oppression in South Africa. People hoped he was the one leader with the charisma and dignity to facilitate a peaceful transition.

As mentioned on page 116, under Botha's government, Mandela had met government officials already, albeit in secret, to try to compromise on how to rule South Africa. He met de Klerk in May 1989 and both men agreed to work together for a peaceful and lasting settlement.

The unbanning of political parties

In February 1990, in his speech at the official opening of Parliament, de Klerk announced the lifting of the ban on political parties and partial removal of the state of emergency. The death penalty and press censorship, for example, were abolished. The extent of the changes he proposed came as a surprise to many commentators. Archbishop Tutu said, 'he has taken my breath away'. Others were more critical because many of the state of emergency restrictions remained. Nevertheless, the measures were intended to allow the government openly to talk with opposition groups and facilitated democratic elections once a settlement was reached. However, unbanning in itself had little effect on the violence and turmoil into which the country had descended, and equally little effect on political parties being ready to fight elections. The ANC, for example, had no real formal political organisation within South Africa.

SOURCE C

Extract from F.W. de Klerk's speech to Parliament, 2 February 1990 (available at www.sahistory.org.za/archive/fw-de-klerk%E2%80%99s-speech-parliament-2-february-1990).

The steps that have been decided, are the following:

- *The prohibition of the African National Congress, the Pan Africanist Congress, the South African Communist Party and a number of subsidiary organisations is being rescinded.*

- *People serving prison sentence merely because they were members of one of these organisations or because they committed another offence which was merely an offence because a prohibition on one of the organisations was in force, will be identified and released. Prisoners who have been sentenced for other offences such as murder, terrorism or arson are not affected by this.*

- *The media emergency regulations as well as the education emergency regulations are being abolished in their entirety.*

- *The security emergency regulations will be amended to still make provision for effective control over visual material pertaining to scenes of unrest.*

- *The restrictions in terms of the emergency regulations on 33 organisations are being rescinded. The organisations include the following: National Education Crisis Committees, South African National Students' Congress, United Democratic Front, Cosatu, Die Blanke Bevrydingsbeweging van Suid-Afrika.*

- *The conditions imposed in terms of the security emergency regulations on 374 people on their release, are being rescinded and the regulations which provide for such conditions are being abolished.*

- *The period of detention in terms of the security emergency regulations will be limited henceforth to six months. Detainees also acquire the right to legal representation and a medical practitioner of their own choosing.*

> Explain the significance of what de Klerk is proposing in Source C in terms of the abolition of the apartheid regime in South Africa.

Problems for the ANC

The ANC faced dissent within; many of those who had stayed in South Africa disagreed with the moderation of exiles, whom they felt had had it easy while abroad. This was exemplified by the position of Mandela's estranged wife, Winnie, who was accused of involvement in kidnappings and murders of opponents.

Winnie Mandela

Winnie Mandela had been brutally treated during her husband's imprisonment, banned in remote areas such as Brandfort in the Orange Free State, and frequently arrested. When she was allowed back to Soweto, she was a militant activist whose youthful supporters became known as Mandela United Football Club with a reputation for brutal vigilante activity. How far she was involved in their violence and intimidation is still disputed, but her trial and six-year prison sentence (later reduced to a fine, following her appeal) undoubtedly weakened her husband's position – although they were by this time estranged, and later divorced.

Administrative problems

- Many grass-roots members of the ANC had participated in violence and now it was difficult to control them.
- The ANC had been exile for so long that it lacked internal organisation and administrative structures; these had to be quickly developed and suitably skilled and experienced staff found to run them.

The significance of Joe Slovo

Joe Slovo was a Communist who had led the military campaign of the MK (see page 59). In many white people's eyes, he was no more than a terrorist. However, the government accepted him as part of the ANC negotiating team. This was a very shrewd move since, as an exiled fighter, Slovo had the respect of more militant activists. He was possibly more influential than former prisoners such as Nelson Mandela. In the event, Slovo was to make two important interventions to stimulate the peace process:

- In August 1990 he supported the ANC's renunciation of violence.
- He supported the so-called 'sunset clause' in the Declaration of Intent (see page 133), which guaranteed current public servants their jobs and pensions. Forty per cent of Afrikaners worked in some capacity for the government, so this was a significant factor in assuaging their fears concerning any settlement. 'We are not,' he said, in justifying this clause 'dealing with a defeated enemy.'

It is important to realise, moreover, that the National Party and ANC knew they had to work together to reach a lasting settlement and that if they failed the result could be full-scale armed conflict. Their representatives met for the first time to begin negotiations in May 1990, and in August the ANC declared a ceasefire. However, the talks were to proceed in a country which was becoming increasingly volatile.

The impact of unrest and violence

The release of Mandela and unbanning of political parties had little immediate effect on slowing the violence between different African groups and that which was often directed towards white people and other ethnic groups. Over 350 black people alone were killed on commuter trains between 1990 and 1993; often rival groups would ambush them as they crossed through 'their' territory.

Reasons for violence

- Many Africans had given up their education for rebellion during the 1980s and early 1990s and felt too unskilled to succeed in a future South Africa.
- Many Africans remained suspicious of de Klerk – his party and government were still associated with apartheid.
- There was a new mix – violent white groups and Inkhata, both of whom sought to maintain the *status quo*. The 'third force' was aiding Inkhata (see page 111). In March 1990, 230 people lost their lives as a result of the violence between Inkhata and the ANC.
- The military wing of the PAC, and the African People's Liberation Army (APLA, see page 60) targeted white as well as black opponents: they lost some support when in August 1993 they brutally murdered an American aid worker.

White extremist reaction

While many white people supported the reforms in apartheid, others were implacably opposed, in particular those conservative elements who lived mainly in rural areas, and members of the public services and security forces who feared for their livelihoods if apartheid was abolished. Some were prepared to work democratically through the Conservative Party (see page 94) but others supported violence. The Afrikaner Weerstandsbeweging (AWB; Afrikaner Resistance Movement) group, under its leader Eugène Terre'Blanche, threatened violence and committed bombings and acts of intimidation; it also sought to prevent negotiations by storming the halls where meetings were being held. The AWB sought an independent white homeland. Its uniforms, banners and paramilitary paraphernalia attracted many who felt threatened and insecure in the face of changes and wanted to join a group which seemed powerful and strong.

The growth in numbers of poor whites

Many white South Africans had suffered economically by the appearance of more skilled non-white people in the workforce and the dismantling of an apartheid system which often protected their jobs. In 1991, hunger relief agencies were estimated to support over 20,000 white people. This group proved a fertile recruiting ground for white extremist groups such as the AWB.

The dismantling of apartheid

Many were surprised by the extent of de Klerk's February 1990 speech (see Source C, page 123). It did not just focus on the promise to release Mandela – de Klerk laid out a formal commitment to constitutional change and to negotiate a peace process. In addition, in October 1990, the Separate Amenities Act, which had formed the basis for petty apartheid, was repealed, making segregation of facilities illegal. Later, in 1991, the repeal of such apartheid measures which remained, such as the Population Registration Act and Group Areas Act, was facilitated by an Act of Parliament in June 1991.

De Klerk had argued with colleagues that the end had to come quickly and fully rather than gradually or piecemeal. He felt a gradual reduction would lead to mistrust and delays. The speech of February 1990 left no one in doubt as to the scale of his intentions. However, many commentators have suggested that once negotiations got started, de Klerk sought to spin them out in the hope that this would strengthen his own position. Others argued that the ANC, on the other hand, wished to get the deal done as quickly as possible.

CODESA 1991

The transition to democracy was hard and fraught with difficulties. Certain constitutional preconditions gave the discussions an urgency which undoubtedly focused people's attentions, but also raised the question of what might happen if no agreement was reached in the time allowed:

- Any new government had to be agreed by the existing tricameral Parliament, and it had to be a lawful successor. No party, for example, could illegally take power and impose a new regime by force.
- The process had to be completed within five years (the lifespan of the current Parliament).

No doubt, negotiators were also mindful that all the major political groups in South Africa, except the small Democrat Party, had paramilitary wings and the National Party could, of course, turn to its security forces. One major question was how far each group could restrain its military wing. One cannot overemphasise the fear, however real or imagined, that violence could intensify.

🔑 **KEY TERM**

Convention for a Democratic South Africa (CODESA) The organisation charged with preparing for a post-apartheid democratic South Africa. CODESA 1 was created in 1991 and CODESA 2 in 1992: both faced difficult negotiations.

December 1991 saw the creation of the **Convention for a Democratic South Africa (CODESA)**, charged with preparing the ground for a new constitution. Inkhata, the PAC and the conservatives refused to attend, and negotiations were bad-tempered among those who did.

Declaration of intent

This was the most significant achievement of CODESA 1. It was a statement committing the government to the creation of a non-racial, gender-inclusive, multi-party democracy in South Africa. Elections would be on the basis of universal adult suffrage, and proportional representation was likely to ensure that all parties with sufficient support were represented in Parliament. It committed the government to obeying the constitution, which was to be overseen by an independent judiciary. Although vaguely worded at times, because the details had still to be worked out, the declaration was sufficiently robust to enable de Klerk to seek a referendum to be held in March 1992 among white voters to see whether they supported the reform process: 69 per cent did so and gave him the mandate to continue.

Key debate: How far did the continued violence impact on the peace-making process in the years 1990–94?

Commentators agree that there was considerable violence in the period 1990–94, but disagree on how far it impacted on the peace process. Some feel the government had lost control of many areas and the violence could spread, while others feel it actually acted as a stimulus to make the politicians more determined to reach a peaceful settlement.

Undeclared war

Journalist Daniel Reed believed South Africa was actually involved in an undeclared civil war in the period. His 1994 book, *Beloved Country*, accompanied a BBC TV series that reported continued violence and bloodshed in many African settlements. However, these conflicts largely went unreported.

EXTRACT I

Extract from Daniel Reed, *Beloved Country*, BBC Books, 1994, page 1.

South Africa is in the grip of a bitter civil war, but only on Sundays. That's the way it often seems in this schizophrenic country, for the factional violence in Black townships becomes newsworthy only if two dozen or more people are slaughtered in a single incident. By some bizarre co-incidence these massacres usually take place on a Sunday.

Reed argues that in fact as many as 60,000 people died as a result of the conflict, yet both the authorities and political organisations such as the ANC were reluctant to talk of war. The ANC blamed the government and its 'puppets', such as Inkhata, while the government itself played it down in order to seem in control. The media meanwhile did not inform the white population, who were relatively unaffected. The vast majority of the violence was perpetrated by Africans on Africans. Nevertheless, Reed asserts that both the government authorities and political organisations had lost control in the areas of conflict and feared for the impact this violence would have, for example, if it escalated into other areas.

Historian James Barber, writing in 1999, reminds us of the ANC commitment to violence and the tenuous nature of its ceasefire in August 1990. He argues that the security forces discovered evidence of Operation Vula, which they initially believed was a planned ANC *coup d'état*. Instead, it dated from 1988 when MK cadres had secretly been infiltrated into South Africa, but remained in position to strike if negotiations failed. Barber goes on to emphasise the widespread distaste among the ANC and MK, in particular, for the leadership decision to abandon the armed struggle. Senior officials, such as ANC Youth Leader Peter Mokaba and ANC chief in Natal Harry Gwala, openly called for an end to negotiations and resumption of the armed struggle. In other words, the ANC remained armed in the event that the peace settlement should fail and were ready to resume hostilities almost immediately should that happen.

EXTRACT 2

Extract from James Barber, *South Africa in the Twentieth Century*, Blackwell, 1999, page 287, referring to the ANC's renunciation of violence.

They decided that Slovo should introduce the idea because his revolutionary credentials were impeccable. Even so it met strong opposition before it was carried to the executive: and then it provoked a furore in the movement with Slovo himself admitting that 90 per cent of ANC supporters saw it as a 'sellout'.

Determination to reach a settlement

Writing in 1999, historian Robert Ross felt that, however violent the period had been, it could have been worse. Both the ANC and government were determined to reach a negotiated settlement and instances of violence simply made them more determined to succeed.

EXTRACT 3

Extract from Robert Ross, *A Concise History of South Africa*, Cambridge University Press, 1999, page 189.

In fact the breakdown of CODESA and the Boipatong and slightly later the Bisho massacres forced both the National Party and the ANC to realise that, come what may, a negotiated settlement had to be found.

Other historians seem to agree that the politicians were determined to reach a settlement. Frank Welsh, writing in 2000, felt that the Boipatong killings concentrated efforts, with leading negotiators holding 40 meetings between June and September 1992 and arriving at the Record of Understanding within three weeks of the Bisho atrocity. In his short history of the ANC published in 2000, Saul Dubow also emphasises that it was the fear of social and political breakdown which stimulated the determination to succeed in reaching a peaceful settlement.

The government perspective

Afrikaner historian Hermann Giliomee has considered the period from the perspective of the government. He feels in particular that President de Klerk genuinely sought a settlement acceptable to all, and that he lacked the ruthlessness to order repression in the way, for example, Vorster may have done. He was a peacemaker – a point Ross would probably have agreed with.

EXTRACT 4

Extract from Hermann Giliomee, *The Afrikaners: Biography of a People*, Hurst & Company, 2003, page 637.

He was not prepared to walk over corpses to retain power. He had no stomach for a show of force. To those who advocated shooting it out he answered in the stark terms he used in an address to senior police officers just before unbanning the liberation movements: 'For if this Armageddon takes place – and blood flows ankle deep in our streets and four to five million people lie dead – the problem will remain exactly the same as it did before the shooting started'.

How well do Extracts 1–4 cover the issue of the impact of continued violence on the peace process in the years 1990–94?

It would appear then that while the violence was widespread and terrible events occurred, the weight of opinion is that the negotiators were determined to do their best to reach a peaceful settlement and the news of atrocities only prompted them further to achieve this. However, there was always the fear that if they failed, there could indeed be an escalation of violence, which no reasonable people wanted. It would seem that the threat of this escalation was always lurking in the background, helping to focus the determination to reach a peaceful settlement.

Summary diagram: Negotiation and compromise, 1989–91

National Party
Realised only a negotiated settlement was possible

F.W. de Klerk's New Course, February 1990

Political activists released, political parties unbanned

Apartheid dismantled by 1991

ANC
Realised only a negotiated settlement possible but …

Disagreements between radicals and moderates

Lacking effective administrative structures

Difficult to control radicals opposing negotiation, but …

Threats
- Continuing violence in townships
- Suspicions of National Party motives
- Extremist white and black groups, for example AWP, APLA
- Suspicions of security forces, for example 'third force'

Threats continued despite negotiations

Negotiations on transition to democracy:
- CODESA 1: 1991
- Declaration of intent: 1991

4 A new political settlement, 1992–94

▶ *How successful was the political settlement?*

The period 1992–94 saw hard bargaining and many challenges, but the determination of both the National Party and the ANC helped towards a new political settlement.

CODESA negotiations

The Declaration of Intent and the success in the resulting referendum led to the creation of CODESA 2 in May 1992. It was charged with creating a working model for the new constitution. In the event, it failed: Mandela accused the National Party of seeking to hold on to power, while de Klerk was involved in battles within his own party to hold on to as much power as possible for as long as possible. However, even in the face of escalating violence, political leaders of the ANC and National Party knew this was the only hope for a peaceful settlement.

SOURCE D

? How well do Sources D and E (see page 131) illustrate the tensions and lack of trust between Nelson Mandela and President de Klerk?

Extract from a memorandum from Nelson Mandela to F.W. de Klerk during the course of the CODESA negotiations, 26 June 1992 (available at www.nelsonmandela.org/omalley/index.php/site/q/03lv02039/04lv02046/05lv02092/06lv02093.htm).

Introduction

1. The Declaration of intent which we adopted at Codesa I committed us to the establishment of a 'democratic South Africa'. On the basis of this commitment many would have been led to believe that it would have been possible to overcome many obstacles in the path of realising this goal.

2. Our country is on the brink of disaster. First there is the crisis in the negotiation process itself. The central blockage stems from the refusal of the NP [National Party] government to move together with all of us in the process of truly democratising South Africa. Secondly, the continuing direct and indirect involvement of the NP government, the state security forces and the police in the violence as well as your unwillingness to act decisively to bring such violence to an end has created an untenable and explosive situation.

3. The NP government persists in portraying the crisis as a creation of the ANC. This attitude is unhelpful and extremely dangerous. The NP government is placing party political interests above national interests by trying to minimise the seriousness of this crisis.

SOURCE E

Extract from de Klerk's reply to Nelson Mandela, 2 July 1992 (available at https://omalley.nelsonmandela.org/omalley/index.php/site/q/03lv02039/04lv02046/05lv02092/06lv02094.htm).

23 June 1992

Dear Mr Mandela

I acknowledge receipt of your memorandum dated 26 June 1992. However, an exchange of memoranda is no substitute for face-to-face talks. I was therefore disappointed that you did not accept my invitation to immediate discussions. Every day that is lost will make the resumption of the process more difficult and may lead to the loss of further lives.

… There are however a number of fundamental issues which need to be addressed urgently at a meeting between us.

i. Violence

Contrary to the ANC's accusations, the Government has not, and will not plan, conduct, orchestrate or sponsor violence in any form whatsoever against any political organisation or community. The lie that the Government is sponsoring and promoting violence remains a lie no matter how often it is repeated. Where elements in state structures err in this regard, the Government will not hesitate to take appropriate measures. There are prosecutions and convictions on record to prove this.

The second interim report of the Goldstone Commission showed that the causes of violence are numerous and complicated. The fact remains that most political violence occurs between supporters of the ANC and the IFF [Inkhata]. This question must therefore be urgently addressed by the leaders of the ANC and the IFF, and the Government, in view of its responsibility for the maintenance of order. I therefore propose that you, Dr Buthelezi and I meet as soon as possible for this purpose. The agenda for this meeting could be to consider: an active full-time monitoring mechanism on the adequacy, efficacy and performance of all the instruments and processes already in place to combat violence and intimidation; and [on] the advisability of a joint monitoring body through which the three parties could act to defuse and solve problems that could give rise to violence. The role of the international community in an observer capacity could be considered, especially in relation to this item.

It was widely felt that the National Party and de Klerk, in particular, had no coherent agenda. It leaked out that during meetings with advisers he would on occasion refuse to countenance various suggestions for future non-racial democracy only to publicly advocate them later without having apparently consulted any of his supporters. With this degree of dissension within the National Party itself, the discussions with all the other groups involved were bound to be fraught. One issue, for example, was the insistence of the ANC on a centralised state, while the National Party had often considered some kind of federation based on the different provinces. Buthelezi, of course, sought more power for the homelands, particularly KwaZulu.

Specifically, however, the difficulties in discussions seemed to be over technical issues which could, with compromise, be overcome. Both the ANC and National Party, for example, supported the idea of a multi-party interim government. However, the National Party argued that all the parties involved should have the right of veto, while the ANC felt that decisions taken by a majority in cabinet should be accepted by all. In the event, this disagreement led to stalemate on 16 May 1992, and only under pressure from US President Clinton did meetings resume. It was decided to deploy a Multi-Party Negotiating Forum (MPNF) which allocated the issue to eleven technical experts to solve. It was they who advocated the creation of a Transitional Executive Council to facilitate the election and instillation of a new interim government.

Relationship between Mandela and de Klerk

Talks often broke down and relations between Mandela and de Klerk were always tense. Even when they jointly won the Nobel Peace Prize in 1993, commentators felt a tension between them, despite Mandela praising de Klerk's role at the ceremony. Although they agreed a new constitution for South Africa, they would nevertheless be political opponents in the ensuing elections. However, negotiators at lower levels often worked well together, and principal delegates Cyril Ramaphosa from the ANC and Roelf Meyer from the National Party developed a particularly good rapport. Mandela once said that he and de Klerk did not have to like each other to work together. Any personal hostilities were undoubtedly overshadowed by the determination to reach an accord within the time frame.

Record of Understanding

On 26 September 1992, a Record of Understanding was issued based on three principles:

KEY TERM

Pangas Heavy knives.

- the release of all political prisoners
- physical restrictions on Zulu hostel dwellers who were held responsible for many of the Inkhata-inspired murders and attacks
- a banning of traditional weapons such as **pangas**, which many people carried openly.

In return, a future government was to guarantee employment and pension rights for existing public employees (see page 133) and power sharing between the leading parties.

In February 1993, Mandela conceded that a future government would be one of 'National Unity' and would include members of all parties which received more than five per cent of the vote. With these agreements in place, it was relatively easy to negotiate a final settlement. It was not so easy to sell it to members of the ANC or the National Party, who continued to distrust each other, let alone the Conservative Party or Inkhata, both of which refused to have anything to do with it.

Nationalist divisions and communal violence

De Klerk had difficulties persuading members of his own party to agree to a settlement. Many white people naturally feared for the future and many had already lost their livelihoods (see page 132):

- They were concerned for their safety in the event of an African backlash. Many PAC members, for example, had been chanting, 'One settler, one bullet'.
- Many feared for their livelihoods as Africans became more skilled and could compete openly for jobs.
- Many relied on the bureaucracy of apartheid or the security forces for employment. The **'sunset clause'**, proposed by Joe Slovo, offered some reassurance as to future employment and pensions.

> 🔑 **KEY TERM**
>
> **Sunset clause** Guarantee of continued employment, and pension rights for those nearing retirement.

The AWB continued its terror campaign while it was joined politically by the Conservatives, led by General Constand Viljoen, and Inkhata to form a Freedom Alliance. However, an incompetent military incursion into Bophuthatswana by the AWB to support the anti-settlement leader led to the Conservatives' withdrawal from the Freedom Alliance. The Conservative Party split but most members agreed to join in with the settlement process.

Incursion into Bophuthatswana

On 10 March 1994, 600 AWB members raided Bophuthatswana to rescue and reinstate the chief, Lucas Mangope. He had opposed the peace settlement and been arrested by the local forces who supported the ANC. The raid was unstructured: participants fired randomly at suspected ANC supporters before they themselves were routed by Bophuthatswana forces. The fiasco saw the demise of the AWB, and the arrest of Mangope.

Continued communal violence

Violence continued throughout the period. While hundreds were being killed each month, three events in particular threatened to derail the settlement process:

- On 17 June 1992, Inkhata members killed 46 suspected ANC supporters in Boipatong. The security forces did nothing to prevent this. It was after this atrocity that Mandela suspended negotiations with de Klerk. COSATU and SACP meanwhile organised mass protests, which brought South Africa to a halt. A march of 100,000 protesters, led by Nelson Mandela, demonstrated outside government headquarters in Pretoria.

SOURCE F

? What does the
photograph in Source F
suggest about the extent
of popular response to
the assassination of Chris
Hani on 10 April 1993?

Demonstrators in central Johannesburg on 17 April 1993 marching to protest against the assassination of Chris Hani.

- On 7 September 1992, 70,000 ANC supporters marched to Bisho, capital of Ciskei, whose leader Oupa Gqozo wished to maintain independence. Ciskei forces opened fire, killing 30.
- On 10 April 1993, the charismatic leader of MK, Chris Hani, was murdered by a white extremist. This was potentially an incendiary event as Hani was a hero to many, particularly young people, because of his efforts to maintain the armed struggle from exile. It was calmed only when it was known that the culprit had been caught on the evidence of a white witness. The ANC leadership, moreover, sought to deflect any possible retaliatory violence by organising rallies and demonstrations in which people would have the opportunity to vent their frustrations in a controlled environment. De Klerk meanwhile condemned white extremists.

However, those working for a settlement continued. The result was a promise to hold elections the following April. There was, therefore, a deadline set for an agreement to be reached.

Constitutional agreement and elections

The new political settlement was lasting and helped bring about the success of the rainbow nation.

In September 1993, the Transitional Executive Council was set up, with its role enhanced, to facilitate the new political system in South Africa. Its principal goal was to ensure protection for minorities while accepting majority rule; in other words, the creation of a rainbow nation in which everyone would be valued irrespective of race – again, the principles of the Freedom Charter of 1955.

Withdrawal of Inkhata

Following the Declaration of Intent, the ANC and National Party, as by far the most influential participants, agreed to reach agreement between themselves before taking proposals to minority parties. Buthelezi pulled Inkhata out in protest and did not return until days before the election for the interim government, which was finally ratified by the MPNF on 18 November 1993.

The new constitution

The new constitution offered a centralised state as an interim system for five years:

- South Africa would be divided into nine provinces, each with its own elected government and civil service.
- A Bill of Rights would be protected by a Constitutional Court.
- The new system could only be amended by a two-thirds majority of the popular vote.
- Guaranteed power sharing for five years.
- While the president would come from the leading party, the deputy president could come from any party with over twenty per cent of the vote.
- Any party with more than five per cent could have a minister appointed from it.

The system was fully democratic with appropriate checks and balances on the power of government. An independent judiciary could prevent any abuses or actions in excess of their legal powers by governments.

Elections

Elections were held on 27 April 1994. They were hugely anticipated:

- As expected, the ANC won convincingly, with 62.5 per cent of the vote.
- The National Party won 20.5 per cent so de Klerk became deputy president.
- Inkhata gained 10.5 per cent so Buthelezi became a government minister.
- The PAC, the party which had advocated continuing violence, won only 1.25 per cent.

The evidence seemed overwhelming that most people had voted for a peaceful and enduring settlement.

The Government of National Unity

Nelson Mandela became president in a Government of National Unity. However, South Africa faced huge problems: 45 years of apartheid could not simply be effaced by a new constitution. Many Africans were frustrated by the slow pace of change: they lacked the education and skills to access most opportunities. Crime remained high. Many white people opted to leave. Newly appointed public servants were accused of corruption.

SOURCE G

? What does Source G suggest about voter interest in the 1994 election?

'Vote here'. People queuing to vote in 1994.

SOURCE H

? What concerns about the future is Archbishop Tutu highlighting in Source H?

Extract from Archbishop Desmond Tutu, 'A Miracle Unfolding', in *The Rainbow People of God: South Africa's Victory over Apartheid*, Doubleday, 1994, pages 258–9.

Apartheid has left us a horrendous legacy represented by massive homelessness, with seven million living in ghetto shacks, a huge educational crisis, unemployment, inadequate health care largely inaccessible to the most needy. The rural areas are poverty stricken, without running water, electricity or proper sewerage, so that cholera epidemics happen in a country that pioneered the heart transplant. It is quite bizarre.

People have perhaps unrealistically high expectations that democracy will mean a good job and a good home overnight. Unfortunately no-one possesses a magic wand to bring paradise immediately. But the new government will have to move quickly to improve the quality of life of the most disadvantaged to make it quite clear that there is [was] a qualitative difference between living under an unjust dispensation and living in a democracy. Resources that were wantonly wastefully invested in the defence budget to engage in unnecessary military adventures in Angola or destabilise our neighbours will, with a drastically reduced defence budget, be available for this necessary social spending. But people will also need to be told to be patient and reduce their expectations to more realistic levels.

The transition to democracy was successful: there were no serious threats to the new system. Indeed, the ANC increasingly lacked any effective opposition; the National Party, for example, fragmented, especially after the retirement of de Klerk in 1997. It was effectively too burdened with the past to offer a new profile.

Mandela's main task was to unify the country: one way was to galvanise country-wide support for the national rugby team, which won the 1995 World Cup to great acclaim. A Truth and Reconciliation Committee was also set up in 1996 under the leadership of Archbishop Tutu. Its role was to investigate wrongdoing by all sides, not to exact retribution but to confront the past and move forward peacefully.

International recognition

Representatives of 170 nations attended Nelson Mandela's inauguration as president in April 1994. South Africa enjoyed widespread international support, not least through the goodwill engendered by the personality of Mandela himself, who became a world elder statesman applauded everywhere. However, it was not just about Mandela. When he retired, his legacy continued despite the problems which remained unsolved. Countries recognised the considerable achievement in moving peacefully to democracy after so many years of conflict. While tensions were evident, few rejected the settlement. The vast majority of people of all races continued to applaud it. The rainbow nation, it seemed, had become an example for the world.

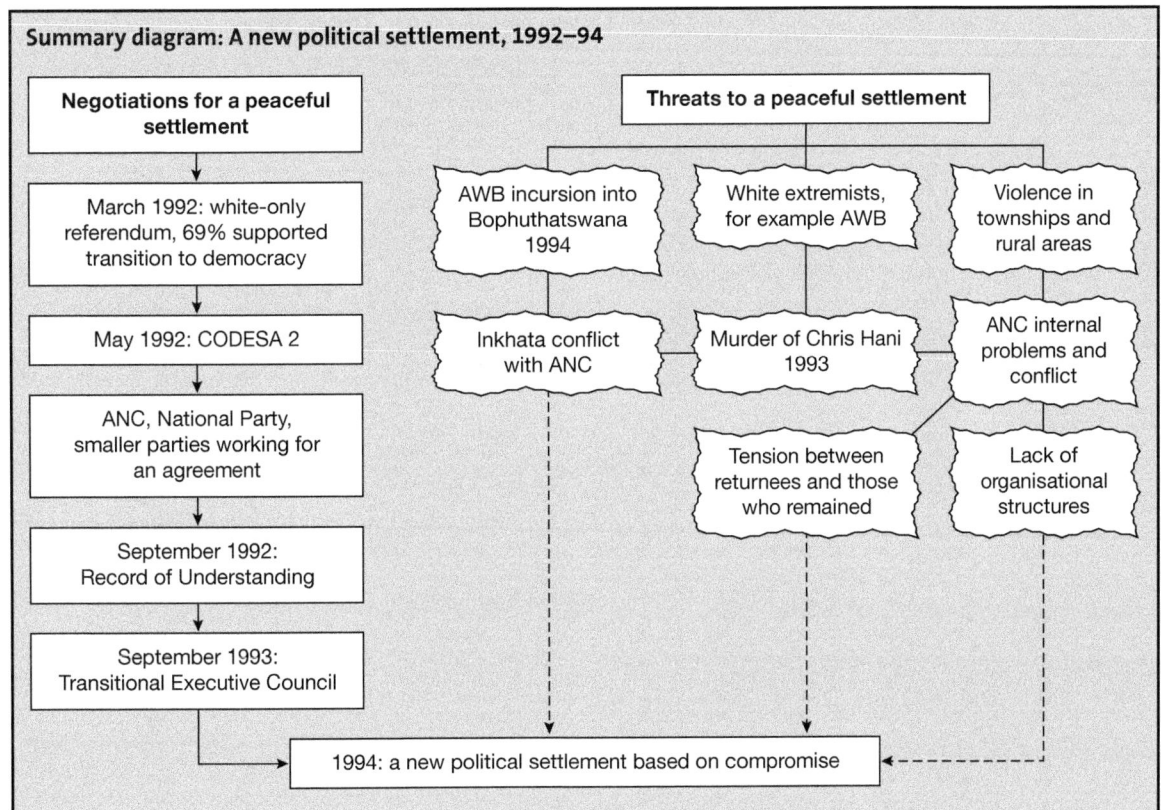

Summary diagram: A new political settlement, 1992–94

Negotiations for a peaceful settlement	Threats to a peaceful settlement

- **Negotiations for a peaceful settlement**
  - March 1992: white-only referendum, 69% supported transition to democracy
  - May 1992: CODESA 2
  - ANC, National Party, smaller parties working for an agreement
  - September 1992: Record of Understanding
  - September 1993: Transitional Executive Council

- **Threats to a peaceful settlement**
  - AWB incursion into Bophuthatswana 1994
  - White extremists, for example AWB
  - Violence in townships and rural areas
  - Inkhata conflict with ANC
  - Murder of Chris Hani 1993
  - ANC internal problems and conflict
  - Tension between returnees and those who remained
  - Lack of organisational structures

1994: a new political settlement based on compromise

Chapter summary

By 1984, violence and unrest had escalated throughout the townships. Much of this was uncoordinated and spontaneous, making it difficult for the security forces to single out leaders. In 1983, the non-racial United Democratic Front was created to co-ordinate protests and develop community awareness in the fight against apartheid. This had a close relationship with the exiled ANC. However, it embraced over 500 separate organisations, some more militant than others, and was criticised for not being able to control more volatile elements. In particular, local courts gained a reputation for intimidation and spreading fear: one common vigilante punishment was 'necklacing' or effectively setting the victim on fire. Meanwhile, government repression continued without any noticeable impact on the protests. Minister P.W. Botha had originally spoken of a 'Total Onslaught' on South Africa to be met by a 'Total Strategy' including military intervention in countries known to be harbouring organisations such as the ANC.

However, Botha also sought to reform apartheid in order to win the support of more non-white South Africans without compromising white superiority. To this end, most petty apartheid was removed and more guarantees were offered to Africans with the right to live in South Africa, but existing laws were enforced ruthlessly.

A new constitution appeared in 1983, creating new parliaments for coloured and Indian voters, but leaving Africans unrepresented. The powers of the presidency were enhanced and Botha became the first executive president. Meanwhile, economic sanctions and international criticisms continued and South Africa became increasingly isolated. This led to significant downturns in the economy, and coincided with the end of the Cold War which reduced South Africa's value to the West as an ally against communism. Botha's successor, F.W. de Klerk, realised apartheid could not continue and began negotiations with the ANC to create a new settlement. This was alongside increasing violence which many feared might escalate into civil war. In particular, the Zulu group Inkhata were accused of much violence and suspected of being aided by a 'third force' made up of members of the security forces who did not wish for a settlement. White extremist groups such as AWB also perpetrated violence. After four years of protracted negotiations, however, a new constitution was created and the first fully democratic elections took place in April 1994. South Africa became a non-racial democratic nation.

Refresher questions

Use these questions to remind yourself of the key material covered in this chapter.

1 What was the purpose of the United Democratic Front?

2 How important was Chief Buthelezi in the struggle against apartheid?

3 To what extent were the security forces accused of involvement in covert activities against anti-apartheid groups?

4 What was 'Inkhatagate'?

5 Why did President Botha decide to negotiate with anti-apartheid groups after 1985?

6 How effective was the 1986 state of emergency in preventing protest and violence?

7 What was President de Klerk's New Course?

8 What was the significance of the unbanning of political parties and release from prison of activists such as Nelson Mandela?

9 How big a threat to the reform process were the activities of white extremists?

10 What did CODESA I achieve?

11 What was the significance of the September 1992 Record of Understanding on the transition to democracy?

12 How did the 1994 constitution protect democracy and prevent government abuse?

Question practice

ESSAY QUESTIONS

1 'The United Democratic Front enabled peaceful actions against apartheid to be mounted at grass-roots level.' How far do you agree with this statement?

2 'P.W. Botha's reform programme offered real opportunities to change the apartheid state in the years 1985–90.' How far do you agree with this statement?

3 How significant was F.W. de Klerk in the dismantling of apartheid in the years 1989–91?

4 To what extent did the political settlement created in the years 1992–94 resolve the differences between different racial groups in South Africa?

SOURCE-BASED QUESTIONS

1 With reference to Source B (page 118) and Source C (page 123), and your understanding of the historical context, assess the value of these sources to a historian studying the impact of P.W. Botha's reform programme 1983–89.

2 With reference to Source D (page 130) and Source E (page 131), and your understanding of the historical context, assess the value of these sources to a historian studying the difficulties in the CODESA negotiations in the period 1990–94.

Conclusion

The response to apartheid, c1948–59

In 1948, South Africa was dominated politically, economically and socially by its minority white population. The overriding reason for this was the fear of black majority rule. Although there were a few exceptions, only white people could vote. White South Africans themselves were divided into Afrikaners and English speakers, and there was tension between them based on the Afrikaners' resentment of English speakers' hegemony in politics and the economy. The National Party, supported mainly by Afrikaners, won the 1948 election. This was mainly due to their superior organisation and campaigning. However, constituencies were also weighted in their favour. The predominantly English-speaking United Party, which had formed the previous government, moreover campaigned poorly and was vague particularly over the crucial issue of race.

The new government had no such imprecision on racial issues: it supported as far as possible complete separation of races, a policy known as apartheid. While the government went on to implement this policy more and more rigidly, at first it simply built on existing laws and structures. Legislation such as the Group Population Act of 1950 formalised and developed a situation which had already existed. Apartheid itself grew more radical later under the premiership of Hendrik Verwoerd, for example through the creation of Bantustans or tribal homelands where Africans were supposed to reside unless working in white South Africa. The message was that Africans, in particular, had no place in white South Africa beyond that of an unskilled labour force. The authorities supported restrictive legislation by repressive measures such as the Suppression of Communism Act of 1950: communism was widely seen as behind all discontent.

Apartheid had been widely attacked by a variety of groups, notably the African National Congress (ANC). It had deployed peaceful methods such as the Defiance Campaign of 1952. In 1955, many anti-apartheid groups came together to produce a Freedom Charter to act as a blueprint for a non-racial democratic South Africa. However, the authorities fought tenaciously against any attempts at reform and arrested many of the signatories, who spent the next five years involved in a Treason Trial. The ANC, the main anti-apartheid group, remained committed to a multiracial solution, but at the end of the decade a new Africanist force, the Pan-Africanist Congress (PAC), had emerged. Many of its members were anti-white and believed that Africans themselves must control the resistance movements.

Radicalisation of resistance and the consolidation of National Party power, 1960–68

While peaceful resistance to apartheid continued, its effectiveness was increasingly questioned as the government usually responded with brutality and repression, deploying its superiority of force. The Sharpeville Massacre of March 1960 is a case in point. Here, a largely non-violent protest about the imposition of pass books led to security forces killing 69 peaceful protesters. The government responded with a state of emergency which resulted in the banning of most anti-apartheid groups such as the ANC and PAC. This, in turn, led these groups to go underground or into exile. Frustration with the ineffectiveness of peaceful protest and the repression led the ANC to begin its armed struggle led by the newly created *Umkhonto we Sizwe* (MK). This group focused on sabotage of property but Poqo, the military wing of PAC, targeted white people and African 'collaborators'. Meanwhile, in the face of worldwide condemnation of apartheid, South Africa left the Commonwealth and became a republic.

The majority of the ANC leadership was captured and put on trial at Rivonia, where the defendants were sentenced to life imprisonment. However, Nelson Mandela's impassioned attack on apartheid from the dock and hopes for a democratic future received wide publicity. While the anti-apartheid organisations regrouped abroad, they recognised their struggle would be long and difficult. They could not launch any attacks inside South Africa, which was surrounded by friendly countries such as white-governed Rhodesia (present-day Zimbabwe) and the Portuguese colony of Mozambique. The period 1960–68 marked the most confident period of white rule. Following a short downturn after the Sharpeville Massacre, the economy grew substantially and most white South Africans enjoyed prosperous lifestyles. The government extended its apartheid programme with the creation of Bantustans, where Africans not working in white South Africa were supposed to live and which were intended to become independent states. However, most commentators saw them simply as repositories for cheap labour.

The government also extended the role of the security forces and developed a substantial arms industry, so that by the end of the decade South Africa was effectively a well-defended police state.

Redefining resistance and challenges to National Party power, 1968–83

Black Consciousness, a movement originating in the USA which advocated pride in the black races, took over from the absent organisations such as the ANC and PAC as the vanguard of the anti-apartheid organisations in South Africa. It was particularly strong among the young who felt alienated from the apparent failures of their parents' struggles against apartheid. It influenced the creation of the South African Students' Movement (SASM), which organised the protests that were to lead to the 1976 Soweto uprising. While the immediate causes were problems with education for Africans, it reflected wider discontent such as poor social and economic conditions. After Soweto, protests never died away until apartheid was ended in the early 1990s. Meanwhile, the ANC, in particular, was rejuvenated by thousands of young people who fled South Africa to join as cadres committed to the armed struggle.

The ANC in exile developed a new phase of the armed struggle, targeting instillations and government bases in South Africa. It also intensified diplomatic activities to gain international support.

The Soweto uprising and the death in police custody of Black Consciousness activist Steve Biko caused worldwide condemnation for South Africa. It became subject to intensified sanctions and boycotts and the economy weakened partly as a result of the 1973 oil crisis. Meanwhile, increasing expenditure was necessary on defence as South Africa's military commitments grew in the face of hostile regimes on its borders. Portugal had relinquished its colonies of Angola and Mozambique, which were now governed by Marxist regimes, while Rhodesia was increasingly involved in wars with rebel groups.

Living conditions for Africans in the Bantustans were primitive. None could be remotely self-sufficient and none was recognised as an independent nation except by South Africa itself.

The National Party was increasingly divided and faced scandal through Muldergate, in which senior government officials had diverted funds and been involved in covert operations to develop pro-apartheid propaganda. Hard-liners eventually left to form the Conservative Party, which threatened National Party domination. Although there was considerable debate about the efficacy of sanctions and boycotts, international opinion appeared to be turning more in favour. South Africa appeared increasingly isolated in the world, although otherwise hostile neighbours such as Zambia still needed to maintain economic links. Overall, however, in the period 1968–83, as the system came under intensified threats, the confidence of the apartheid regime began to falter.

The end of apartheid and the creation of the 'rainbow nation', 1984–94

By 1984, violence and unrest was rampant throughout the townships. Much of this was uncoordinated and spontaneous, making it difficult for the security forces to single out leaders. In 1983, over 500 separate organisations came together to form the non-racial United Democratic Front (UDF) to co-ordinate protests and develop community awareness in the fight against apartheid. This had a close relationship with the exiled ANC. However, it faced criticism for not being able to control more volatile elements such as vigilantes who gained a reputation for intimidation and fear: one common vigilante punishment was 'necklacing' or effectively setting the victim on fire.

Government repression continued without any noticeable impact on the degree of protests. Minister P.W. Botha had originally spoken of a 'Total Onslaught' on South Africa largely co-ordinated by Communists to crush the regime. His answer was a 'Total Strategy' including military intervention in countries known to be harbouring organisations such as the ANC, but also economic, political and psychological warfare to win hearts and minds to increase support among non-white groups. To this end, he attempted to reform apartheid without compromising white superiority. As a result, most petty apartheid was removed, more guarantees were offered to Africans with the right to live in South Africa; but existing laws were enforced ruthlessly. A new constitution appeared in 1983, creating new parliaments for coloured and Indian voters, but leaving Africans unrepresented. The powers of the presidency were enhanced and Botha became the first executive president.

Nevertheless, South Africa became increasingly isolated as economic sanctions and international criticisms continued. This led to significant downturns in the economy, and coincided with the end of the Cold War, which reduced South Africa's value to the West as an ally against communism. One example of the impact of sanctions was how the obsolescence of much of South Africa's weaponry was exposed during the Battle of Cuito Cuanavale in Angola in 1988. Botha's successor, F.W. de Klerk, realised that apartheid could not continue in its present form and began negotiations, largely with the ANC, to create a new settlement. This was alongside increasing violence which many feared might escalate into a civil war. In particular, the Zulu group Inkhata was accused of much violence and suspected of being aided by a 'third force' made up of members of the security forces who did not wish for a settlement. White extremists group such as the Afrikaner Weerstandsbeweging (AWB) also perpetrated violence. However, after four years of protracted negotiations a new constitution was created; the first fully democratic elections took place in April 1994; and South Africa became a non-racial democratic nation.

Edexcel A level History

Sources guidance

South Africa 1948–94: from apartheid state to rainbow nation is assessed by an exam comprising two sections:

- Section A tests the depth of your historical knowledge through source analysis.
- Section B requires you to write one essay from a choice of two from your own knowledge (see page 150 for guidance on this).

The following advice relates to Paper 2, Section A. It is relevant to A level and AS level questions. Generally, the AS exam is similar to the A level exam. Both examine the same content and require similar skills; nonetheless, there are differences, which are discussed below.

The questions in Paper 2, Section A, are structured differently in the A level and AS exams.

AS examination	Full A level examination
Section A – contains one compulsory question divided into two parts. **Part (a)** is worth 8 marks. It focuses on the value of a single source for a specific enquiry. **Part (b)** is worth 12 marks. It asks you to weigh the value of a single source for a specific enquiry. Together, the two sources will comprise about 350 words.	**Section A** – contains a single compulsory question worth 20 marks. The question asks you to evaluate the usefulness of two sources for a specific historical enquiry. Together, the two sources will comprise about 400 words.
Questions will start with the following stems: (a) Why is Source 1 valuable to the historian for an enquiry about … (b) How much weight do you give the evidence of Source 2 for an enquiry into …	Questions will start with the following stem: 1 How far could the historian make use of Sources 1 and 2 together to investigate …

Edexcel style questions

AS style question

(a) Study Sources 1 and 2 before you answer this question. Why is Source 1 valuable to the historian for an enquiry about Prime Minister Botha's reforms? Explain your answer using the source, the information given about it and your own knowledge of the historical context.

(b) How much weight do you give the evidence of Source 2 for an enquiry into the extent of Botha's reforms to apartheid in the 1980s? Explain your answer using the source, the information given about it and your own knowledge of the historical context.

A level style question

Study Sources 1 and 2 before you answer this question. How far could the historian make use of Sources 1 and 2 together to investigate the extent of Botha's reform to apartheid in the 1980s? Explain your answer, using both sources, the information given about them and your own knowledge of the historical context.

Sources 1 and 2

SOURCE I

Extract from a dispatch from J.H.G. Leahy, an official at the British Embassy in Pretoria, to the British Foreign and Commonwealth Office on the progress of P.W. Botha's projected reforms and the prospects for the future, 15 December 1980.

Complicated new legislation affecting urban blacks is coming forward … Suffice it to say here that the South African Government claim to accept that the South African economy is going to need many more millions of skilled and semi-skilled black workers in the years ahead and that these people will want better conditions and wider trade unions rights. But Dr Koornhof's [the Government minister responsible] new legislation, though well intentioned, does not in practice change the essentials of influx control, which is at the heart of the matter; and … Botha's new legislation on trade unions, while making several concessions, is designed to direct trade union development into acceptable channels rather than to allow it to develop on natural lines to a position of real economic, still less of political, power.

The new political season beginning next month looks like being a busy one. But the crucial question remains the same – is P.W. Botha any nearer to solving the problem which matters more than all the rest – how to find a lasting and mutually acceptable accommodation between blacks and whites? If I had to answer that question myself I would say that while the propellor is rotating quite fast and churning up the water the ship of state does not seem to be making much headway.

SOURCE 2

Extract from David Harrison, *The White Tribe of Africa*, BBC Books, 1981, page 276.

In fact by the time Botha had become Prime Minister Apartheid was far more than a policy which could be repealed, an ugly aspect of an otherwise normal society. It was a total way of life, written into the constitution and enshrined in law. Apartheid had developed an unstoppable momentum of its own. As John Kane-Berman reported to the Guardian in 1980, 'Botha and his generals may now see some of the folly but Apartheid is greater than they are.'

In schools the Broederbond machine continued to print its racist pattern on youthful minds. In the civil service the Afrikaner bureaucracy remorselessly enforced the laws of the land. If Botha really had abandoned the chimera of homeland independence and the strict territorial separation of the races, the forced removal of Africans from 'white man's land' might have been expected to drop away … But in the absence of legislation that told them to do otherwise, the civil servants in government and local administration went on doing what they had always done. So black South Africans continued to be dumped in the 'closer settlements' where they had no prospect of making a living and where, as the eighties commenced, their children continued to die from diseases contracted through malnutrition.

Prosecutions under the Group Areas Act also continued. Coloureds and Indians caught living illegally in the central Johannesburg area were fined and evicted.

Understanding the questions

- To answer successfully you must understand how the question works.
- The question is written precisely in order to make sure that you understand the task. Each part of the question has a specific meaning.
- You must use the source, the information given about the source, and your own knowledge of historical context when answering the question.

Understanding the AS question

Why is Source 1 valuable to the historian for an enquiry[1] about how far Prime Minister Botha reformed apartheid in the 1980s[2]?

1 You must focus on the reasons why the source could be helpful to a historian. Indeed, you can get maximum marks without considering the source's limitations.
2 The final part of the question focuses on a specific topic that a historian might investigate (how far Prime Minister Botha reformed apartheid in the 1980s).

How much weight do you give the evidence of Source 2[1] for an enquiry[2] into how far Prime Minister Botha reformed apartheid in the 1980s[3]?

1 This question focuses on evaluating the extent to which the source contains evidence. Therefore, you must consider the ways in which the source is valuable and the limitations of the source.
2 This is the essence of the task: you must focus on what a historian could legitimately conclude from studying this source.
3 This is the specific topic that you are considering the source for: how far Prime Minister Botha reformed apartheid in the 1980s.

Understanding the A level question

How far[1] could the historian make use of Sources 1 and 2[2] together[3] to investigate how far Prime Minister Botha reformed the system of apartheid in the early 1980s[4]. Explain your answer, using both sources, the information given about them and your own knowledge of the historical context[5].

1 You must evaluate the extent of something, rather than giving a simple 'yes' or 'no' answer.
2 This is the essence of the task: you must focus on what a historian could legitimately conclude from studying these sources.
3 You must examine the sources as a pair and make a judgement about both sources, rather than simply making separate judgements about each source.
4 The final part of the question focuses on a specific topic that a historian might investigate. In this case, the extent of Botha's reforms to apartheid in the 1980s.
5 This instruction lists the resources you should use: the sources, the information given about the sources and your own knowledge of historical context that you have learnt during the course.

Source skills

Generally, Section A of Paper 2 tests your ability to evaluate source material. More specifically, the sources presented in Section A will be taken from the period that you have studied: 1948–94, or be written by people who witnessed these events. Your job is to analyse the sources by reading them in the context of the values and assumptions of the society and the period that produced them.

Examiners will mark your work by focusing on the extent to which you are able to:

- Interpret and analyse source material:
  - At a basic level, this means you can understand the sources and select, copy, paraphrase and summarise the source or sources to help answer the question.
  - At a higher level, your interpretation of the sources includes the ability to explain, analyse and make inferences based on the sources.
  - At the highest levels, you will be expected to analyse the source in a sophisticated way. This includes the ability to distinguish between information, opinions and arguments contained in the sources.
- Deploy knowledge of historical context in relation to the sources:
  - At a basic level, this means the ability to link the sources to your knowledge of the context in which the source was written, using this knowledge to expand or support the information contained in the sources.
  - At a higher level, you will be able to use your contextual knowledge to make inferences, and to expand, support or challenge the details mentioned in the sources.
  - At the highest levels, you will be able to examine the value and limits of the material contained in the sources by interpreting the sources in the context of the values and assumptions of the society that produced them.

- Evaluate the usefulness and weight of the source material:
  - At a basic level, evaluation of the source will be based on simplistic criteria about reliability and bias.
  - At a higher level, evaluation of the source will be based on the nature and purpose of the source.
  - At the highest levels, evaluation of the source will based on a valid criterion that is justified in the course of the essay. You will also be able to distinguish between the values of different aspects of the sources.

Make sure your source evaluation is sophisticated. Avoid crude statements about bias, and avoid simplistic assumptions such as that a source written immediately after an event is reliable, whereas a source written years later is unreliable.

Try to see things through the eyes of the writer:

- How does the writer understand the world?
- What assumptions does the writer have?
- Who is the writer trying to influence?
- What views is the writer trying to challenge?

Basic skill: comprehension

The most basic source skill is comprehension: understanding what the source means. There are a variety of techniques that you can use to aid comprehension. For example, you could read the sources included in this book and in past papers:

- Read the sources out loud.
- Look up any words that you don't understand and make a glossary.
- Make flash cards containing brief biographies of the writers of the sources.

You can demonstrate comprehension by copying, paraphrasing and summarising the sources. However, keep this to the minimum as comprehension is a low-level skill and you need to leave room for higher-level skills.

Advanced skill: contextualising the sources

First, to analyse the sources correctly you need to understand them in the context in which they were written. People in the 1980s may have seen the world differently from people in twenty-first century Britain: the sources reflect this. Your job is to understand the values and assumptions behind the source.

- One way of contextualising the sources is to consider the nature, origins and purpose of the sources. However, this can lead to formulaic responses.
- An alternative is to consider two levels of context. First, you should establish the general context. In this case, Sources 1 and 2 refer to a period in which Botha was trying to maintain the apartheid state by conceding some reforms in order to win the support of some non-white groups.

Second, you can look for specific references to contemporary events or debates in the sources. For example:

Sources 1 and 2 both refer to how far Botha reformed apartheid but view them differently. Source 1 asserts that Botha was influenced by the need for more skilled black workers if the economy was to grow, and that these workers would demand better working conditions and trade union representation. However, the author feels that reform may falter because the crucial issue of influx control, or the limitations on blacks being able to settle in white South Africa was not being addressed. Any legislation on the legalising of black trade unions therefore would only very partially address the essential issues in black and white relations. Source 2, on the other hand, which is dated 1981, after some of the projected reforms have taken place, questions their extent. It shows, for example, that Africans are continuing to be removed to their barren homelands, an issue which was questioned in Source 1. It argues moreover that apartheid was so fundamental a structure that it could not simply be legislated away. The fundamentals which underpin it, for example racist education and the tireless bureaucracy, seem unstoppable.

Use context to make judgements

- Start by establishing the general context of the source:
  - Ask yourself, what was going on at the time when the source was written, or the time of the events described in the source?
  - What are the key debates that the source might be contributing to?
- Next, look for key words and phrases that establish the specific context. Does the source refer to specific people, events or books that might be important?
- Make sure your contextualisation focuses on the question.
- Use the context when evaluating the usefulness and limitations of the source.

For example:

Source 1 is valuable to the historian studying the extent of Botha's reforms in the 1980s because it reports the reasons for his actions, that South Africa needed more skilled black workers. It shows more than cosmetic reforms are envisaged, for example the legalisation of trade unions, but did not address other key issues such as influx control. Source 2 on the other hand shows how the reforms are limited not least because the apartheid state is so entrenched that it has a momentum of its own. With a wide-ranging bureaucracy and race-based education, it provided a comprehensive and far-reaching societal system and lifestyle, which could not be simply legislated away. The source goes on to show that despite any rhetoric, principles of apartheid such as removals of those without the right to live in 'white' areas continued remorselessly.

Essay guidance

Edexcel's Paper 2 Option 2F.2: South Africa 1948–94: from apartheid state to 'rainbow nations' is assessed by an exam comprising two sections:

- Section A tests the depth of your historical knowledge through source analysis (see pages 144–9 for guidance on this).
- Section B requires you to write one essay from a choice of two from your own knowledge.

The following advice relates to Paper 2, Section B. It is relevant to A level and AS level questions. Generally, the AS exam is similar to the A level exam. Both examine the same content and require similar skills; nonetheless, there are differences, which are discussed below.

Essay skills

In order to get a high grade in Section B of Paper 2 your essay must contain four essential qualities:

- focused analysis
- relevant detail
- supported judgement
- organisation, coherence and clarity.

This section focuses on the following aspects of exam technique:

- understanding the nature of the question
- planning an answer to the question set
- writing a focused introduction
- deploying relevant detail
- writing analytically
- reaching a supported judgement.

The nature of the question

Section B questions are designed to test the depth of your historical knowledge. Therefore, they can focus on relatively short periods, or single events, or indeed on the whole period from 1948 to 1994. Moreover, they can focus on different historical processes or 'concepts'. These include:

- cause
- consequence
- change/continuity
- similarity/difference
- significance.

These different question focuses require slightly different approaches:

Cause	1 How far were the Sharpeville Massacre and the government response to it the main reasons for the decision of the ANC to move to an armed struggle in 1961?
Consequence	2 To what extent did the National Party electoral victory of 1948 lead to the implementation of the apartheid state by 1959?
Continuity and change	3 'P.W. Botha's reforms in the 1980s led to major changes in the nature of the apartheid state.' How far do you agree with this statement?
Similarities and differences	4 'The beliefs and strategies of the Africanist and integrationist wings of the anti-apartheid movement were fundamentally different in the period from 1948 to 1994.' How far do you agree with this statement?
Significance	5 'The Soweto uprising of 1976 had great significance in changing the nature of anti-apartheid opposition.' How far do you agree with this statement?

Some questions include a 'stated factor'. The most common type of stated factor question would ask how far one factor caused something. For example, for the first question in the table:

> How far were the Sharpeville Massacre and the government response to it main reasons for the decision of the ANC to move to an armed struggle in 1961?

In this type of question you would be expected to evaluate the importance of the 'Sharpeville Massacre and government response to it' – the 'stated factors' – compared to other factors.

AS and A level questions

AS level questions are generally similar to A level questions. However, the wording of AS questions will be slightly less complex than the wording of A level questions.

A level question	AS level question	Differences
'P.W. Botha's reforms in the 1980s led to major changes in the nature of the apartheid state.' How far do you agree with this statement?	To what extent did the reforms of P.W. Botha improve the political representation for non-white groups?	The A level question focuses on the complex notion of 'changes in the nature of the apartheid state' (for example, how real were the reforms, how far were non-white people affected by them) whereas the AS question focuses on the relatively simple issue of how far the political representation for non-white people was improved
'F.W. de Klerk's New Course was the main reason for the end of white domination of politics in South Africa.' How far do you agree with this statement?	How far did F.W. de Klerk's New Course lead to the end of white domination in South Africa?	The AS question asks how far F.W. de Klerk's policies led to the end of white domination. The A level question asks you to make the more complex judgement: how far it led to the end of white political domination as opposed to other factors (for example, rising violence)

To achieve the highest level at A level, you will have to deal with the full complexity of the question. For example, if you were dealing with question 5 you would need to address the changing nature of anti-apartheid opposition and the various factors which led to its changing, not just the impact of the Soweto uprising on this.

Planning your answer

It is crucial that you understand the focus of the question. Therefore, read the question carefully before you start planning. Check:

- The chronological focus: which years should your essay deal with?
- The topic focus: what aspect of your course does the question deal with?
- The conceptual focus: is this a causes, consequences, change/continuity, similarity/difference or significance question?

For example, for question 4 you could point these out as follows:

> 'The beliefs and strategies of the Africanist and integrationist wings of the anti-apartheid movement[1] were fundamentally different[2] in the period from 1948 to 1994[3].' How far do you agree with this statement?

1 Topic focus: the beliefs and strategies of the Africanist and integrationist wings of the anti-apartheid movement.
2 Conceptual focus: similarity/difference.
3 Chronological focus: 1948–94.

Your plan should reflect the task that you have been set. Section B asks you to write an analytical, coherent and well-structured essay from your own knowledge, which reaches a supported conclusion in around 40 minutes:

- To ensure that your essay is coherent and well structured, your essay should comprise a series of paragraphs, each focusing on a different point.
- Your paragraphs should come in a logical order. For example, you could write your paragraphs in order of importance, so you begin with the most important issues and end with the least important.
- In essays where there is a 'stated factor' it is a good idea to start with the stated factor before moving on to the other points.
- To make sure you keep to time, you should aim to write three or four paragraphs plus an introduction and a conclusion.

Writing a focused introduction

The opening paragraph should do four main things:

- answer the question directly
- set out your essential argument
- outline the factors or issues that you will discuss
- define key terms used in the question – where necessary.

Different questions require you to define different terms, for example:

A level question	Key terms
2 To what extent did the National Party electoral victory of 1948 lead to the implementation of the apartheid state?	Here it is worth defining what is meant by 'the implementation of the apartheid state'
5 'The Soweto uprising of 1976 had great significance in changing the nature of anti-apartheid opposition.' How far do you agree with this statement?	In this example you should define what is meant by 'the nature of anti-apartheid opposition'

Here's an example introduction in answer to question 1 in the table on page 151:

The Sharpeville Massacre and the government response to it were important reasons for the ANC decision to move to an armed struggle in 1961 but they weren't the only ones[1]. The massacre and the government response horrified opinion both in South Africa and in the wider world, but the ANC decision to implement the armed struggle may already have been taken – largely in the face of the ineffectiveness of peaceful protest, and the government's ruthless responses to this[2]. It had certainly been extensively discussed. It might be argued that the Sharpeville Massacre and government response simply ended an ongoing debate about the movement to an armed struggle for which plans had already been laid[3].

1 The essay starts with a clear answer to the question.
2 This sentence simultaneously defines and sets out the four key areas the essay will consider.
3 Finally, the essential argument is stated.

The opening paragraph: advice

- Don't write more than a couple of sentences on general background knowledge. This is unlikely to focus explicitly on the question.
- After defining key terms, refer back to these definitions when justifying your conclusion.
- The introduction should reflect the rest of the essay. Don't make one argument in your introduction, then make a different argument in the essay.

Deploying relevant detail

Paper 2 tests the depth of your historical knowledge. Therefore, you will need to deploy historical detail. In the main body of your essay your paragraphs should begin with a clear point, be full of relevant detail and end with explanation or evaluation. A detailed answer might include statistics, proper names, dates and technical terms. For example, if you are writing a paragraph about the conditions within the Bantustans, you might include details about poverty, health and employment.

Writing analytically

The quality of your analysis is one of the key factors that determines the mark you achieve. Writing analytically means clearly showing the relationships between the ideas in your essay. Analysis includes two key skills: explanation and evaluation.

Explanation

Explanation means giving reasons. An explanatory sentence has three parts:

- a claim: a statement that something is true or false
- a reason: a statement that justifies the claim
- a relationship: a word or phrase that shows the relationship between the claim and the reason.

Imagine you are answering question 1 in the table on page 151:

> How far were the Sharpeville Massacre and the government response to it the main reasons for the decision of the ANC to move to an armed struggle in 1961?

Your paragraph on the Sharpeville Massacre and the government response to it should start with a clear point, which would be supported by a series of examples. Finally, you would round off the paragraph with some explanation:

Therefore, the Sharpeville Massacre and the government response to it were fundamental reasons[1] because[2] they convinced the ANC that the government would never be swayed by peaceful protest and always react ruthlessly to protest, whether peaceful or not[3].

1 Claim.
2 Relationship.
3 Reason.

Make sure:

- that the reason you give genuinely justifies the claim you have made
- your explanation is focused on the question.

Reaching a supported judgement

Finally, your essay should reach a supported judgement. The obvious place to do this is in the conclusion of your essay. Even so, the judgement should reflect the findings of your essay. The conclusion should present:

- a clear judgement that answers the question
- an evaluation of the evidence that supports the judgement
- finally, the evaluation should reflect valid criteria.

Evaluation and criteria

Evaluation means weighing up to reach a judgement. Therefore, evaluation requires you to:

- summarise both sides of the issue
- reach a conclusion that reflects the proper weight of both sides.

So for question 2 in the table on page 151:

> To what extent did the National Party electoral victory of 1948 lead to the implementation of the apartheid state by 1959?

the conclusion might look like this:

In conclusion, the National Party victory of 1948 led in many ways to the establishment of the apartheid state by 1959[1]. Clearly, by this date much of the key apartheid legislation was in place, such as the Population Registration Act of 1950 which categorised South Africans into four racial groups, and the Group Areas Act which designated specific areas for them to live and forced evictions if they were in a 'black spot'. Between 1951 and 1983, for example, 3.5 million Africans were evicted from their homes. The racially mixed town of Sophiatown was emptied between 1955 and 1959[2]. However, much of the foundation of apartheid was in place before 1948, such as the Natives Land Act of 1913 which restricted Africans to their tribal homelands unless they were working in white South Africa, and the Native Labour Regulation Act of 1911 which forced them to carry passes[3]. Therefore, the National Party was able to build on existing structures to implement apartheid and, given that the United Party was just as segregationist as its National Party rivals, it could be argued that the apartheid state was already in process before 1948[4].

1 The conclusion starts with a clear judgement that answers the question.
2 This sentence considers examples of apartheid legislation to show how far it was implemented by 1959.
3 The conclusion also considers evidence how far apartheid legislation pre-dated the National Party victory.
4 The essay ends with a final judgement that is supported by the evidence of the essay.

The judgement is supported in part by evaluating the evidence, and in part by linking it to valid criteria. In this case, the criterion is how far apartheid legislation was already in place. Significantly, this criterion is specific to this essay, and different essays will require you to think of different criteria to help you make your judgement.

Glossary of terms

Africanist   Refers to Africanism, the policy of black Africans to fight against apartheid without help from other ethnic groups.

Africans   The original population of Africa.

Afrikaners   Descendants of immigrants to South Africa, mainly from the Netherlands and Germany.

Agents provocateurs   Government agents tasked with entrapping opponents by planning illegal actions and keeping the authorities informed.

Apartheid   Strict separation of different racial groups. It is an Afrikaans word, meaning 'apart-hood'.

Banning orders   Measures restricting one's movements, limiting one to a certain specifically defined area or house arrest.

Bantus   African people who speak a common group of languages. In the apartheid era white people used the term to refer to Africans in a derogatory manner.

Bantustans   African homelands or tribal reserves.

Betterment   Government-driven improvements in agriculture and living conditions in the homelands.

Black Consciousness   Movement based on Black Power in the USA in which African people took increasing pride in their culture and identity. This was particularly associated in South Africa with Steve Biko and the South African Students' Organisation (SASO).

Black Pimpernel   Referring to the Scarlet Pimpernel, the elusive hero of Baroness D'Orczy's novels set in the French Revolution.

Boers   A Dutch word; the name given to the settlers from the Netherlands and Germany.

Broederbond   Hugely influential Afrikaner organisation promoting apartheid and Afrikaner hegemony.

Bureaucracy   Members of the administration which implemented government policies.

Cape   The southernmost province of South Africa, originally Cape Colony, part of the British Empire.

Cato Manor   A township near Durban where serious riots took place in 1959 as a result of police trying to close down shebeens.

Charterist ideals   Refers to the Freedom Charter of 1955. The ANC still adhered to these goals.

Civil disobedience   Refusal to follow the law, such as refusing to carry passes.

Coalition   A partnership between different political parties to try to win elections together.

Cold War   The hostility between the USA and the Union of Soviet Socialist Republics (USSR, or Soviet Union) in the post-Second World War era; this manifested itself in methods such as propaganda and gaining allies through economic aid.

Colonisation   Settling in an area and taking control over it and its people, often through force and exploitation.

Commonwealth   Association of members and former members of the British Empire.

Commonwealth Conference   Annual meeting of members of the Commonwealth or former British Empire.

Communism   Belief that the planning and control of the economy and society should all be controlled by the state. People should be rewarded according to the value of their contribution to society. Nationalist politicians opposed in particular the belief that all should have equality of opportunity regardless of ethnicity.

Convention for a Democratic South Africa (CODESA)   The organisation charged with preparing for a post-apartheid democratic South Africa. CODESA 1 was created in 1991 and CODESA 2 in 1992: both faced difficult negotiations.

Covenant   Solemn oath or agreement; in this sense, the agreement apparently made between God and the Boers in 1838.

Decolonisation   When former empires relinquished their colonies and gave them independence.

Dominion Largely self-governing country within the British Empire, recognising the monarch as head of state.

Draconian Extreme.

Dutch Reformed Church The Afrikaner Church which supported apartheid.

French Revolutionary and Napoleonic Wars A series of wars fought between France and Britain and their respective allies between 1792 and 1815 in which France was defeated.

Genealogy Study of one's family, to identify one's roots.

Gold rush Rapid migration of people to an area to find gold and become rich.

Grass-roots support Backing at a local level.

Great Trek Movement of Boer farmers into the vast South African interior, away from British rule, which began in 1834.

Gross domestic product (GDP) The value of goods and services produced within the country; one criterion commonly used for determining national wealth.

Guerrilla warfare Fighting using techniques such as ambush and bombings, avoiding direct large-scale conflict.

High treason Plotting to overthrow the state.

Hinterland Land in the interior of a country.

Indigenous Native to an area.

Inkhata Zulu nationalist organisation which developed into the Inkhata Freedom Party in 1990: it opposed the ANC in the 1980s and sought an independent Zulu homeland.

Intaba movement Resistance movement in East Pondoland. *Intaba* is a Zulu word for 'mountain'.

Integrationist One who believes that all races, including white people, should be involved in the fight against apartheid.

Kaffir A derogatory name given by Afrikaners to black Africans.

Knobkerrie A type of club with a head made from wooden roots.

Kraals African collections of farms where families or close members of tribal groups would live together.

Laager mentality The belief among Afrikaners of the need to stick together in the face of outside criticism: the analogy refers to how Boers would defend themselves within camps (laagers) if attacked by Africans during the period of settlement.

Liberal Party Political party made up mainly of white people who opposed apartheid.

Mandate Former colony of the defeated powers after the First World War, given to the victorious powers to prepare for independence. Most powers were reluctant to relinquish control.

Maoris Indigenous peoples of New Zealand.

Miscegenation Mixing of different racial groups through marriage and sexual relations.

Mission schools Schools run by various Churches to educate African children.

Necklaced Vigilante punishment by setting victims on fire by enveloping them in petrol-soaked tyres.

Oil crisis of 1973 A massive increase in the price of oil, threatening the prosperity of many developed nations.

Pangas Heavy knives.

Passive resistance Non-violent opposition.

Pastoral environment Rural life based on small-scale agriculture.

Pickets A method of protest whereby groups of people gather to stop people from going in to an institution or a location.

Polity Used to refer to an organised society.

Poqo Armed wing of the PAC.

Radicalisation Process by which people come to adopt extreme political or religious ideas, often through undue influence from particular groups, in this case the PAC.

Rand In 1960, South Africa decimalised its currency, moving from British sterling (pounds, shillings and pence) to rands and cents.

Republic Country without a monarch at its head, usually led by a president.

Rubicon 'Crossing the Rubicon' is a term used to describe the taking of a critical decision that cannot be reversed.

Second Boer War   War between Britain and the Boers between 1899 and 1902 with the Boers seeking to assert their complete independence from Britain, which, in turn, wished to extend its influence to gain control over the gold and diamond industries in the Transvaal.

Security Council   The executive of the UN, responsible for international peace keeping.

Security Council Resolution 134   UN resolution condemning the South African government for the Sharpeville Massacre.

Segregation   Separate facilities for members of different races.

Seventh Day Adventists   Religious group who see Saturday as the Sabbath.

Shebeens   Illegal drinking clubs.

Soweto   An acronym for South Western Townships (African townships on the edge of Johannesburg).

Sunset clause   Guarantee of continued employment, and pension rights for those nearing retirement.

Total Onslaught   The fear that there was a total co-ordinated attack orchestrated by Communists to destroy apartheid.

Total Strategy   Botha's response to Total Onslaught. This involved the deployment of every possible means, for example political, economic and military to protect the apartheid regime.

Trade unions   Worker-based organisations which aimed to improve working conditions for their members and sometimes became involved in anti-apartheid activities.

Tricameral   A Parliament comprised of three houses, in this case assembly, representatives and delegates.

***Umkhonto we Sizwe* or Spear of the Nation (MK)**   Armed wing of the ANC.

United Democratic Front (UDF)   Organisation created in 1983 within South Africa to co-ordinate the struggle against apartheid.

United Nations   Formed in 1945, largely to solve international disputes and problems.

United Nations General Council   The legislature of the United Nations.

Vietnam War   Civil war between Communist North and non-Communist South Vietnam. The war escalated after the Communist Vietcong rebelled against the government in the South in the mid to late 1950s, and the North supported them. The USA supported the South, becoming involved full time in their support after 1965. In 1975, the North Vietnamese invaded the South and united the country under communism.

White-collar   Professional jobs such as administrators.

White supremacy   A belief in the right of white people to govern and the inferiority of non-white people.

Whitewash   An official exoneration of an individual or group even though the evidence strongly suggests their guilt or culpability.

Further reading

Books of overall relevance

W. Beinart, *Twentieth Century South Africa* **(Oxford University Press, 1994)**

Readable, informative and particularly strong on social and economic aspects and what was going on in rural areas

N.L. Clark and W.H. Worger, *South Africa: The Rise and Fall of Apartheid* **(Pearson, 2004)**

Thorough account aimed at students, with a useful collection of documents

S. Dubow, *Apartheid 1948–1994* **(Oxford Histories, 2014)**

A thorough account which contextualises apartheid in a global and local perspective and considers resistance within the context of governmental power

H. Giliomee, *The Last Afrikaner Leaders: A Supreme Test of Power* **(Tafelburg/University of Virginia Press, 2012)**

A leading Afrikaner historian's account of the role of political leaders in the development and demise of apartheid

P. Hain, *Mandela* **(Octopus Books, 2010)**

A short but thorough biography of Nelson Mandela

D. Harrison, *The White Tribe of Africa: South Africa in Perspective* **(BBC Books, 1981)**

Very readable and engaging account of the Afrikaners and their relationship with the Broederbund: the basis of a BBC TV series

N. Mandela, *Long Walk to Freedom* **(Abacus, 2013)**

Essential background reading; a very well-written autobiography, exhaustive in its coverage of the fight against apartheid in the period covered by this book

F. Meli, *A History of the ANC: South Africa Belongs to Us* **(James Currey, 1989)**

A history of the ANC by one of its leaders in the 1980s

A. Sparks, *The Mind of South Africa: The Story of the Rise and Fall of Apartheid* **(Heinemann, 1990)**

Excellent account of apartheid seem in terms of the Afrikaner mind-set

L. Thompson, *A History of South Africa* **(Yale University Press, 1990)**

Thorough and comprehensive history

F. Welsh, *A History of South Africa* **(HarperCollins 2000)**

Thorough and authoritative, offering challenging perspectives on many aspects of South African history

Chapter 1

H. Giliomee, *The Afrikaners: Biography of a People* **(University of Virginia Press, 2013)**

Highly praised history, particularly useful for seeing apartheid from the Afrikaner perspective

J. Gunther, *Inside Africa* **(Hamish Hamilton, 1955)**

Thorough account of South Africa in the mid-1950s, including interviews with most of the government and opposition leaders

P. Hain, *Sing the Beloved Country* **(Pluto Press, 1996)**

Highly readable account from a former anti-apartheid activist

Chapter 2

L. Callinicos, *Oliver Tambo: Beyond the Engeli Mountains,* **second edition (David Philip, 2004)**

Detailed and authorised biography of a key figure whose contribution is often underestimated outside of South Africa

S. Dubow, *The African National Congress* **(Sutton Pocket Histories, 2000)**

A short but comprehensive history of the ANC

P. Frankel, *An Ordinary Atrocity: Sharpeville and its Massacre* **(Yale University Press, 2001)**

A reconstruction of the events at Sharpeville through interviews with both perpetrators and demonstrators

H. Joseph, *Side by Side* **(Zed Books, 1986)**

Autobiography by one of the most noted anti-apartheid activists

T. Lodge, *Sharpeville: An Apartheid Massacre and its Consequences* **(Oxford University Press, 2011)**

The massacre seen in a wider context and therefore thorough in its coverage of many of the issues facing South Africa at the time of the massacre and in the years afterwards: essential reading

D. McKinley, *The ANC and the Liberation Struggle: A Critical Political Biography* (Pluto Press, 1997)

A controversial analysis of the activities of the ANC

A. Reeves, *Shooting at Sharpeville: The Agony of South Africa* (Houghton Mifflin, 1961)

Available at: https://archive.org/details/shootingatsharpe002466mbp

Chapter 3

S. Biko, *I Write What I Like* (Heinemann, 1987)

A compilation of the writings of Steve Biko

V. Brittain, *Hidden Lives, Hidden Deaths: South Africa's Crippling of a Continent* (Faber & Faber, 1988)

An impassioned criticism of South Africa's foreign policy in the 1970s and 1980s

Commonwealth Secretariat, *Racism in Southern Africa: The Commonwealth Stand* (Commonwealth Secretariat, 1989)

The Commonwealth's account of its contribution to the fight against apartheid including valuable material on sanctions

D. McRae, *Under Our Skin: A White Family's Journey Through South Africa* (Simon & Schuster, 2012)

An engrossing account of growing up in South Africa and the tensions caused with his family by the author's increasing opposition to apartheid

D. Woods *Biko* (Paddington Press, 1978)

Impassioned biography of Steve Biko, written in secret while the author was under house arrest: the final section is a devastating indictment of apartheid

D. Woods, *Asking for Trouble: Autobiography of a Banned Journalist* (Victor Gollancz, 1980)

Autobiography of an influential anti-apartheid journalist who befriended Steve Biko

Chapter 4

D. Reed, *Beloved Country: South Africa's Silent Wars* (BBC Books, 1994)

An impassioned account of the violence accompanying the peace process, which formed the basis of a BBC TV series

S. Tollin, *Salute to Senge: A Diary of the Social Situation in South Africa between 1982 and 1987* (Arthur H. Stockwell, 2011)

Extracts from a diary kept by an opponent of apartheid who worked with disadvantaged children in Johannesburg: very useful for a personal perspective on national events and how they impacted an individual people and groups

D. Tutu, *The Rainbow People of God: South Africa's Victory Over Apartheid* (Doubleday, 1994)

Selection of Archbishop Tutu's writings and speeches

Useful websites

www.anc.org.za/

Official ANC site with lots of primary material source relating to the struggle against apartheid

www.bbc.co.uk/archive/apartheid/

Online BBC programmes about apartheid including a *Panorama* documentary from 1957

www.nelsonmandela.org/omalley/index.php/site/q/03lv00000.htm

Thorough coverage in terms of documents, interviews and analysis hosted by journalist Padraig O'Malley

www.sahistory.org.za/

Exhaustive educational site with documents, histories, biographies, timelines and some very useful analytical essays

Films useful for background

A World Apart (1988)

Intensely moving film based in part on the life of anti-apartheid activist Ruth First but focusing on the impact her activities had on her family

Cry Freedom (1987)

Sweeping indictment of apartheid, focusing on the role of Steve Biko in opposing it

Cry the Beloved Country (1952 and 1995)

Both versions are worth seeing

Goodbye Bafana (2007)

A minor masterpiece about Nelson Mandela's developing relationship based on trust with one of his prison warders

Mandela: Long Walk to Freedom (2013)

Big budget biopic based on Nelson Mandela's autobiography

Index